FLAVIA BIONDI

GENERATIONS

LION
FORGE

GENERATIONS

Written & Illustrated by
Flavia Biondi

Publisher's Cataloging-In-Publication Data

(Prepared by The Donohue Group, Inc.)

Names: Biondi, Flavia, author, illustrator. | Roncalli di Montorio, Carla translator. |
    Iacaccia, Anna, designer. | Officine Bolzoni, letterer. | Torsoli, Cosimo, letterer. |
    Foschini, Michele, editor. | Smylie, Mark (Mark S.), editor.

Title: Generations / written and illustrated by Flavia Biondi ; translated by Carla
    Roncalli Di Montorio ; original book design, Anna Iacaccia ; letters by Officine
    Bolzoni & Cosimo Torsoli ; edited for Bao Publishing by Michele Foschini ;
    edited by Mark Smylie.

Other Titles: Generazione. English

Description: [St. Louis, Missouri] : The Lion Forge, LLC, [2017] | Translation of: La
    Generazione. Milano : BAO, ©2016.

Identifiers: ISBN 978-1-941302-50-7

Subjects: LCSH: Young gay men--Family relationships--Italy--Comic books, strips,
    etc. | Families--Italy--Comic books, strips, etc. | LCGFT: Graphic novels.

Classification: LCC PN6767.B56 G46 2017 | DDC 741.5973--dc23

10 9 8 7 6 5 4 3 2 1

"To my Nan Ada, who couldn't write letters,
Or numbers, but could draw turtle-doves..."

Translated by
Carla Roncalli Di Montorio

Original editors (Italian edition)
Caterina Marietti & Leonardo Favia

Original book design
Anna Iacaccia

Letters by
Officine Bolzoni & Cosimo Torsoli

Edited for Bao Publishing by
Michele Foschini

Edited by
Mark Smylie

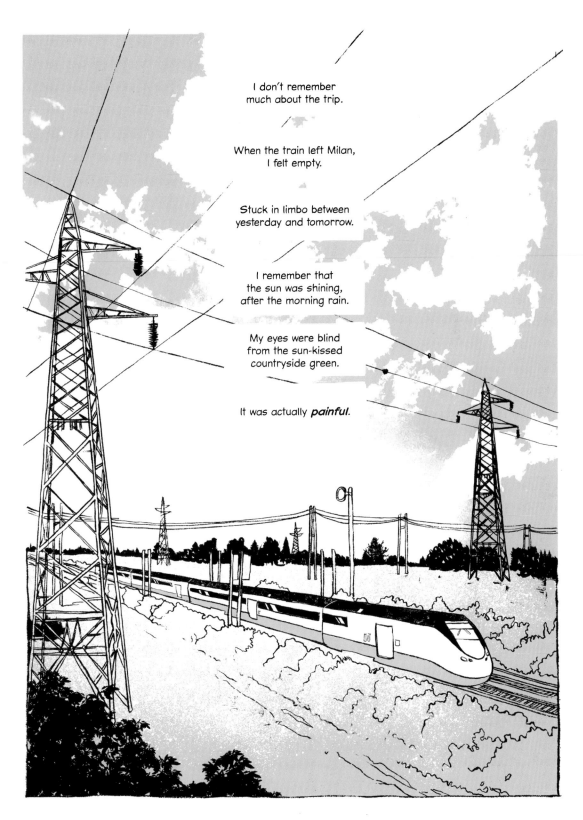

I don't remember
much about the trip.

When the train left Milan,
I felt empty.

Stuck in limbo between
yesterday and tomorrow.

I remember that
the sun was shining,
after the morning rain.

My eyes were blind
from the sun-kissed
countryside green.

It was actually *painful*.

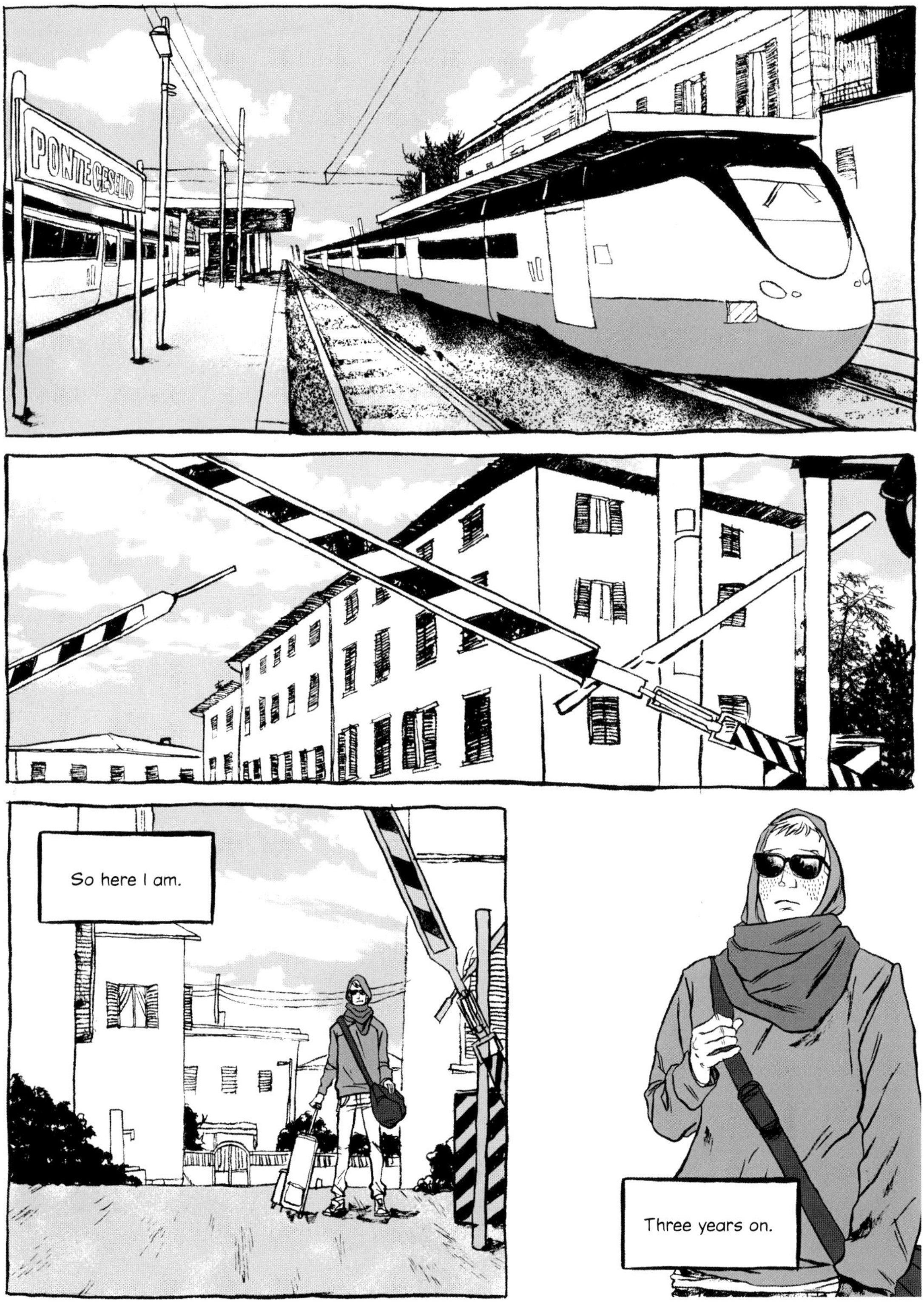
PONTE CESELLO
So here I am.
Three years on.

Nothing seems to have changed.

I can't go back to my Father's.

Not after what happened.

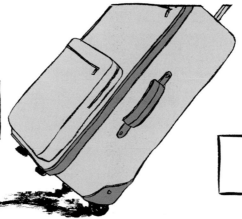

Not after three years of silence.

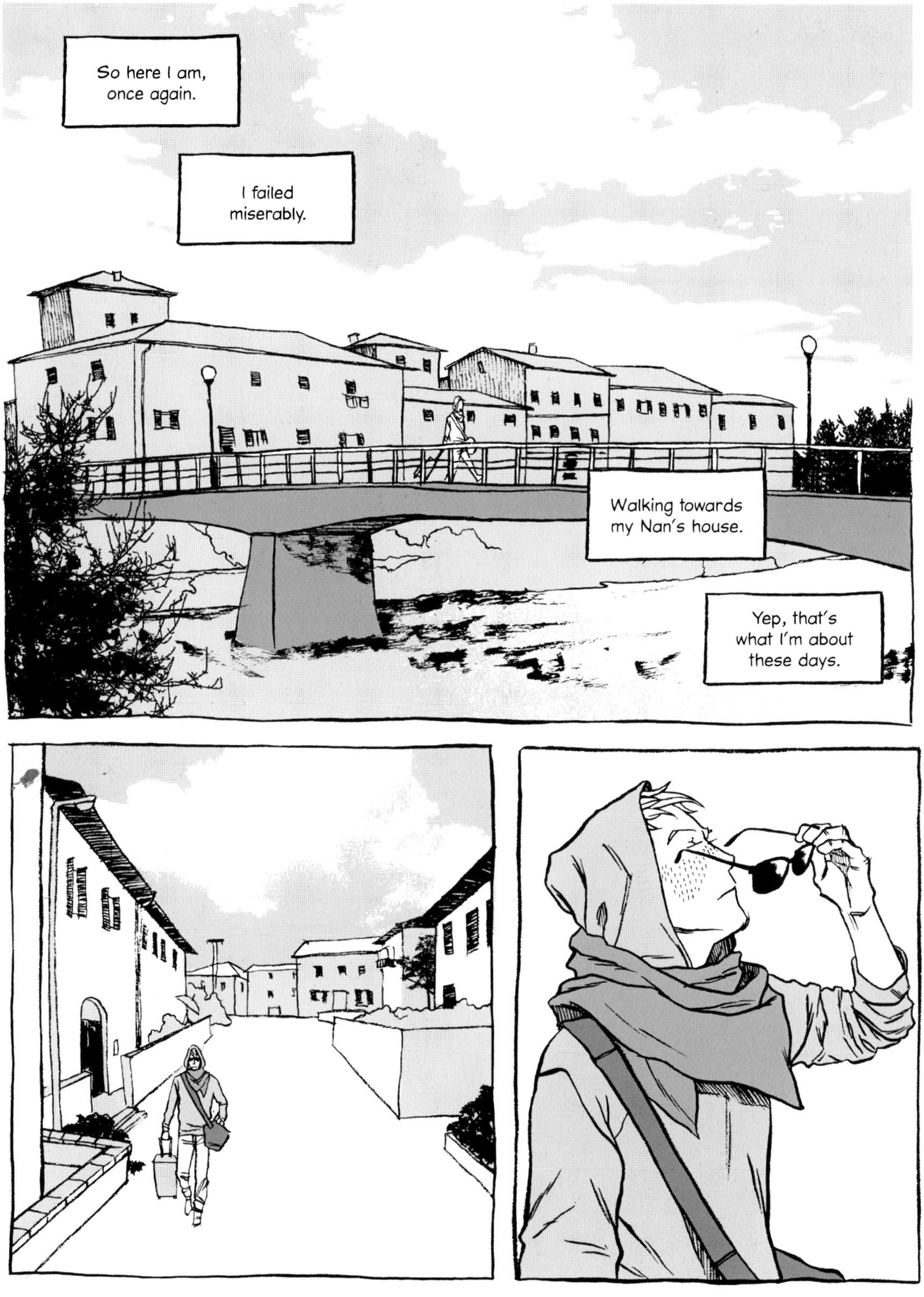
So here I am, once again.
I failed miserably.
Walking towards my Nan's house.
Yep, that's what I'm about these days.

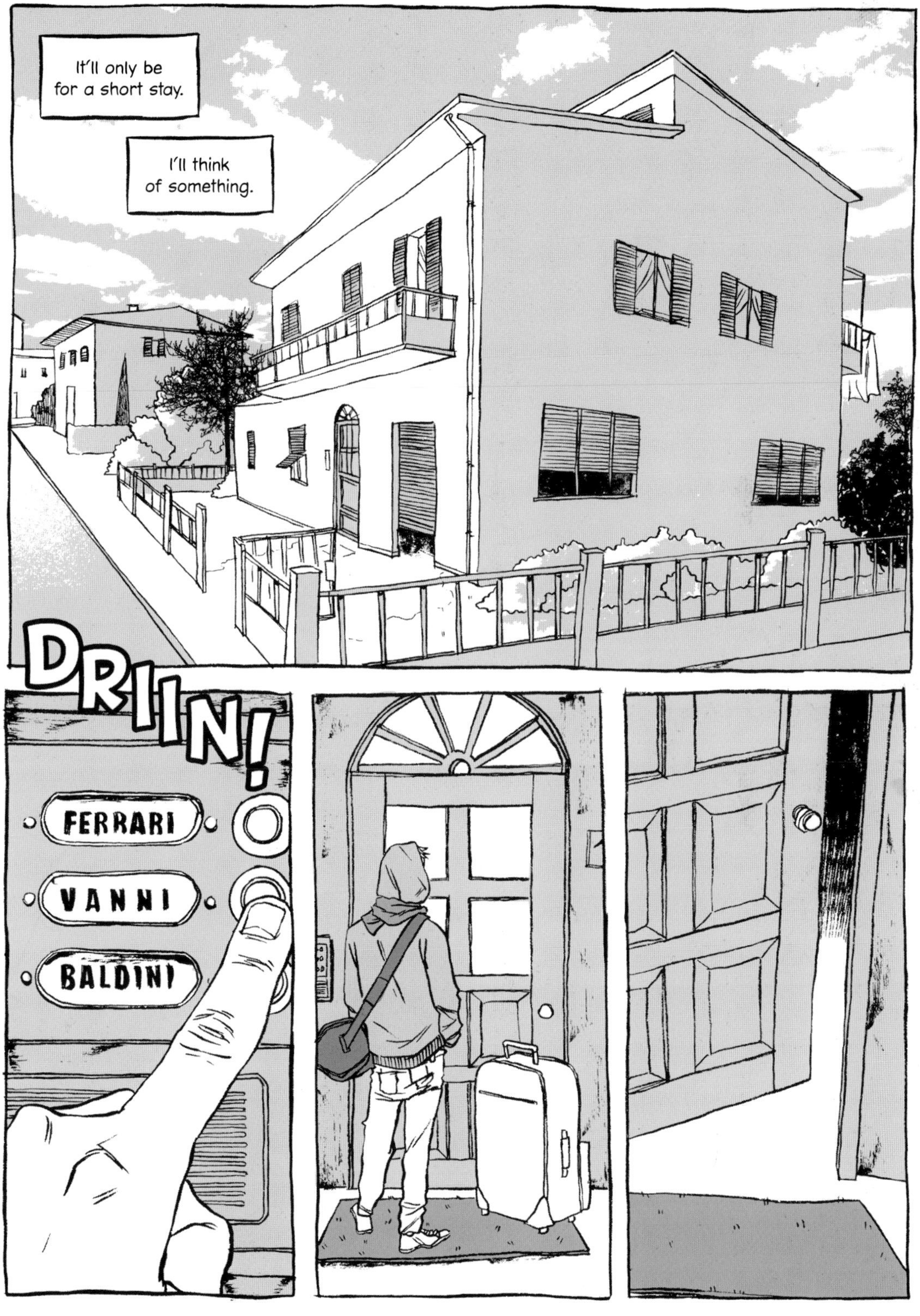

It'll only be for a short stay.
I'll think of something.
DRIIN!
FERRARI
VANNI
BALDINI

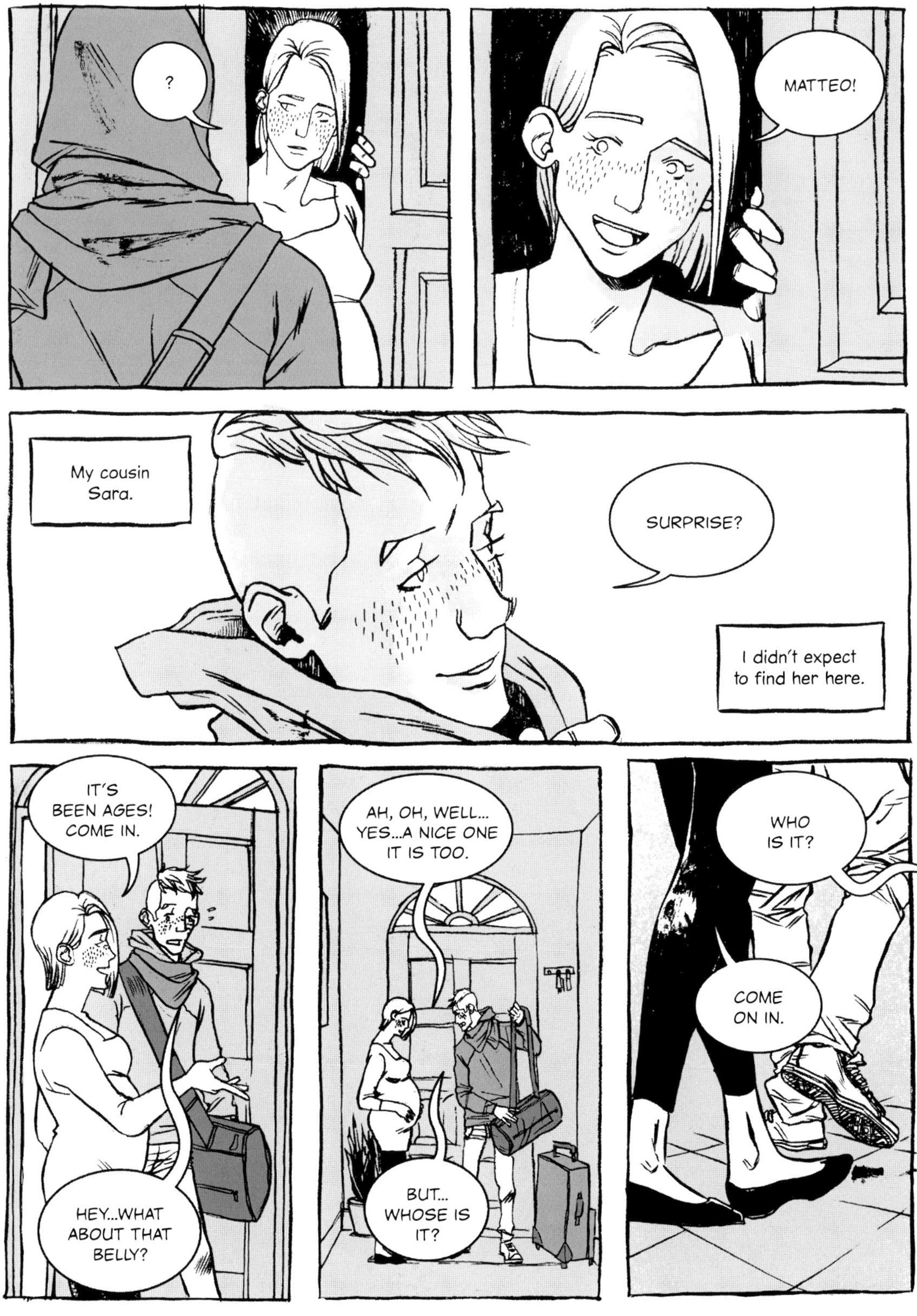
?
MATTEO!
My cousin Sara.
SURPRISE?
I didn't expect to find her here.
IT'S BEEN AGES! COME IN.
HEY...WHAT ABOUT THAT BELLY?
AH, OH, WELL... YES...A NICE ONE IT IS TOO.
BUT... WHOSE IS IT?
WHO IS IT?
COME ON IN.

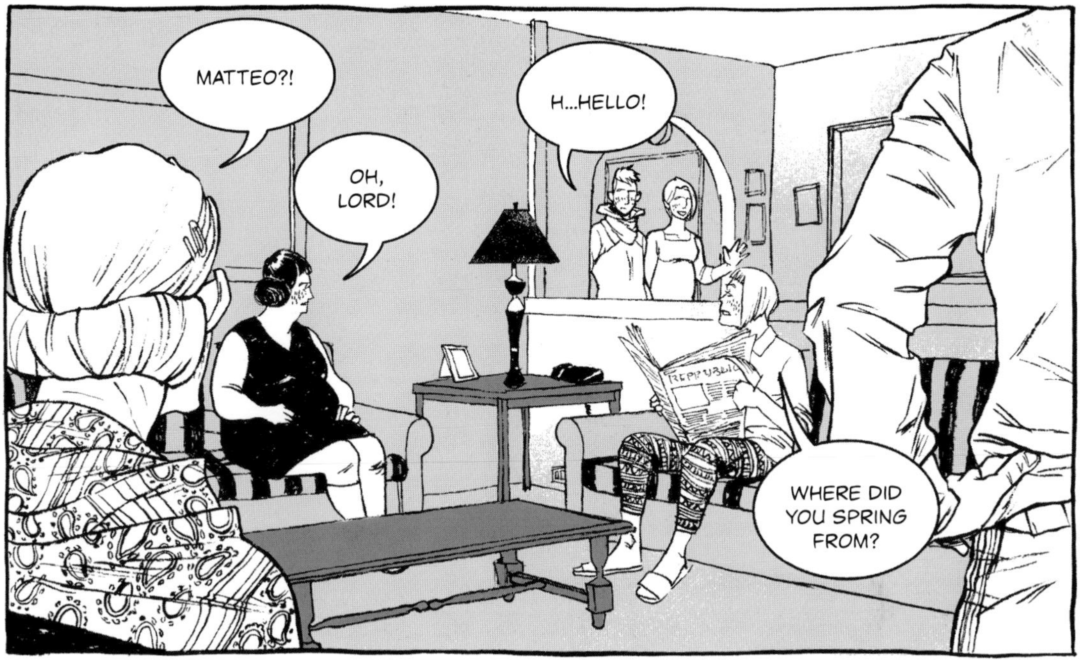
MATTEO?!
OH, LORD!
H...HELLO!
WHERE DID YOU SPRING FROM?

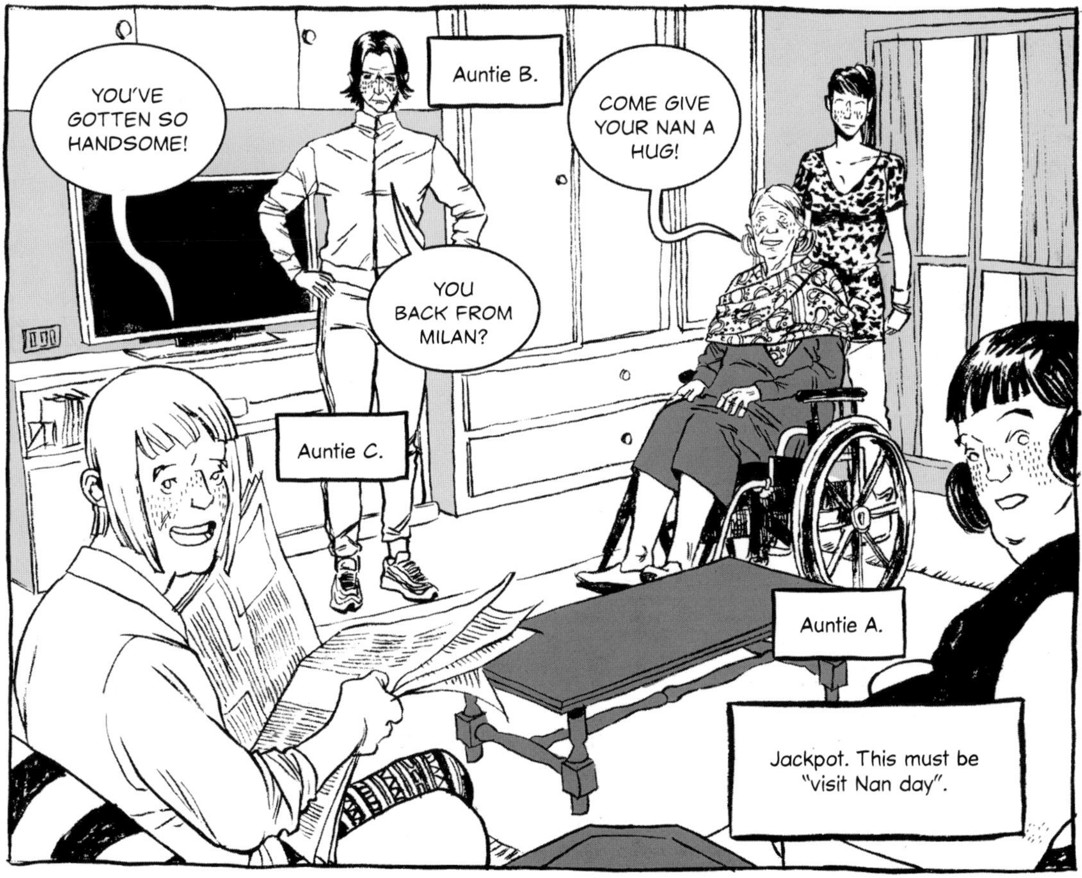
YOU'VE GOTTEN SO HANDSOME!
Auntie B.
YOU BACK FROM MILAN?
COME GIVE YOUR NAN A HUG!
Auntie C.
Auntie A.
Jackpot. This must be "visit Nan day".

HELLO, NAN, HOW ARE YOU?

ARE YOU EATING ENOUGH? YOU'RE ALL SKIN AND BONES!

NO WAY! MY NEPHEW'S JUST HANDSOME!

ANTONIA, MAKE HIM A COFFEE!

I'LL ALSO BRING A SLICE OF MANTOVANA*, I MADE IT THIS MORNING.

IT'S OK! DON'T WORRY, AUNTIE!

WHAT ARE ALL THESE BAGS? HAVE YOU JUST COME BACK?

HAVE YOU NOT BEEN TO YOUR DAD'S?

ER, YEAH, YOU KNOW, ABOUT THAT...

RIGHT, LET ME CALL YOUR DAD, SO WE CAN ALL HAVE LUNCH TOGETHER!

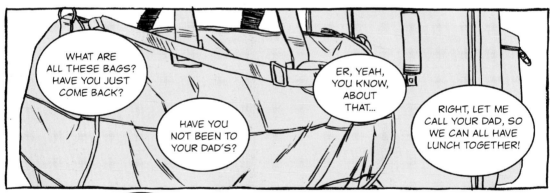

NO, NO, WAIT!

* *MANTOVANA= TUSCAN CAKE, FROM THE PRATO AREA

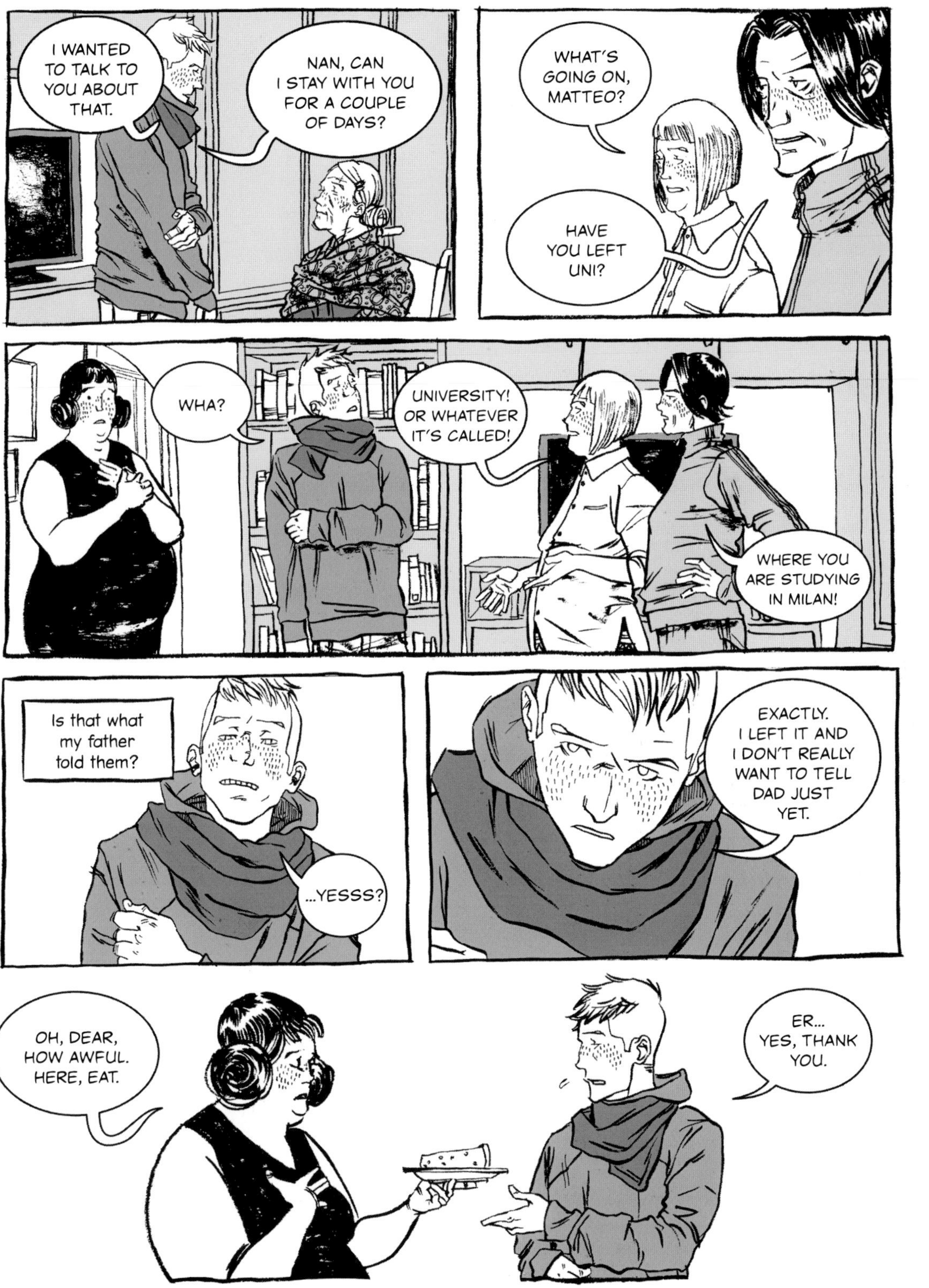
I WANTED TO TALK TO YOU ABOUT THAT.
NAN, CAN I STAY WITH YOU FOR A COUPLE OF DAYS?
WHAT'S GOING ON, MATTEO?
HAVE YOU LEFT UNI?
WHA?
UNIVERSITY! OR WHATEVER IT'S CALLED!
WHERE YOU ARE STUDYING IN MILAN!
Is that what my father told them?
...YESSS?
EXACTLY. I LEFT IT AND I DON'T REALLY WANT TO TELL DAD JUST YET.
OH, DEAR, HOW AWFUL. HERE, EAT.
ER... YES, THANK YOU.

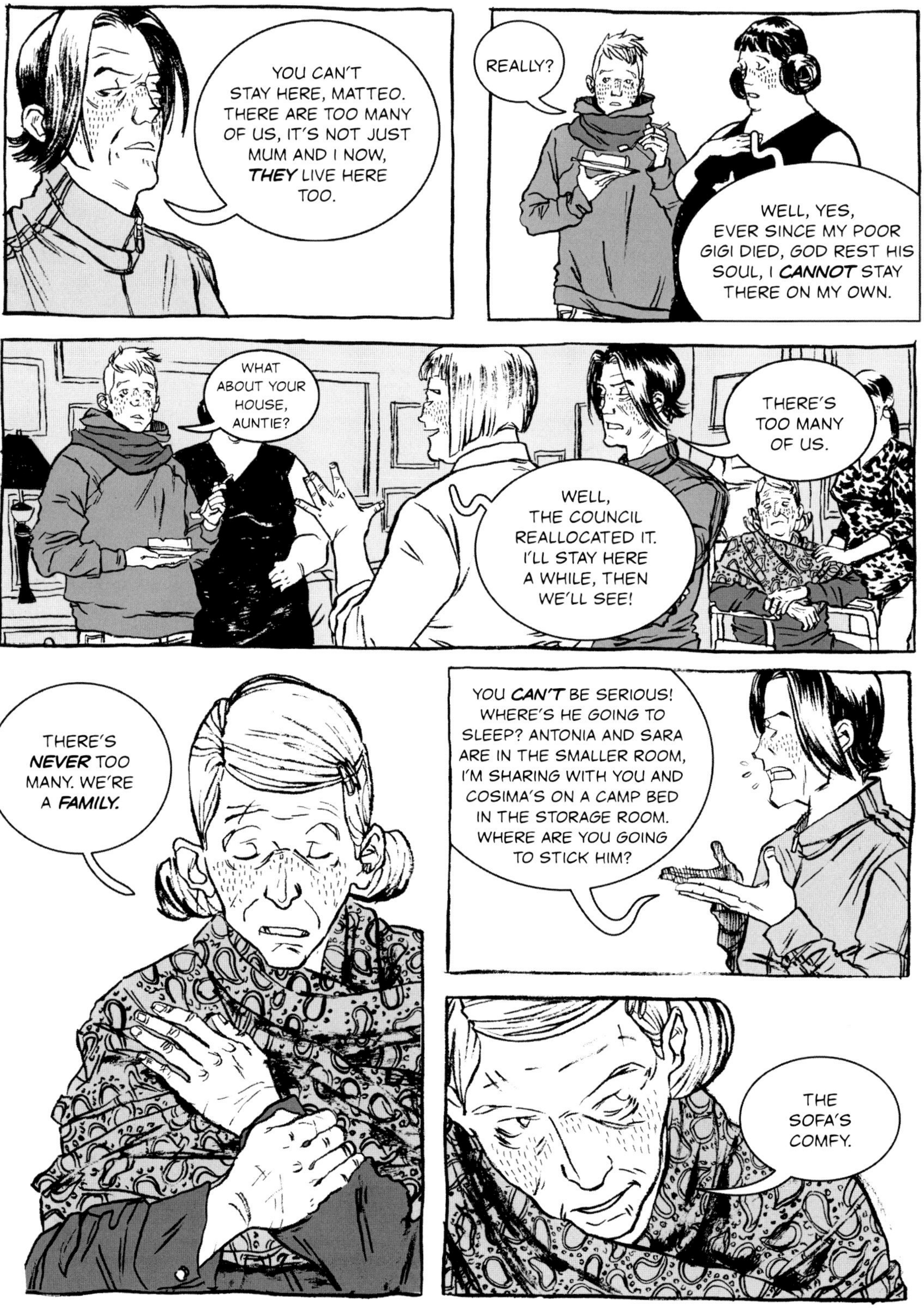
YOU CAN'T STAY HERE, MATTEO. THERE ARE TOO MANY OF US, IT'S NOT JUST MUM AND I NOW, ***THEY*** LIVE HERE TOO.
REALLY?
WELL, YES, EVER SINCE MY POOR GIGI DIED, GOD REST HIS SOUL, I ***CANNOT*** STAY THERE ON MY OWN.
WHAT ABOUT YOUR HOUSE, AUNTIE?
WELL, THE COUNCIL REALLOCATED IT. I'LL STAY HERE A WHILE, THEN WE'LL SEE!
THERE'S TOO MANY OF US.
THERE'S ***NEVER*** TOO MANY. WE'RE A ***FAMILY.***
YOU ***CAN'T*** BE SERIOUS! WHERE'S HE GOING TO SLEEP? ANTONIA AND SARA ARE IN THE SMALLER ROOM, I'M SHARING WITH YOU AND COSIMA'S ON A CAMP BED IN THE STORAGE ROOM. WHERE ARE YOU GOING TO STICK HIM?
THE SOFA'S COMFY.

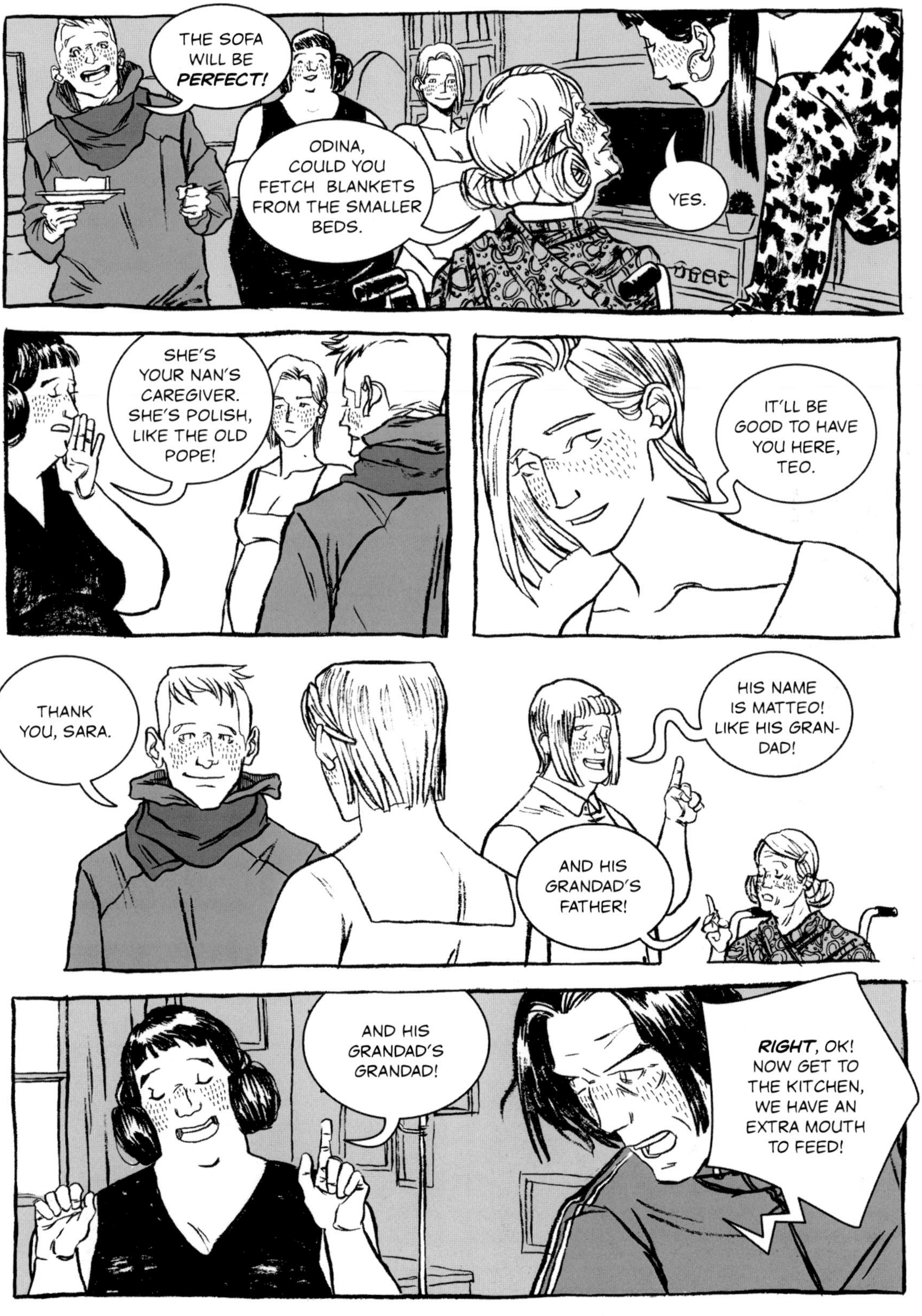
THE SOFA WILL BE **PERFECT!**
ODINA, COULD YOU FETCH BLANKETS FROM THE SMALLER BEDS.
YES.
SHE'S YOUR NAN'S CAREGIVER. SHE'S POLISH, LIKE THE OLD POPE!
IT'LL BE GOOD TO HAVE YOU HERE, TEO.
THANK YOU, SARA.
HIS NAME IS MATTEO! LIKE HIS GRAN-DAD!
AND HIS GRANDAD'S FATHER!
AND HIS GRANDAD'S GRANDAD!
RIGHT, OK! NOW GET TO THE KITCHEN, WE HAVE AN EXTRA MOUTH TO FEED!

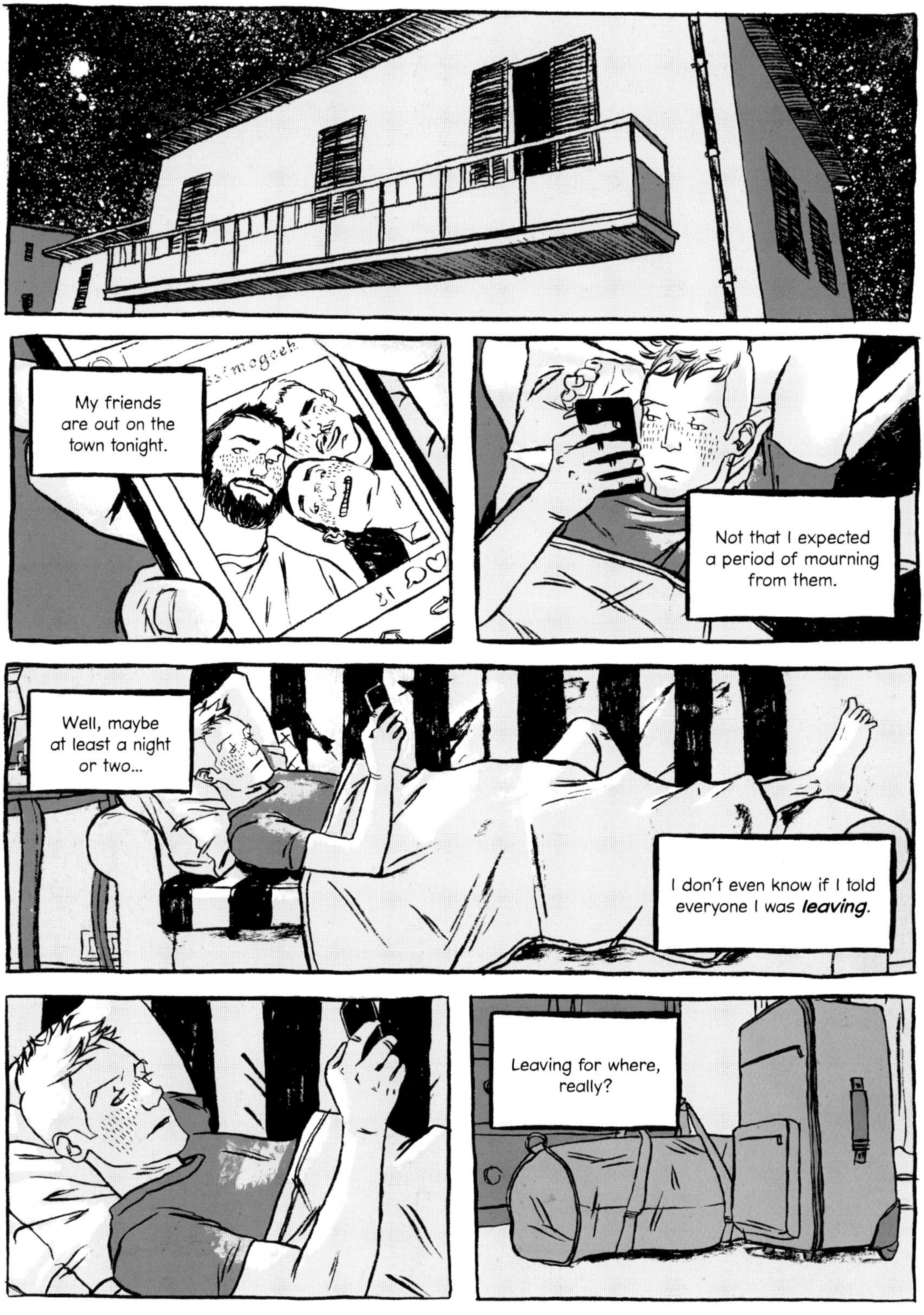
My friends are out on the town tonight.
Not that I expected a period of mourning from them.
Well, maybe at least a night or two...
I don't even know if I told everyone I was ***leaving***.
Leaving for where, really?

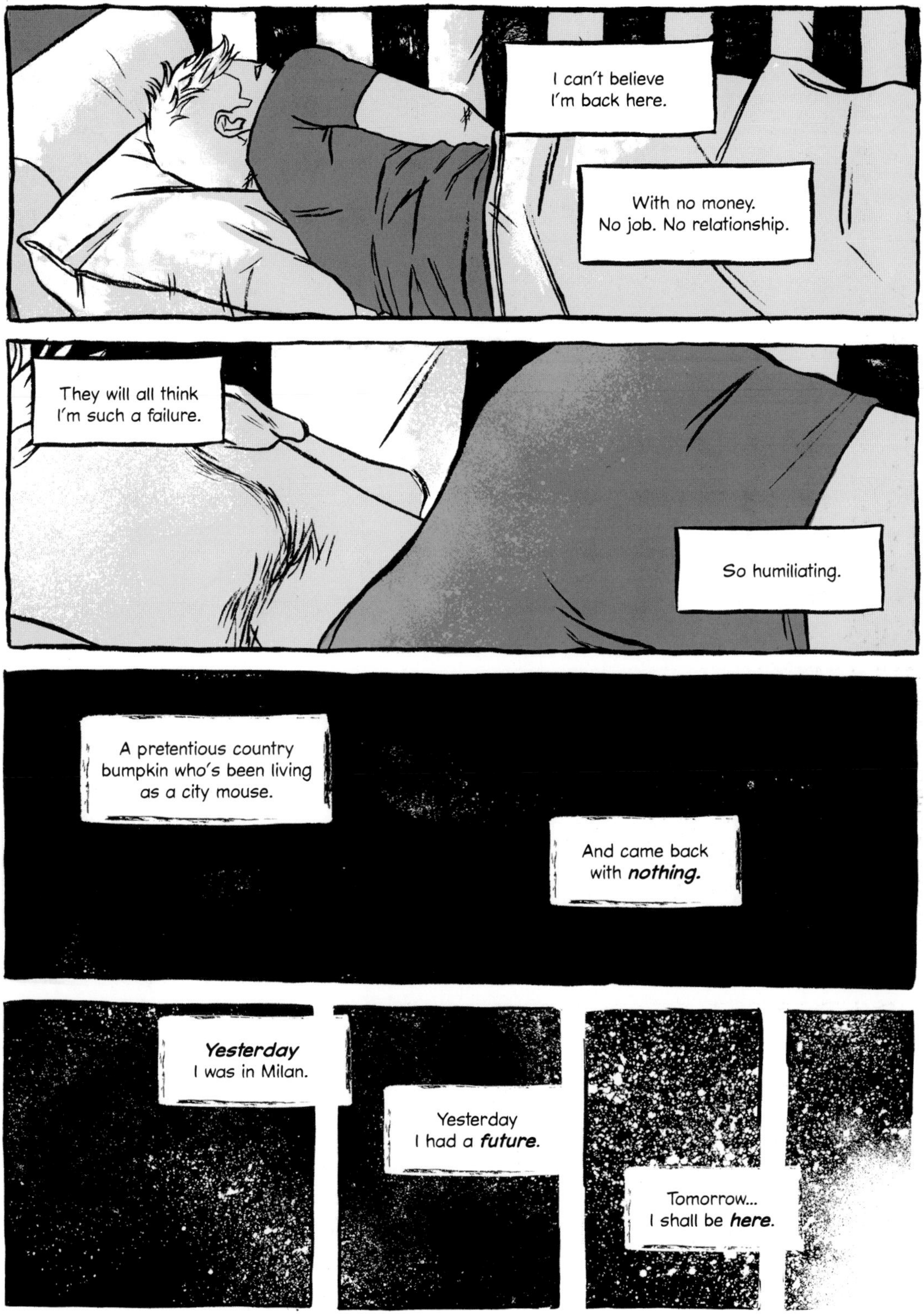
I can't believe I'm back here.
With no money. No job. No relationship.
They will all think I'm such a failure.
So humiliating.
A pretentious country bumpkin who's been living as a city mouse.
And came back with ***nothing.***
Yesterday I was in Milan.
Yesterday I had a ***future.***
Tomorrow... I shall be ***here.***

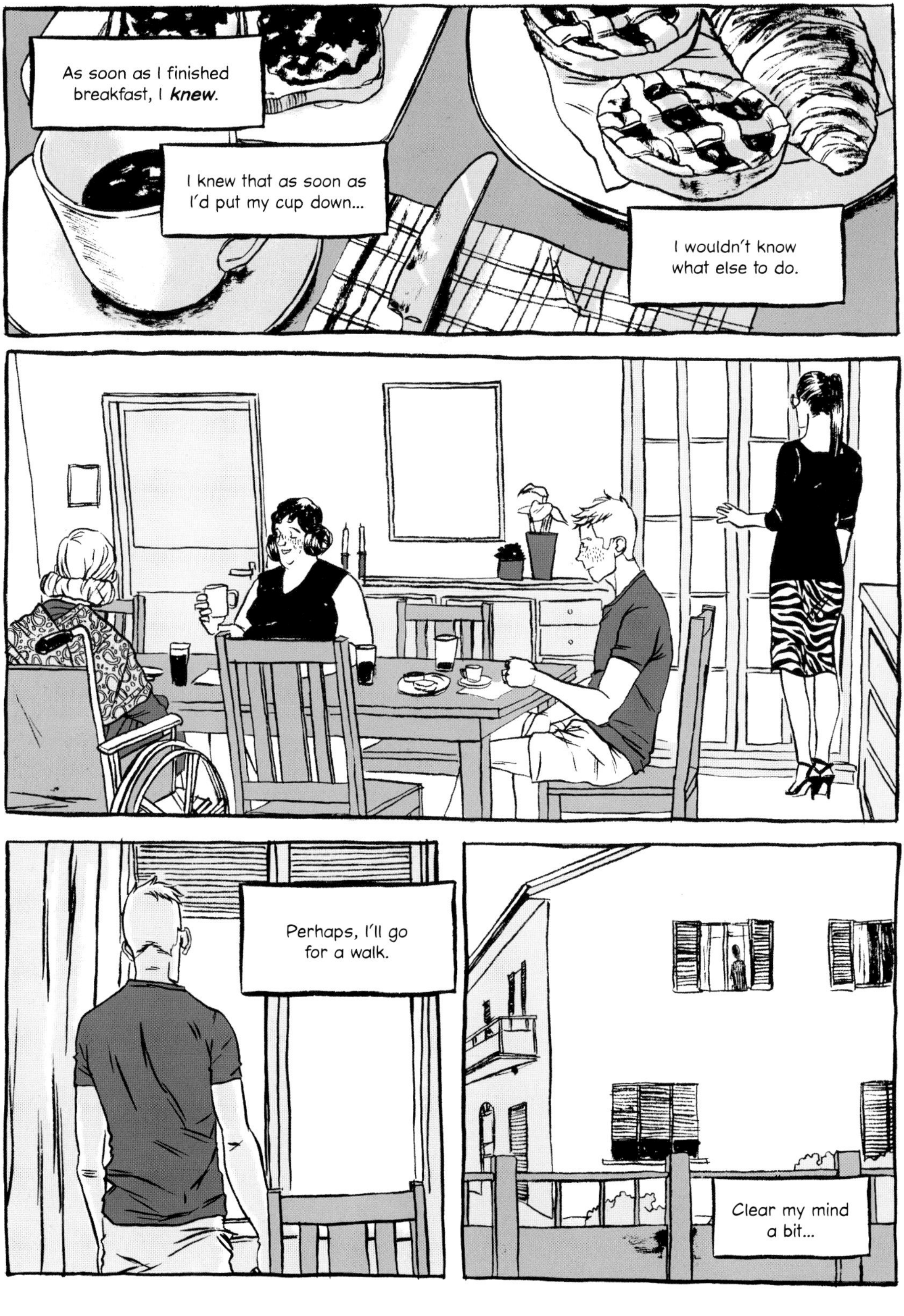
As soon as I finished breakfast, I ***knew***.
I knew that as soon as I'd put my cup down...
I wouldn't know what else to do.
Perhaps, I'll go for a walk.
Clear my mind a bit...

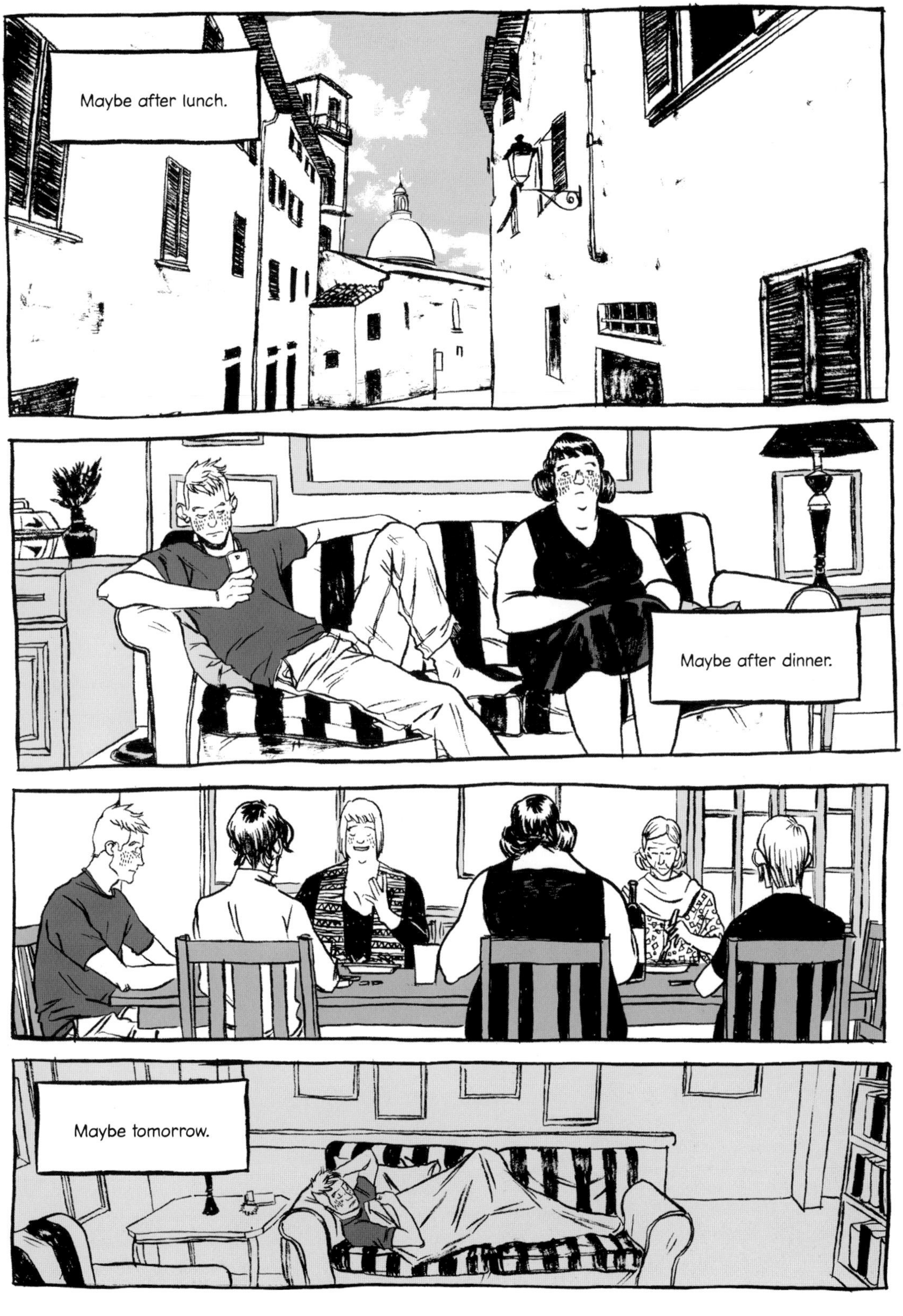
Maybe after lunch.
Maybe after dinner.
Maybe tomorrow.

Tomorrow.

Tomorrow.

Tomorrow.

I hate everyone else's life.

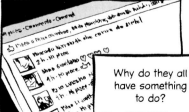

Why do they all have something to do?

Not me, *I* am a *failure*, all I can do is sleep and eat like the elderly.

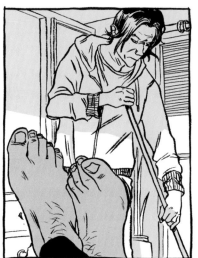

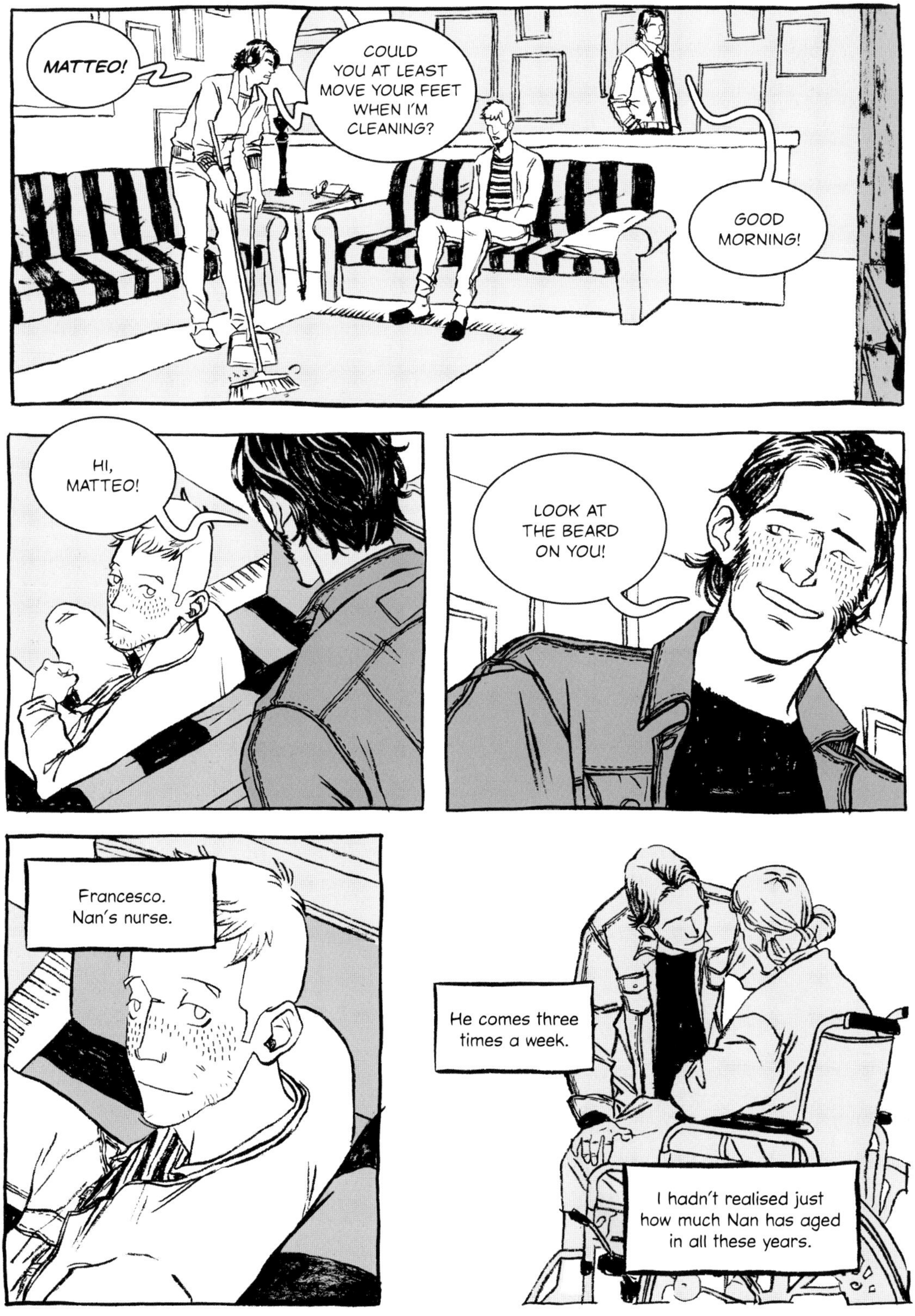
MATTEO!
COULD YOU AT LEAST MOVE YOUR FEET WHEN I'M CLEANING?
GOOD MORNING!
HI, MATTEO!
LOOK AT THE BEARD ON YOU!
Francesco. Nan's nurse.
He comes three times a week.
I hadn't realised just how much Nan has aged in all these years.

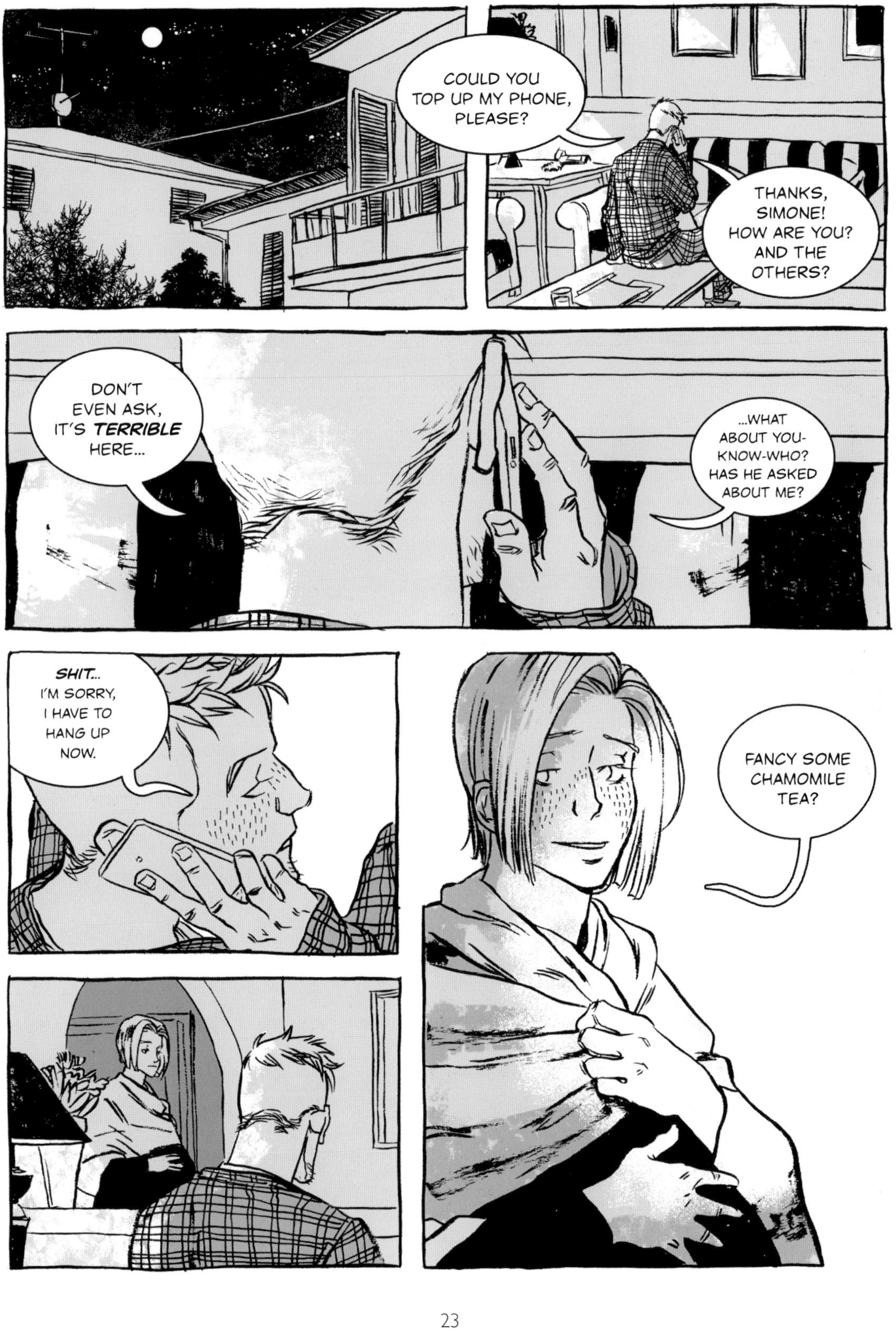
COULD YOU TOP UP MY PHONE, PLEASE?
THANKS, SIMONE! HOW ARE YOU? AND THE OTHERS?
DON'T EVEN ASK, IT'S TERRIBLE HERE...
...WHAT ABOUT YOU-KNOW-WHO? HAS HE ASKED ABOUT ME?
SHIT... I'M SORRY, I HAVE TO HANG UP NOW.
FANCY SOME CHAMOMILE TEA?

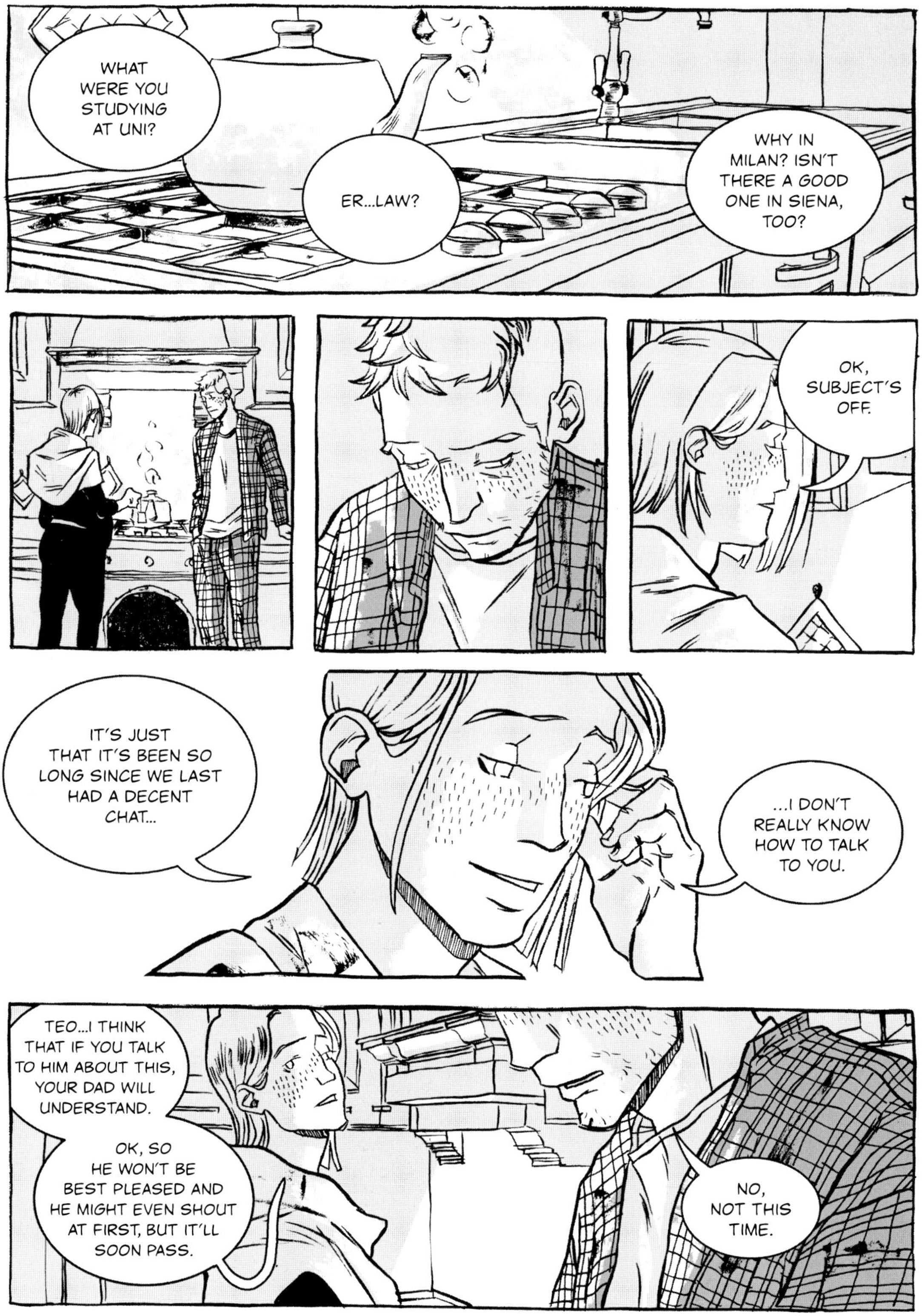
WHAT WERE YOU STUDYING AT UNI?
ER...LAW?
WHY IN MILAN? ISN'T THERE A GOOD ONE IN SIENA, TOO?
OK, SUBJECT'S OFF.
IT'S JUST THAT IT'S BEEN SO LONG SINCE WE LAST HAD A DECENT CHAT...
...I DON'T REALLY KNOW HOW TO TALK TO YOU.
TEO...I THINK THAT IF YOU TALK TO HIM ABOUT THIS, YOUR DAD WILL UNDERSTAND.
OK, SO HE WON'T BE BEST PLEASED AND HE MIGHT EVEN SHOUT AT FIRST, BUT IT'LL SOON PASS.
NO, NOT THIS TIME.

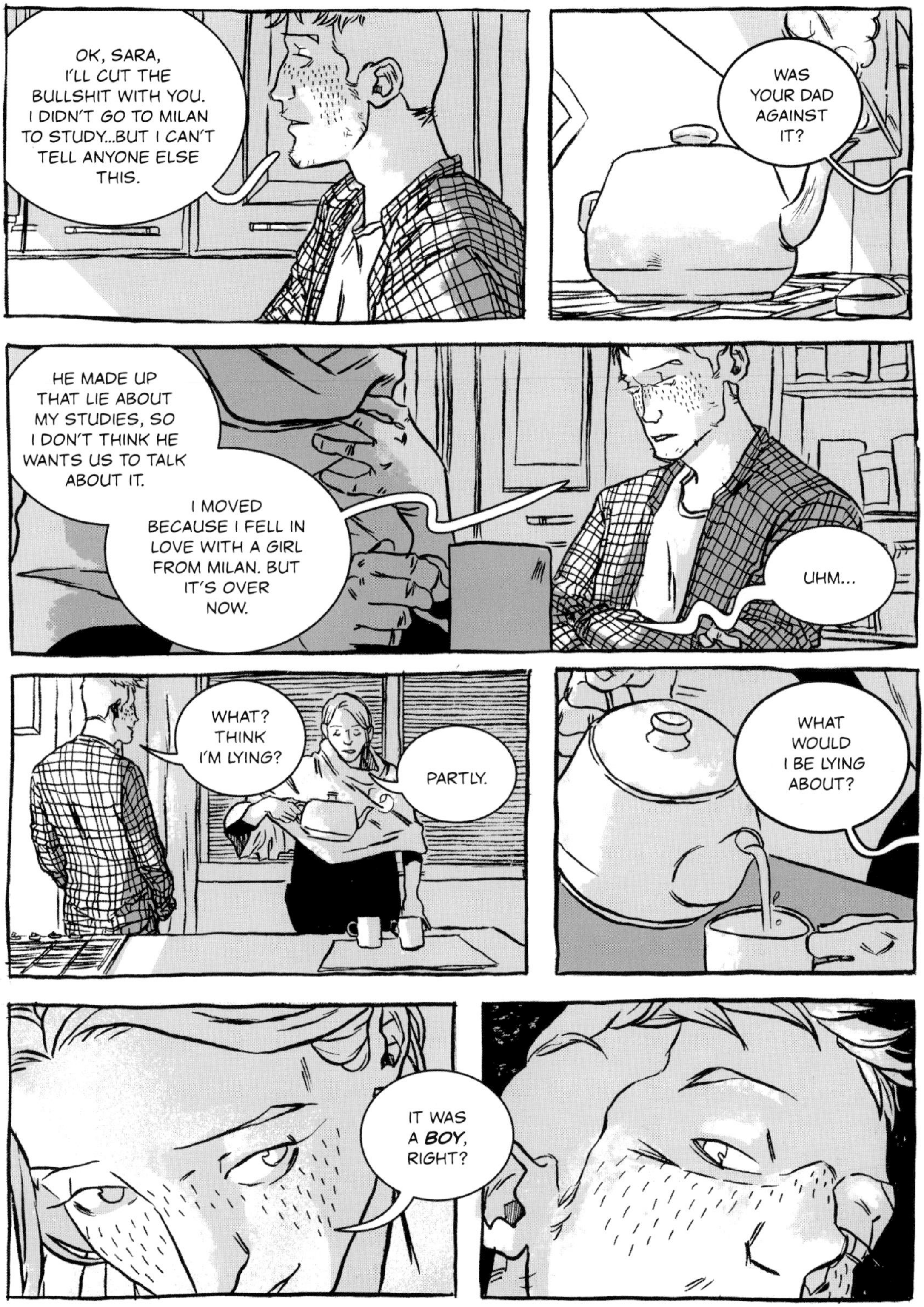
OK, SARA, I'LL CUT THE BULLSHIT WITH YOU. I DIDN'T GO TO MILAN TO STUDY...BUT I CAN'T TELL ANYONE ELSE THIS.
WAS YOUR DAD AGAINST IT?
HE MADE UP THAT LIE ABOUT MY STUDIES, SO I DON'T THINK HE WANTS US TO TALK ABOUT IT.
I MOVED BECAUSE I FELL IN LOVE WITH A GIRL FROM MILAN. BUT IT'S OVER NOW.
UHM...
WHAT? THINK I'M LYING?
PARTLY.
WHAT WOULD I BE LYING ABOUT?
IT WAS A **BOY**, RIGHT?

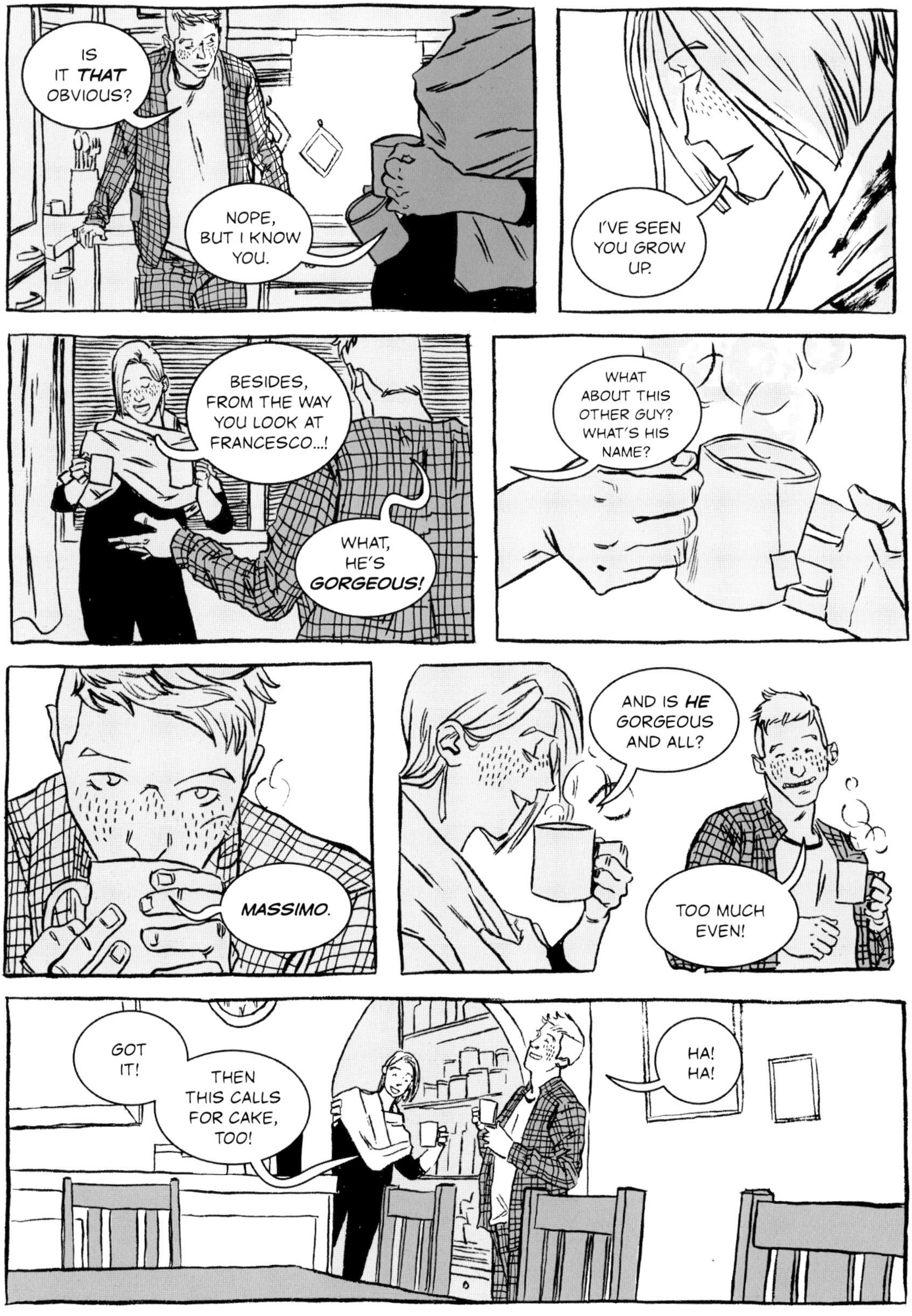
IS IT THAT OBVIOUS?
NOPE, BUT I KNOW YOU.
I'VE SEEN YOU GROW UP.
BESIDES, FROM THE WAY YOU LOOK AT FRANCESCO...!
WHAT, HE'S GORGEOUS!
WHAT ABOUT THIS OTHER GUY? WHAT'S HIS NAME?
MASSIMO.
AND IS HE GORGEOUS AND ALL?
TOO MUCH EVEN!
GOT IT!
THEN THIS CALLS FOR CAKE, TOO!
HA! HA!

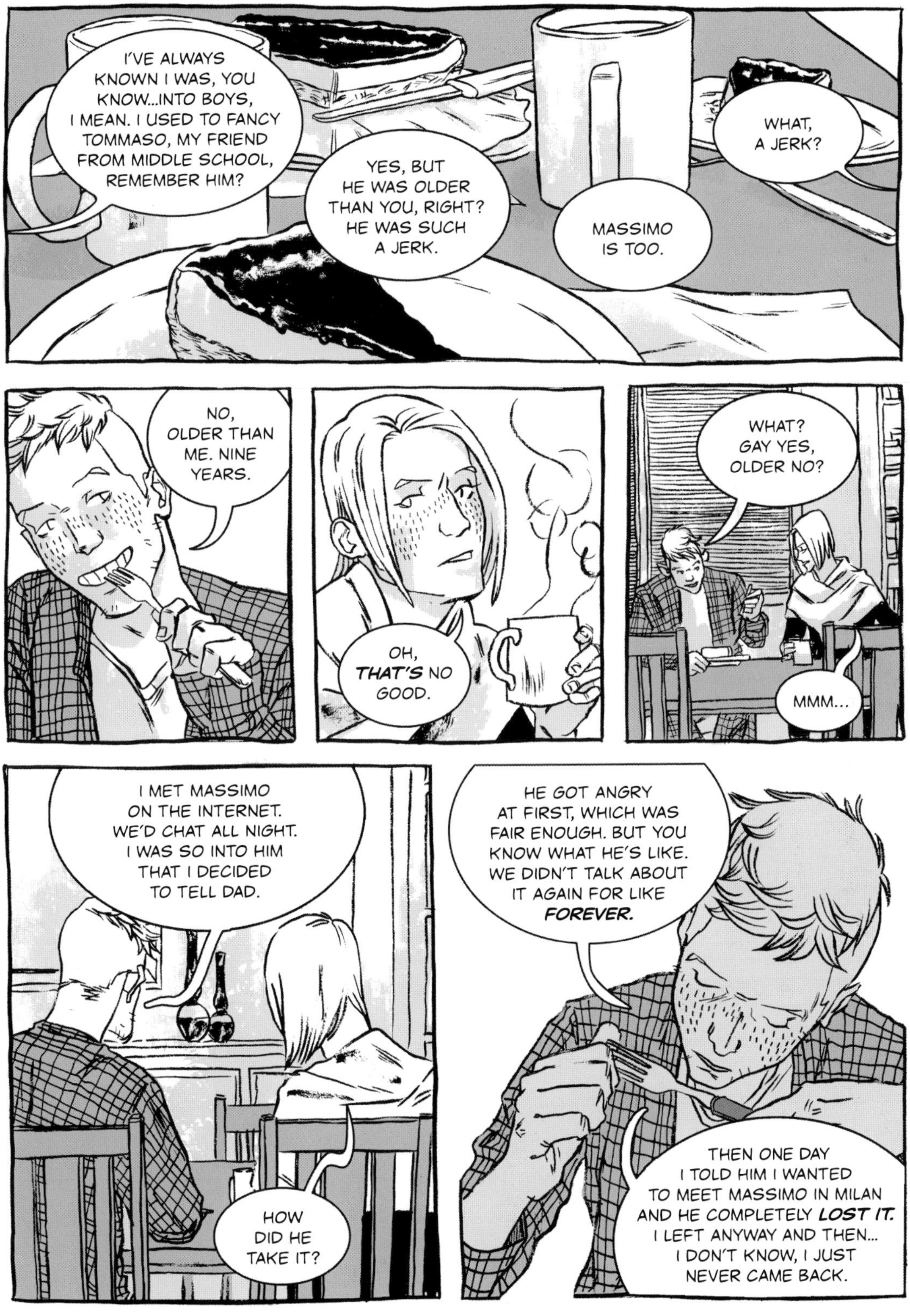
I'VE ALWAYS KNOWN I WAS, YOU KNOW...INTO BOYS, I MEAN. I USED TO FANCY TOMMASO, MY FRIEND FROM MIDDLE SCHOOL, REMEMBER HIM?
YES, BUT HE WAS OLDER THAN YOU, RIGHT? HE WAS SUCH A JERK.
MASSIMO IS TOO.
WHAT, A JERK?
NO, OLDER THAN ME. NINE YEARS.
OH, ***THAT'S*** NO GOOD.
WHAT? GAY YES, OLDER NO?
MMM...
I MET MASSIMO ON THE INTERNET. WE'D CHAT ALL NIGHT. I WAS SO INTO HIM THAT I DECIDED TO TELL DAD.
HOW DID HE TAKE IT?
HE GOT ANGRY AT FIRST, WHICH WAS FAIR ENOUGH. BUT YOU KNOW WHAT HE'S LIKE. WE DIDN'T TALK ABOUT IT AGAIN FOR LIKE ***FOREVER.***
THEN ONE DAY I TOLD HIM I WANTED TO MEET MASSIMO IN MILAN AND HE COMPLETELY ***LOST IT.*** I LEFT ANYWAY AND THEN... I DON'T KNOW, I JUST NEVER CAME BACK.

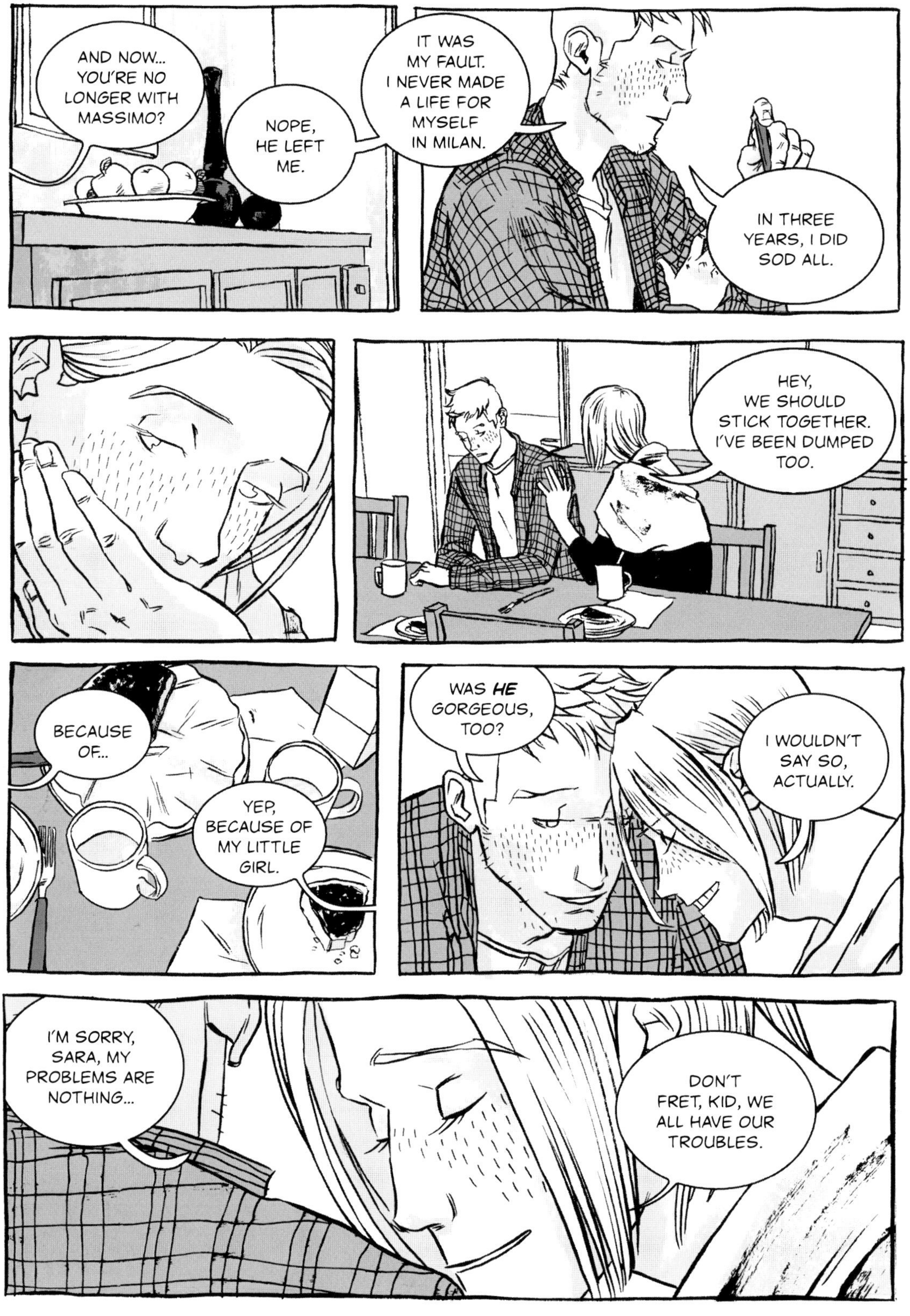
AND NOW... YOU'RE NO LONGER WITH MASSIMO?
NOPE, HE LEFT ME.
IT WAS MY FAULT. I NEVER MADE A LIFE FOR MYSELF IN MILAN.
IN THREE YEARS, I DID SOD ALL.
HEY, WE SHOULD STICK TOGETHER. I'VE BEEN DUMPED TOO.
BECAUSE OF...
YEP, BECAUSE OF MY LITTLE GIRL.
WAS **HE** GORGEOUS, TOO?
I WOULDN'T SAY SO, ACTUALLY.
I'M SORRY, SARA, MY PROBLEMS ARE NOTHING...
DON'T FRET, KID, WE ALL HAVE OUR TROUBLES.

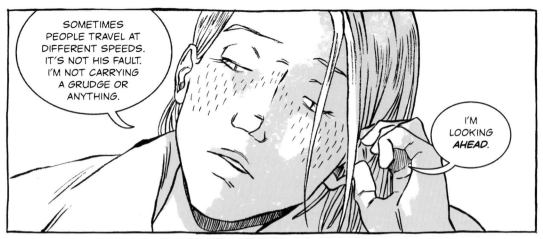

SOMETIMES PEOPLE TRAVEL AT DIFFERENT SPEEDS. IT'S NOT HIS FAULT. I'M NOT CARRYING A GRUDGE OR ANYTHING.

I'M LOOKING *AHEAD*.

PUT YOUR HAND HERE, TEO.

IT'S THIS LITTLE TROUBLEMAKER'S FAULT IF I CAN'T SLEEP TONIGHT.

SHE'S MOVING...

TOMORROW'S ALL ABOUT *HER*.

29

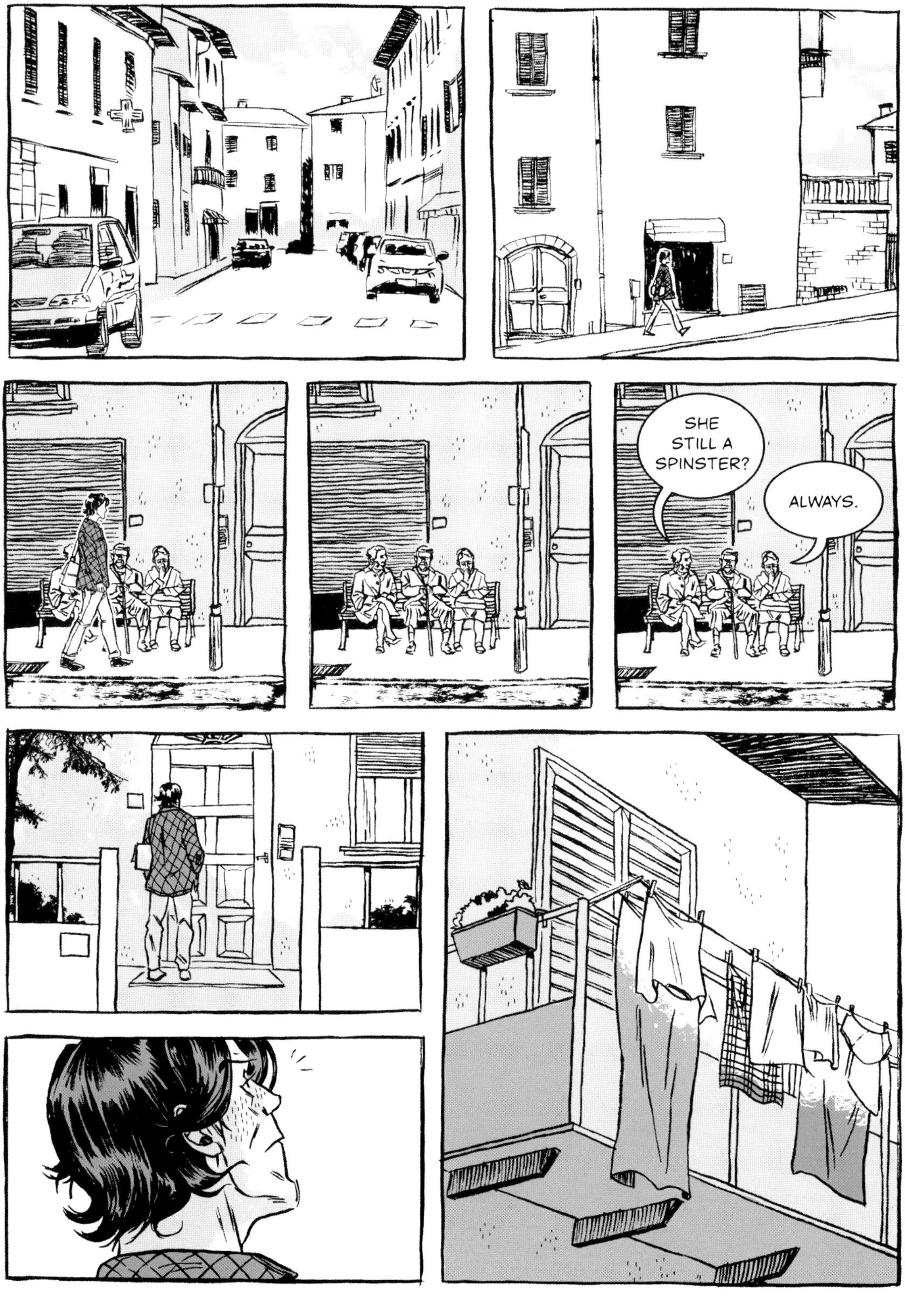
SHE STILL A SPINSTER?
ALWAYS.

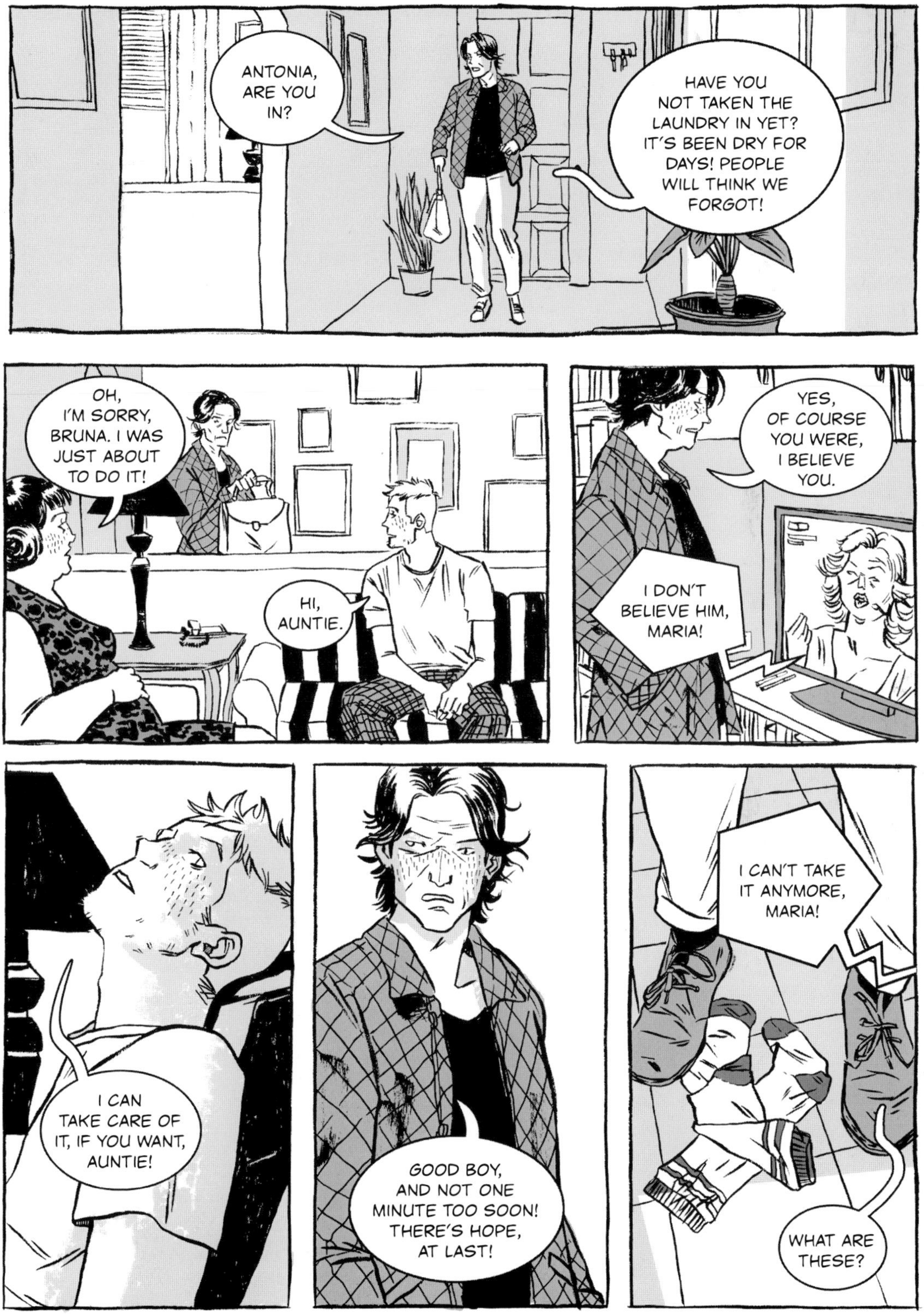
ANTONIA, ARE YOU IN?
HAVE YOU NOT TAKEN THE LAUNDRY IN YET? IT'S BEEN DRY FOR DAYS! PEOPLE WILL THINK WE FORGOT!
OH, I'M SORRY, BRUNA. I WAS JUST ABOUT TO DO IT!
HI, AUNTIE.
YES, OF COURSE YOU WERE, I BELIEVE YOU.
I DON'T BELIEVE HIM, MARIA!
I CAN TAKE CARE OF IT, IF YOU WANT, AUNTIE!
GOOD BOY, AND NOT ONE MINUTE TOO SOON! THERE'S HOPE, AT LAST!
I CAN'T TAKE IT ANYMORE, MARIA!
WHAT ARE THESE?

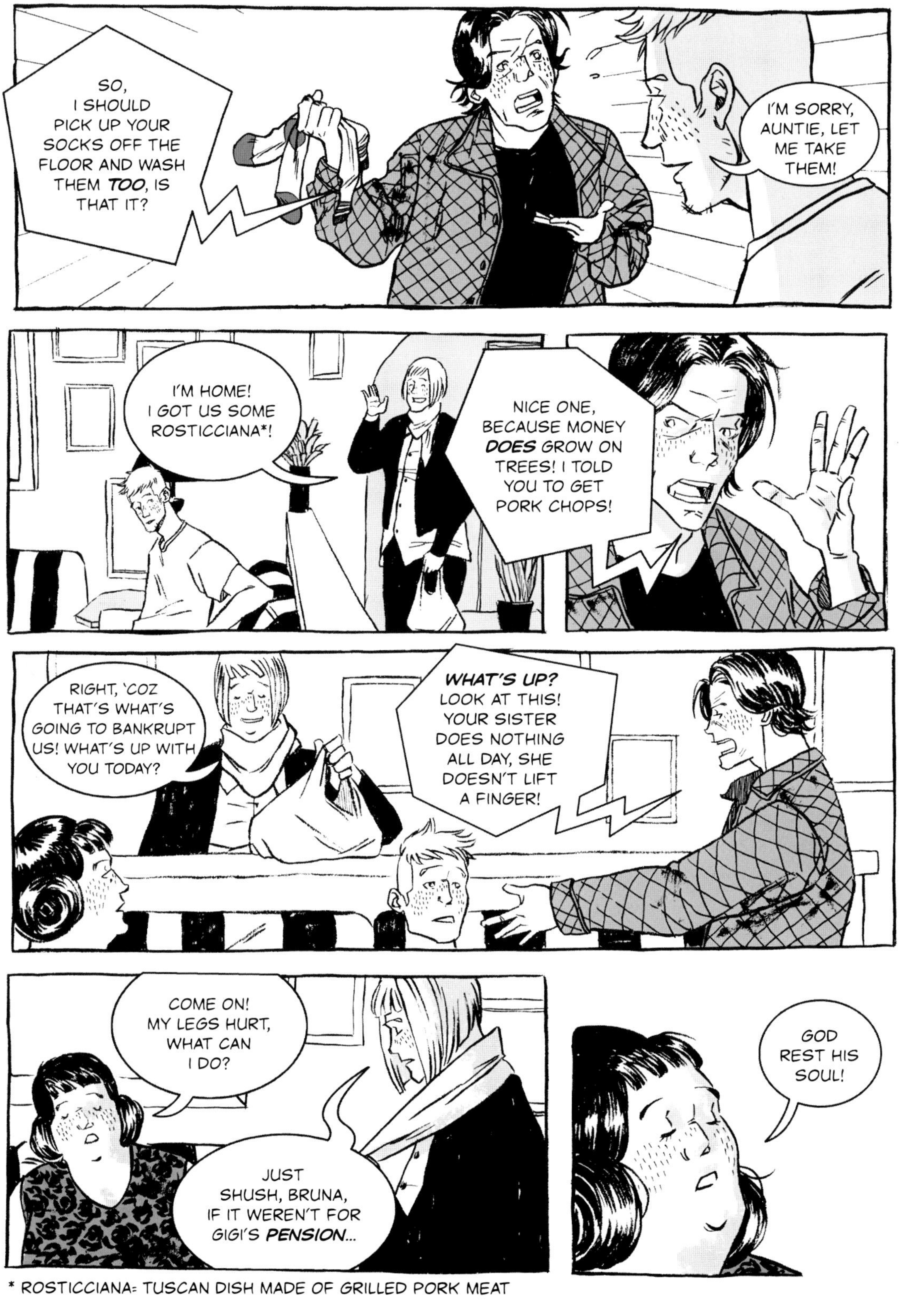
SO, I SHOULD PICK UP YOUR SOCKS OFF THE FLOOR AND WASH THEM ***TOO***, IS THAT IT?
I'M SORRY, AUNTIE, LET ME TAKE THEM!
I'M HOME! I GOT US SOME ROSTICCIANA*!
NICE ONE, BECAUSE MONEY ***DOES*** GROW ON TREES! I TOLD YOU TO GET PORK CHOPS!
RIGHT, 'COZ THAT'S WHAT'S GOING TO BANKRUPT US! WHAT'S UP WITH YOU TODAY?
WHAT'S UP? LOOK AT THIS! YOUR SISTER DOES NOTHING ALL DAY, SHE DOESN'T LIFT A FINGER!
COME ON! MY LEGS HURT, WHAT CAN I DO?
JUST SHUSH, BRUNA, IF IT WEREN'T FOR GIGI'S ***PENSION***...
GOD REST HIS SOUL!

* ROSTICCIANA= TUSCAN DISH MADE OF GRILLED PORK MEAT

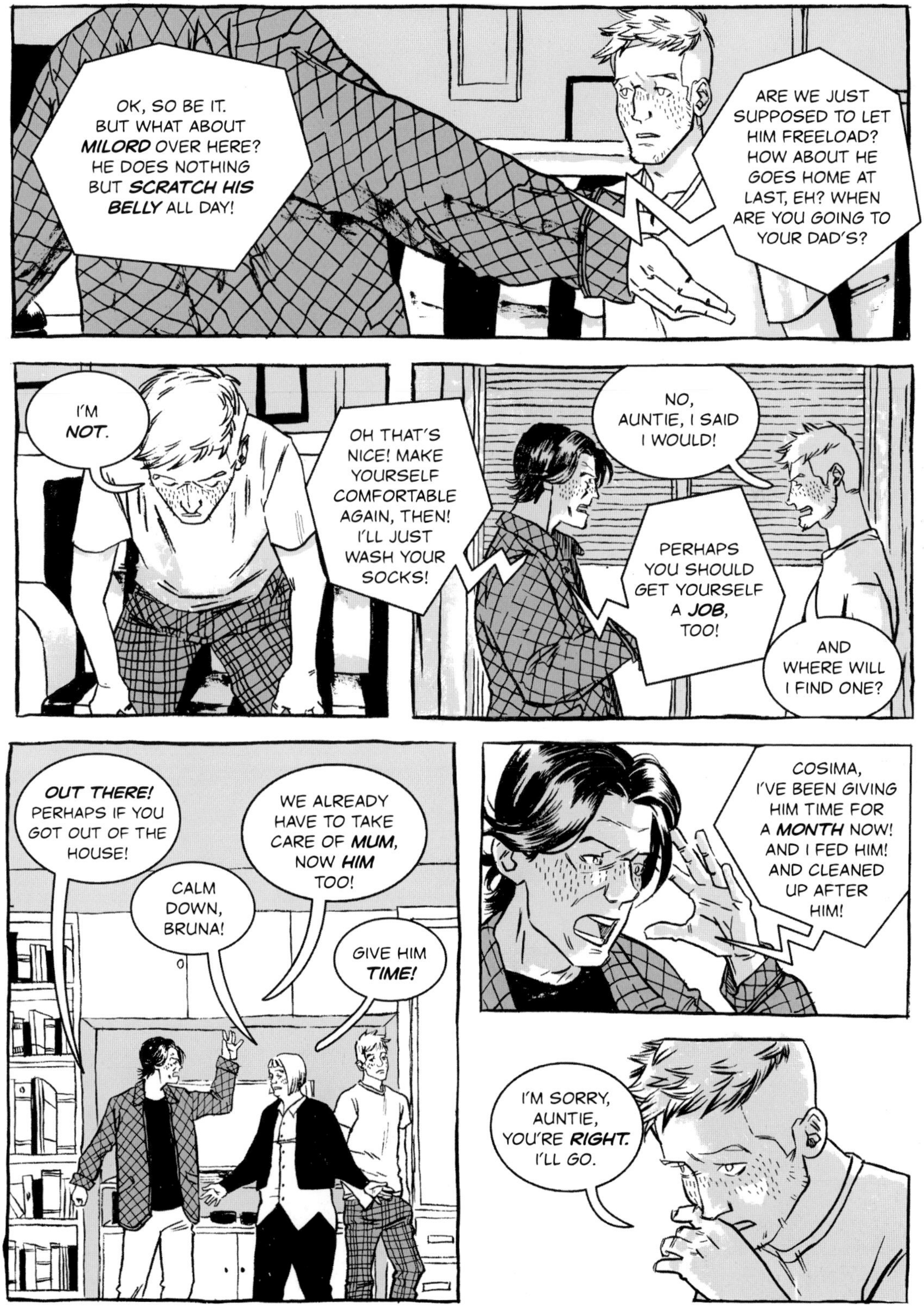
OK, SO BE IT. BUT WHAT ABOUT MILORD OVER HERE? HE DOES NOTHING BUT SCRATCH HIS BELLY ALL DAY!
ARE WE JUST SUPPOSED TO LET HIM FREELOAD? HOW ABOUT HE GOES HOME AT LAST, EH? WHEN ARE YOU GOING TO YOUR DAD'S?
I'M NOT.
OH THAT'S NICE! MAKE YOURSELF COMFORTABLE AGAIN, THEN! I'LL JUST WASH YOUR SOCKS!
NO, AUNTIE, I SAID I WOULD!
PERHAPS YOU SHOULD GET YOURSELF A JOB, TOO!
AND WHERE WILL I FIND ONE?
OUT THERE! PERHAPS IF YOU GOT OUT OF THE HOUSE!
WE ALREADY HAVE TO TAKE CARE OF MUM, NOW HIM TOO!
CALM DOWN, BRUNA!
GIVE HIM TIME!
COSIMA, I'VE BEEN GIVING HIM TIME FOR A MONTH NOW! AND I FED HIM! AND CLEANED UP AFTER HIM!
I'M SORRY, AUNTIE, YOU'RE RIGHT. I'LL GO.

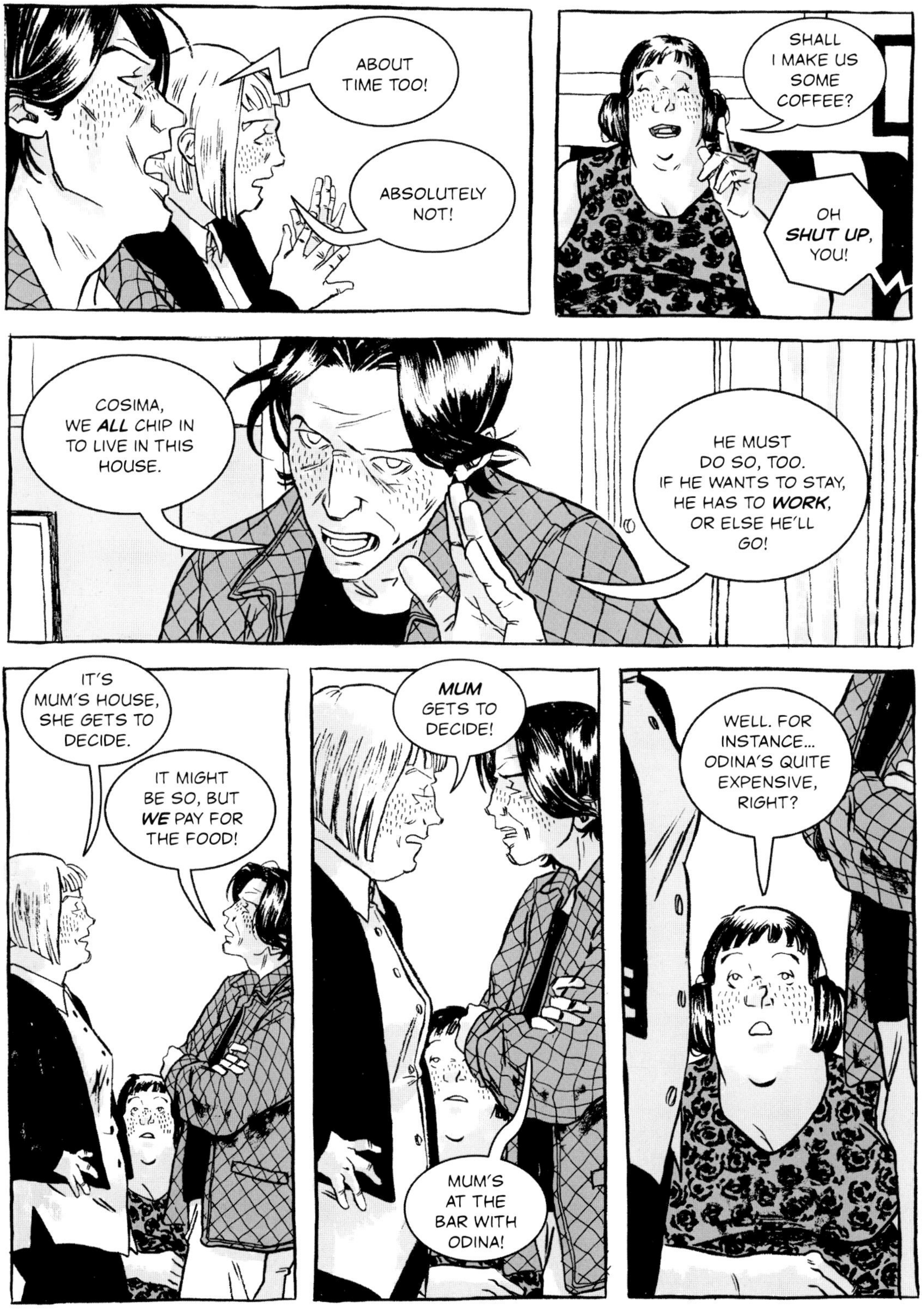
ABOUT TIME TOO!
ABSOLUTELY NOT!
SHALL I MAKE US SOME COFFEE?
OH **SHUT UP**, YOU!
COSIMA, WE **ALL** CHIP IN TO LIVE IN THIS HOUSE.
HE MUST DO SO, TOO. IF HE WANTS TO STAY, HE HAS TO **WORK**, OR ELSE HE'LL GO!
IT'S MUM'S HOUSE, SHE GETS TO DECIDE.
IT MIGHT BE SO, BUT **WE** PAY FOR THE FOOD!
MUM GETS TO DECIDE!
MUM'S AT THE BAR WITH ODINA!
WELL. FOR INSTANCE... ODINA'S QUITE EXPENSIVE, RIGHT?

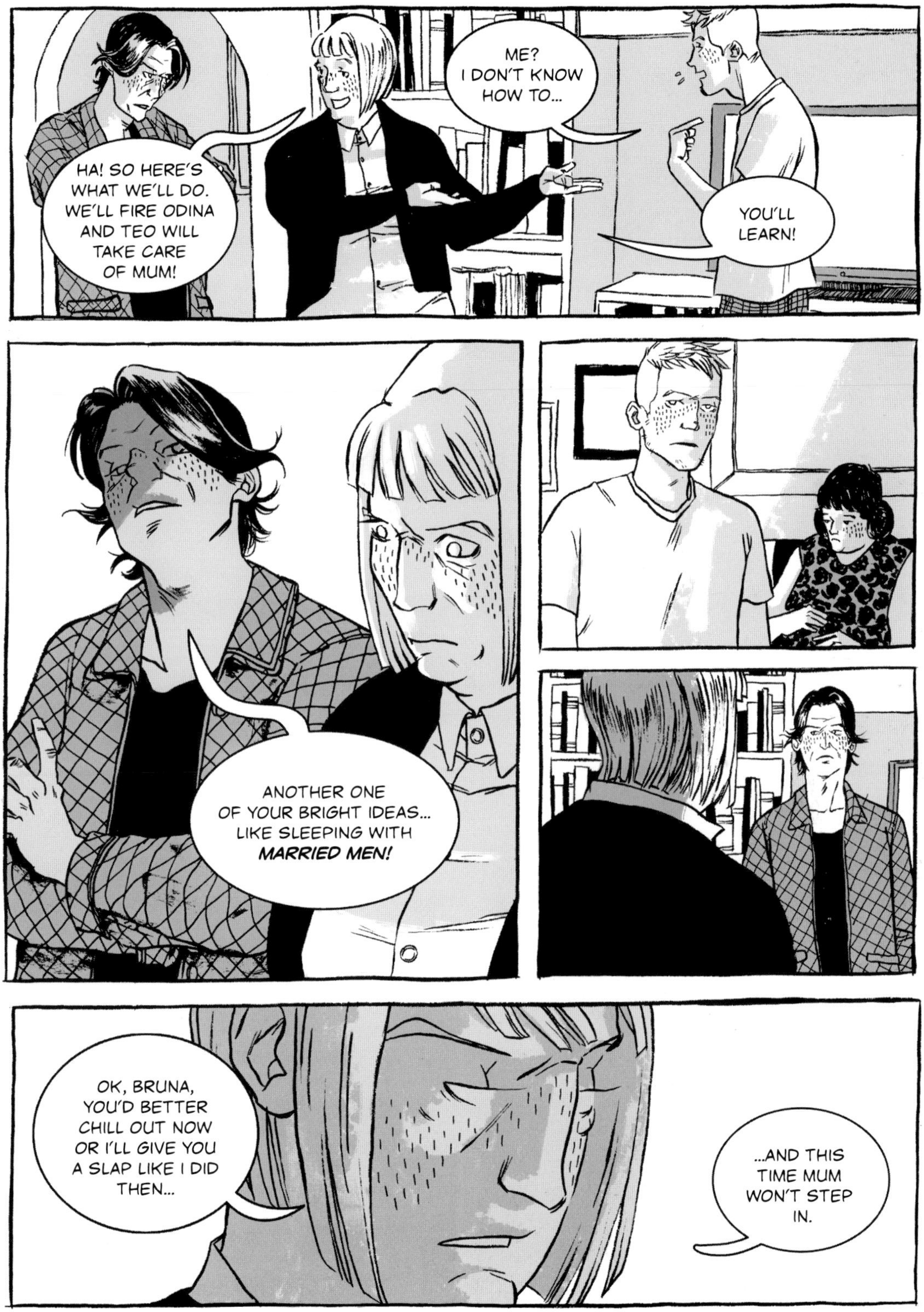
ME? I DON'T KNOW HOW TO...
HA! SO HERE'S WHAT WE'LL DO. WE'LL FIRE ODINA AND TEO WILL TAKE CARE OF MUM!
YOU'LL LEARN!
ANOTHER ONE OF YOUR BRIGHT IDEAS... LIKE SLEEPING WITH ***MARRIED MEN!***
OK, BRUNA, YOU'D BETTER CHILL OUT NOW OR I'LL GIVE YOU A SLAP LIKE I DID THEN...
...AND THIS TIME MUM WON'T STEP IN.

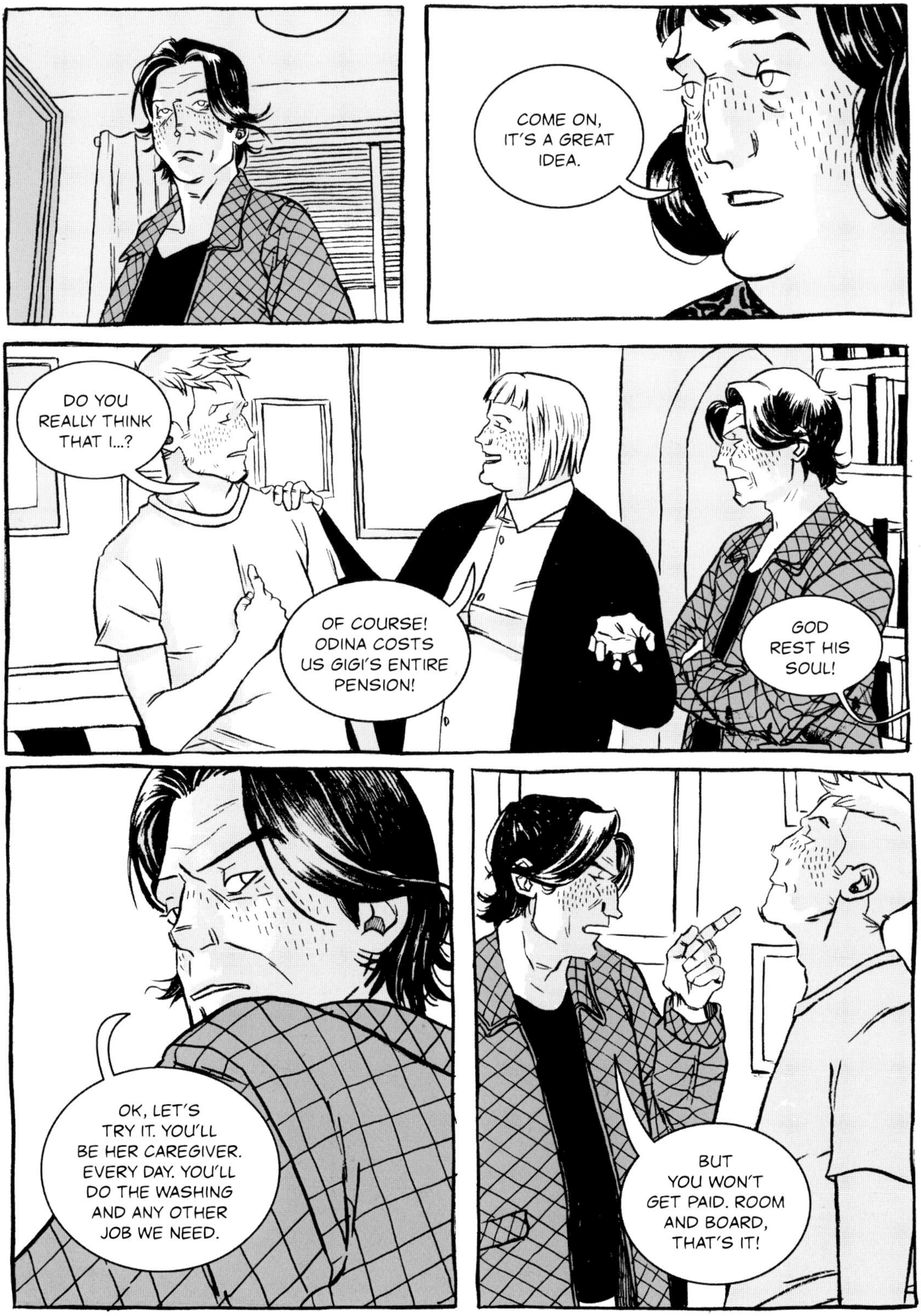
COME ON, IT'S A GREAT IDEA.
DO YOU REALLY THINK THAT I...?
OF COURSE! ODINA COSTS US GIGI'S ENTIRE PENSION!
GOD REST HIS SOUL!
OK, LET'S TRY IT. YOU'LL BE HER CAREGIVER. EVERY DAY. YOU'LL DO THE WASHING AND ANY OTHER JOB WE NEED.
BUT YOU WON'T GET PAID. ROOM AND BOARD, THAT'S IT!

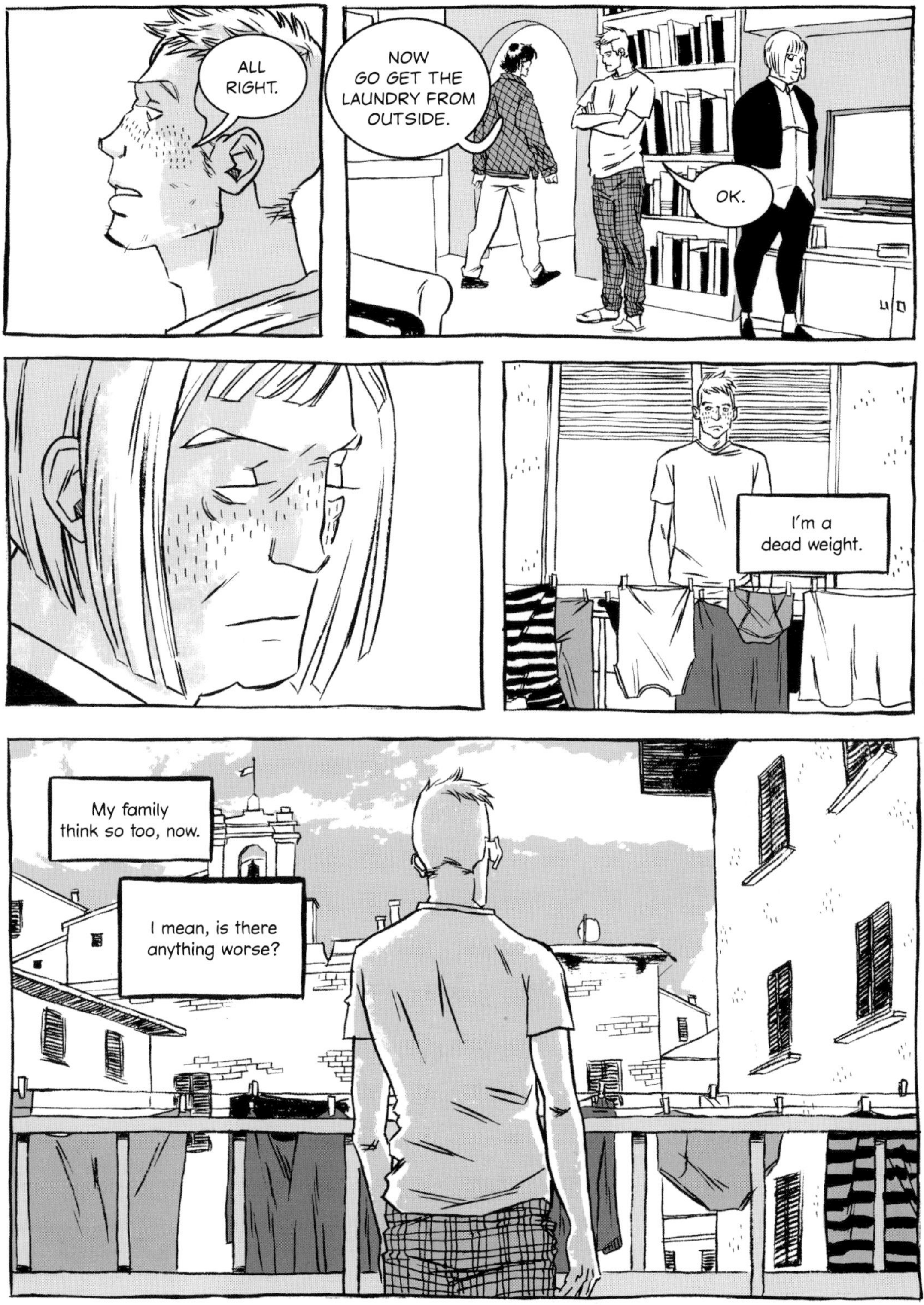
ALL RIGHT.
NOW GO GET THE LAUNDRY FROM OUTSIDE.
OK.
I'm a dead weight.
My family think so too, now.
I mean, is there anything worse?

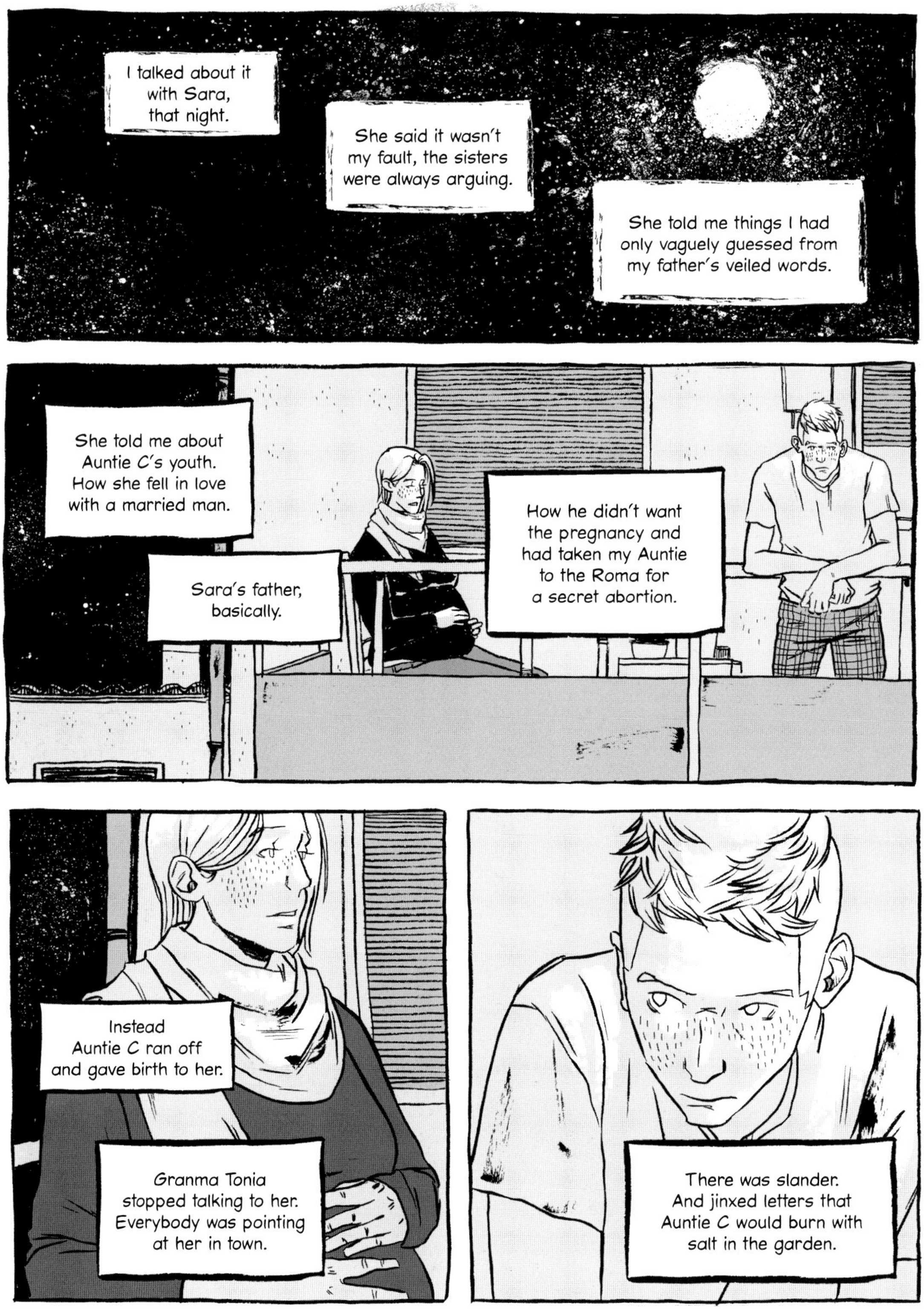
I talked about it with Sara, that night.
She said it wasn't my fault, the sisters were always arguing.
She told me things I had only vaguely guessed from my father's veiled words.
She told me about Auntie C's youth. How she fell in love with a married man.
Sara's father, basically.
How he didn't want the pregnancy and had taken my Auntie to the Roma for a secret abortion.
Instead Auntie C ran off and gave birth to her.
Granma Tonia stopped talking to her. Everybody was pointing at her in town.
There was slander. And jinxed letters that Auntie C would burn with salt in the garden.

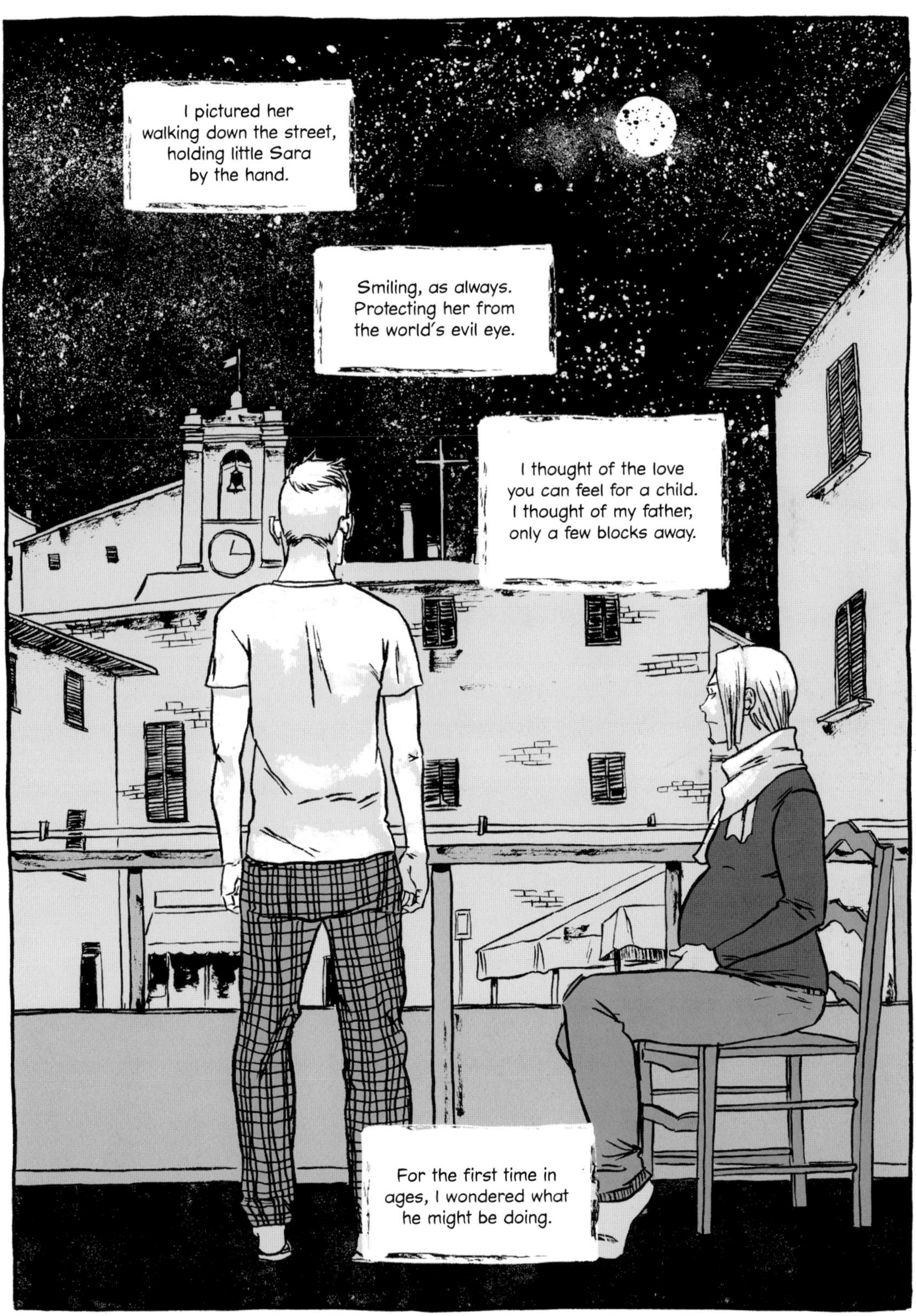
I pictured her walking down the street, holding little Sara by the hand.
Smiling, as always. Protecting her from the world's evil eye.
I thought of the love you can feel for a child. I thought of my father, only a few blocks away.
For the first time in ages, I wondered what he might be doing.

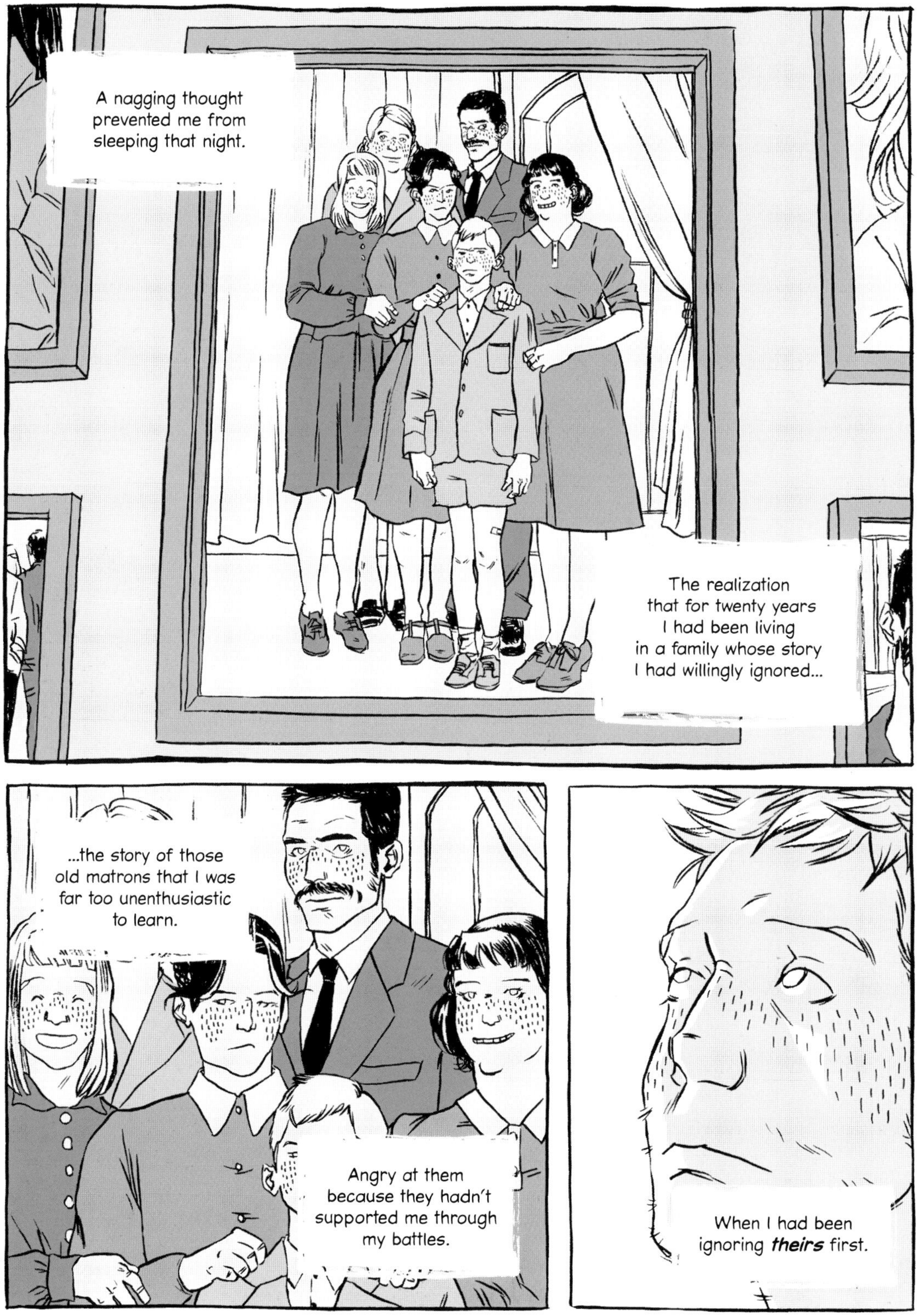
A nagging thought prevented me from sleeping that night.
The realization that for twenty years I had been living in a family whose story I had willingly ignored...
...the story of those old matrons that I was far too unenthusiastic to learn.
Angry at them because they hadn't supported me through my battles.
When I had been ignoring ***theirs*** first.

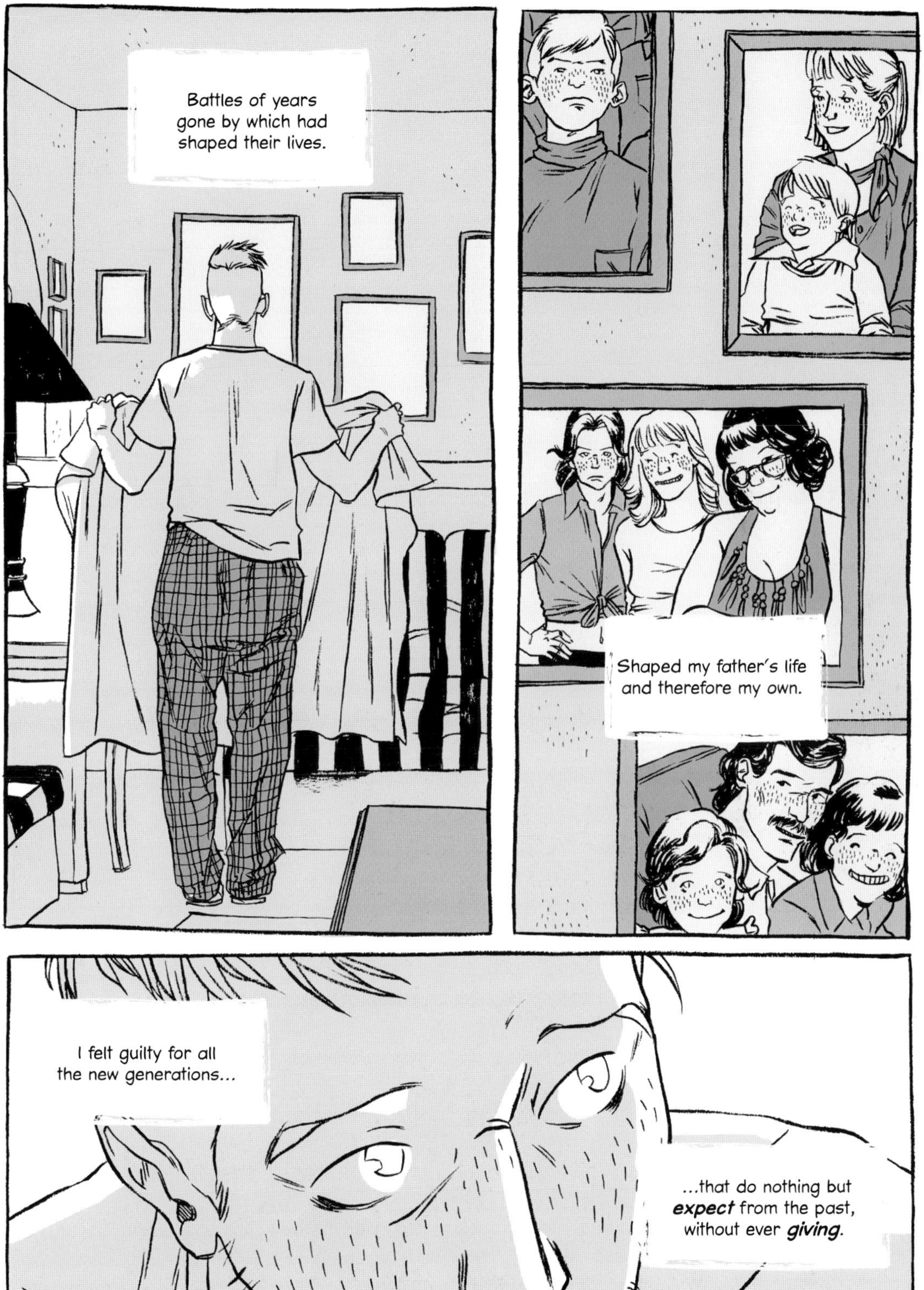
Battles of years gone by which had shaped their lives.
Shaped my father's life and therefore my own.
I felt guilty for all the new generations...
...that do nothing but ***expect*** from the past, without ever ***giving***.

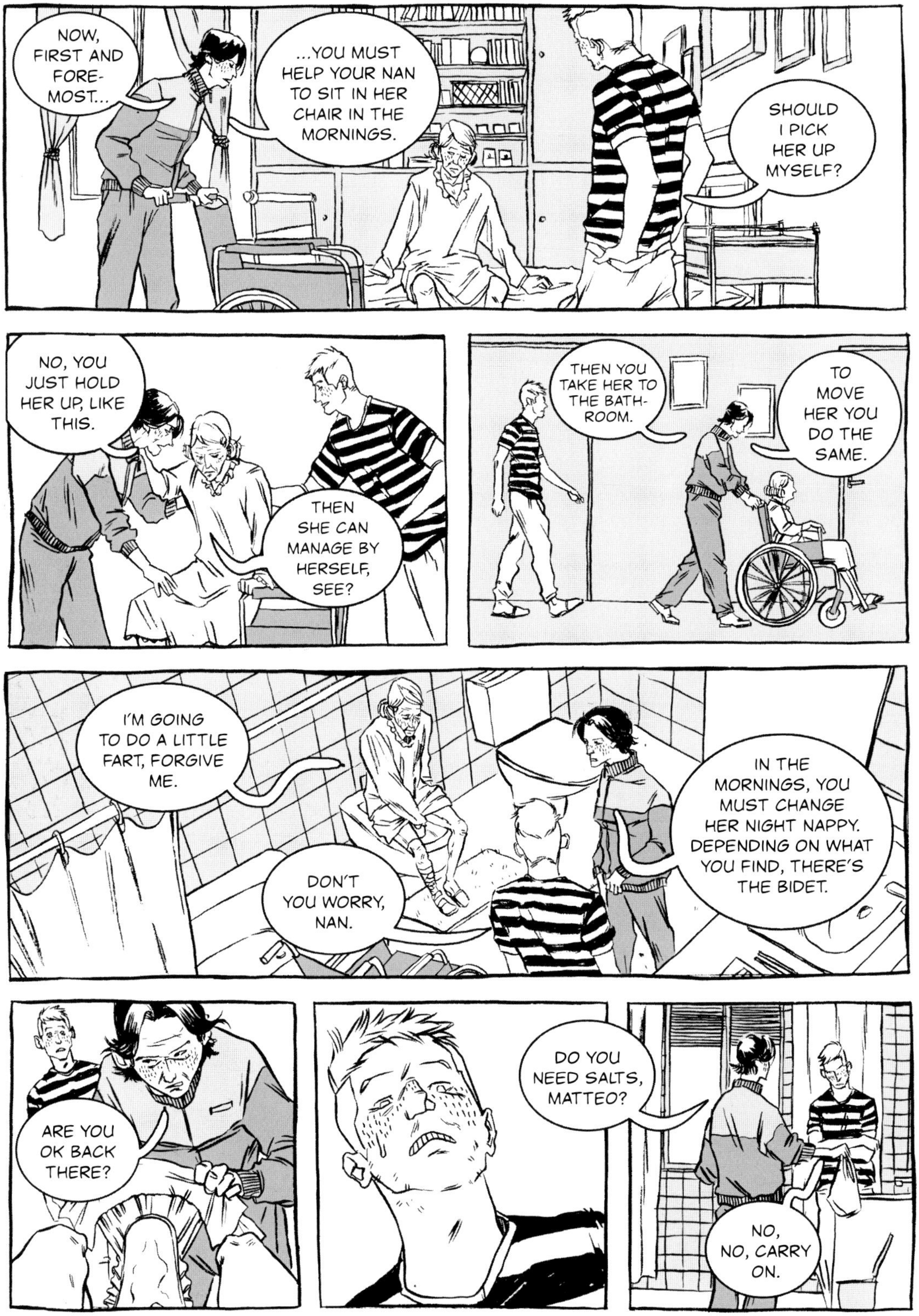
NOW, FIRST AND FORE-MOST...
...YOU MUST HELP YOUR NAN TO SIT IN HER CHAIR IN THE MORNINGS.
SHOULD I PICK HER UP MYSELF?
NO, YOU JUST HOLD HER UP, LIKE THIS.
THEN SHE CAN MANAGE BY HERSELF, SEE?
THEN YOU TAKE HER TO THE BATH-ROOM.
TO MOVE HER YOU DO THE SAME.
I'M GOING TO DO A LITTLE FART, FORGIVE ME.
DON'T YOU WORRY, NAN.
IN THE MORNINGS, YOU MUST CHANGE HER NIGHT NAPPY. DEPENDING ON WHAT YOU FIND, THERE'S THE BIDET.
ARE YOU OK BACK THERE?
DO YOU NEED SALTS, MATTEO?
NO, NO, CARRY ON.

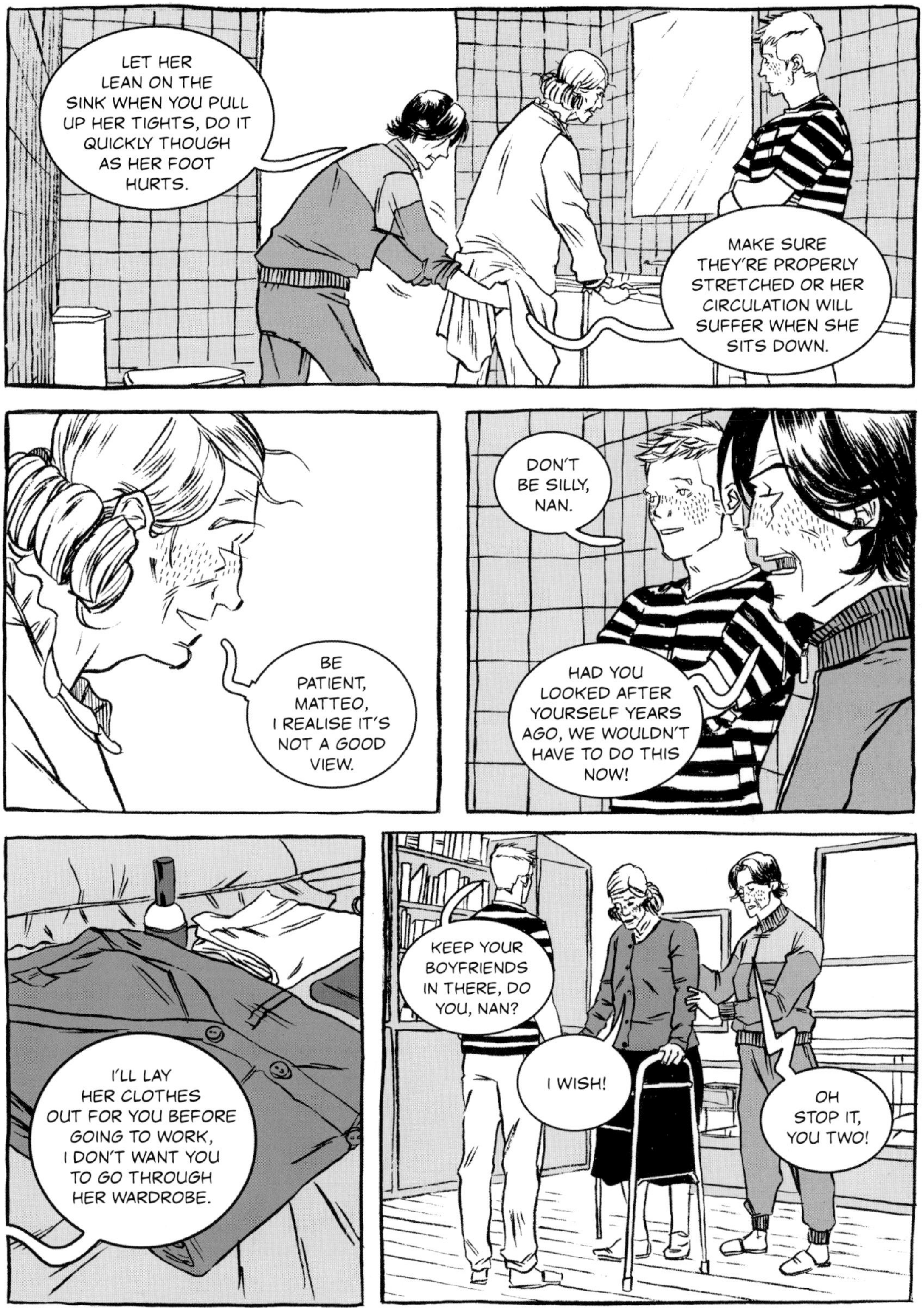
LET HER LEAN ON THE SINK WHEN YOU PULL UP HER TIGHTS, DO IT QUICKLY THOUGH AS HER FOOT HURTS.
MAKE SURE THEY'RE PROPERLY STRETCHED OR HER CIRCULATION WILL SUFFER WHEN SHE SITS DOWN.
BE PATIENT, MATTEO, I REALISE IT'S NOT A GOOD VIEW.
DON'T BE SILLY, NAN.
HAD YOU LOOKED AFTER YOURSELF YEARS AGO, WE WOULDN'T HAVE TO DO THIS NOW!
I'LL LAY HER CLOTHES OUT FOR YOU BEFORE GOING TO WORK, I DON'T WANT YOU TO GO THROUGH HER WARDROBE.
KEEP YOUR BOYFRIENDS IN THERE, DO YOU, NAN?
I WISH!
OH STOP IT, YOU TWO!

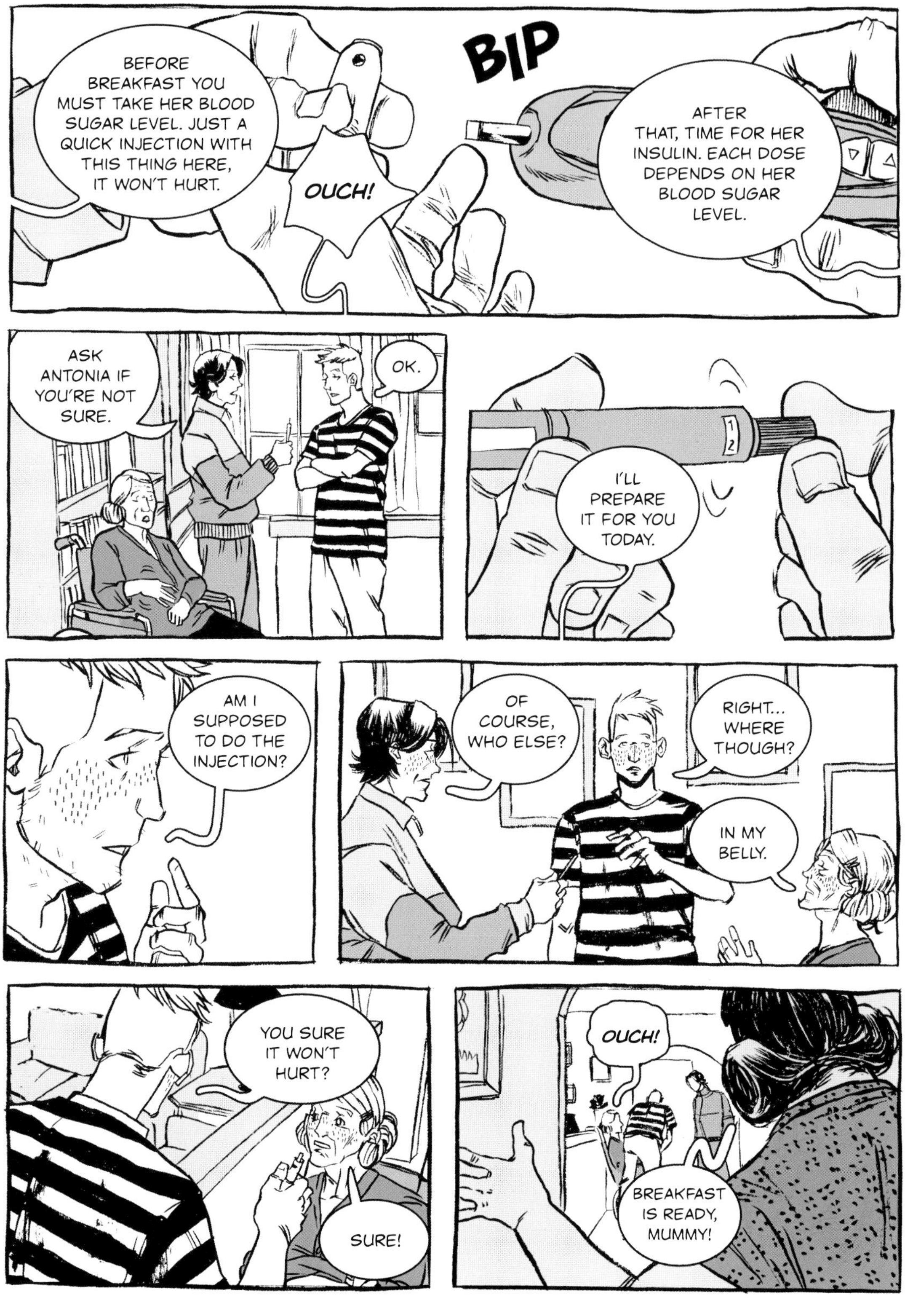
BEFORE BREAKFAST YOU MUST TAKE HER BLOOD SUGAR LEVEL. JUST A QUICK INJECTION WITH THIS THING HERE, IT WON'T HURT.
OUCH!
BIP
AFTER THAT, TIME FOR HER INSULIN. EACH DOSE DEPENDS ON HER BLOOD SUGAR LEVEL.
ASK ANTONIA IF YOU'RE NOT SURE.
OK.
I'LL PREPARE IT FOR YOU TODAY.
AM I SUPPOSED TO DO THE INJECTION?
OF COURSE, WHO ELSE?
RIGHT... WHERE THOUGH?
IN MY BELLY.
YOU SURE IT WON'T HURT?
SURE!
OUCH!
BREAKFAST IS READY, MUMMY!

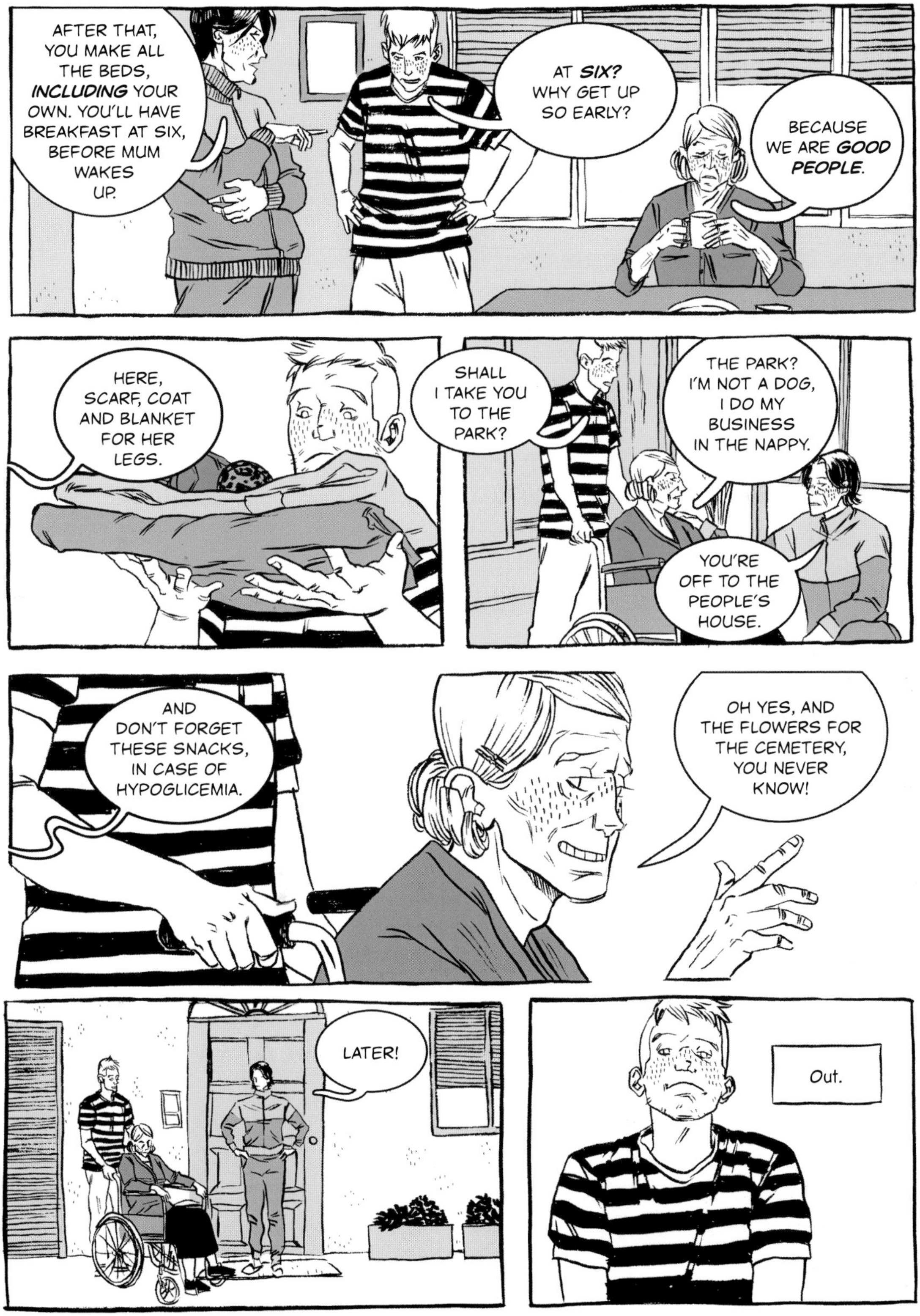
AFTER THAT, YOU MAKE ALL THE BEDS, **INCLUDING** YOUR OWN. YOU'LL HAVE BREAKFAST AT SIX, BEFORE MUM WAKES UP.
AT **SIX?** WHY GET UP SO EARLY?
BECAUSE WE ARE **GOOD PEOPLE**.
HERE, SCARF, COAT AND BLANKET FOR HER LEGS.
SHALL I TAKE YOU TO THE PARK?
THE PARK? I'M NOT A DOG, I DO MY BUSINESS IN THE NAPPY.
YOU'RE OFF TO THE PEOPLE'S HOUSE.
AND DON'T FORGET THESE SNACKS, IN CASE OF HYPOGLICEMIA.
OH YES, AND THE FLOWERS FOR THE CEMETERY, YOU NEVER KNOW!
LATER!
Out.

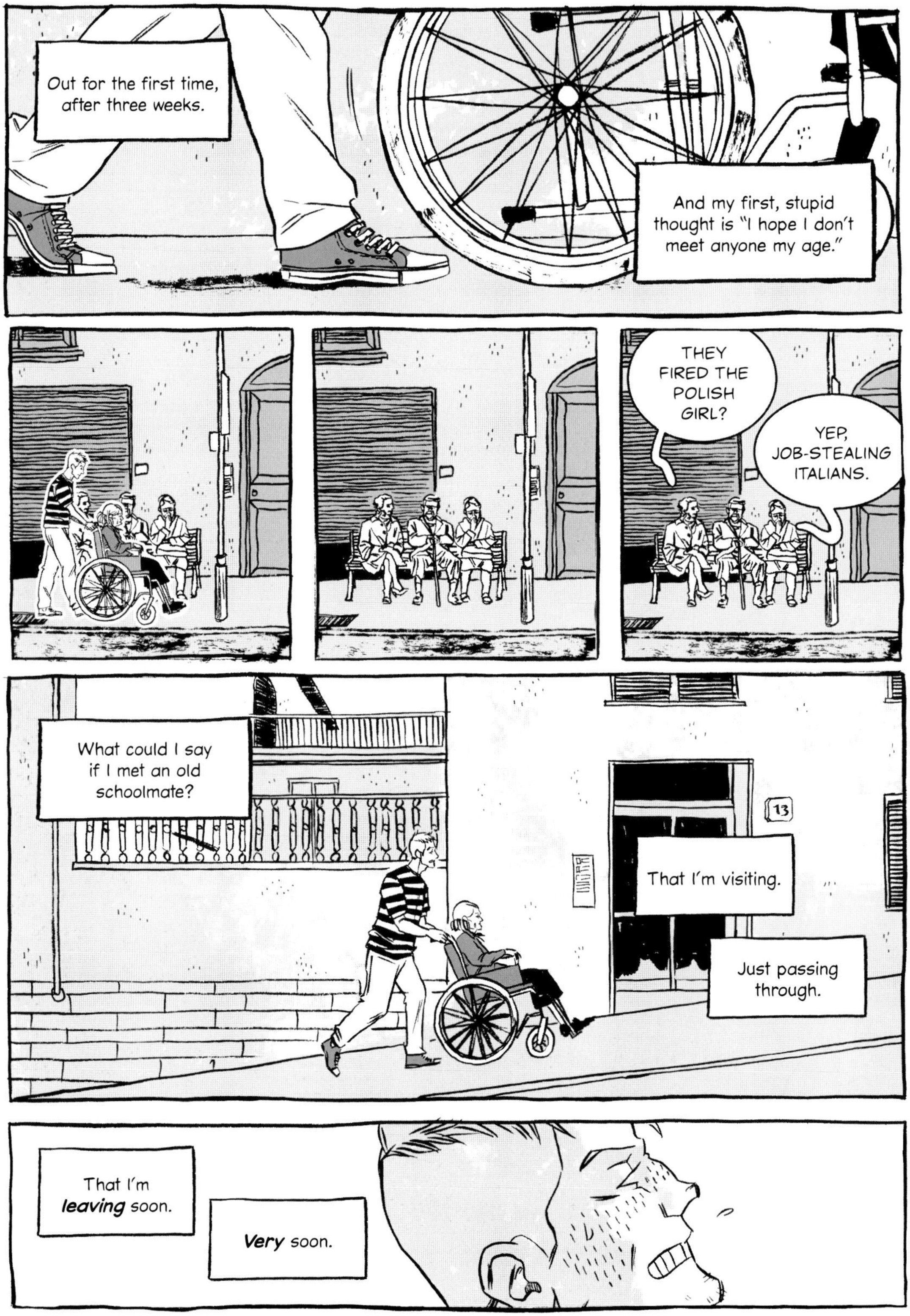
Out for the first time, after three weeks.
And my first, stupid thought is "I hope I don't meet anyone my age."
THEY FIRED THE POLISH GIRL?
YEP, JOB-STEALING ITALIANS.
What could I say if I met an old schoolmate?
13
That I'm visiting.
Just passing through.
That I'm *leaving* soon.
Very soon.

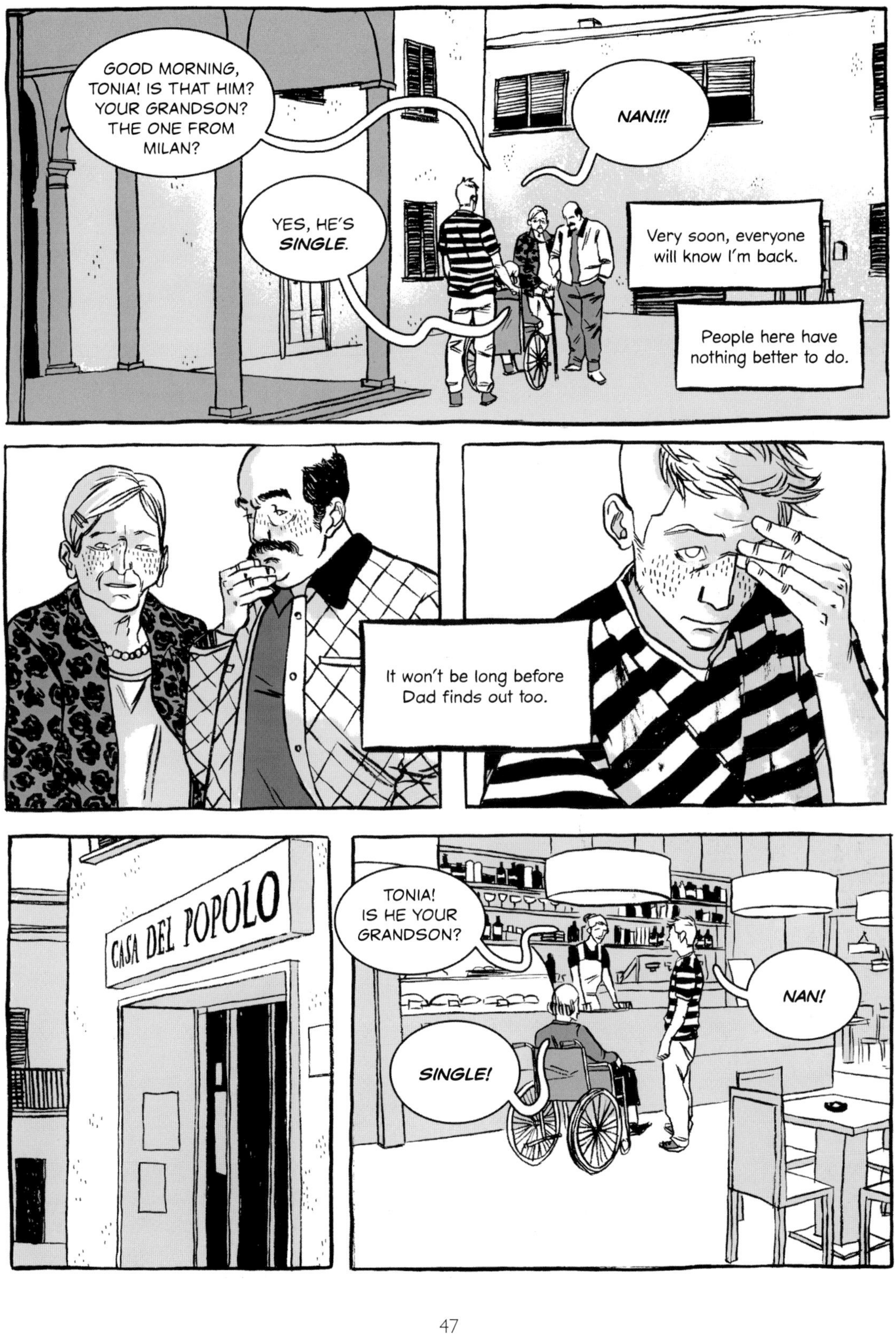
GOOD MORNING, TONIA! IS THAT HIM? YOUR GRANDSON? THE ONE FROM MILAN?
YES, HE'S *SINGLE*.
NAN!!!
Very soon, everyone will know I'm back.
People here have nothing better to do.
It won't be long before Dad finds out too.
CASA DEL POPOLO
TONIA! IS HE YOUR GRANDSON?
SINGLE!
NAN!

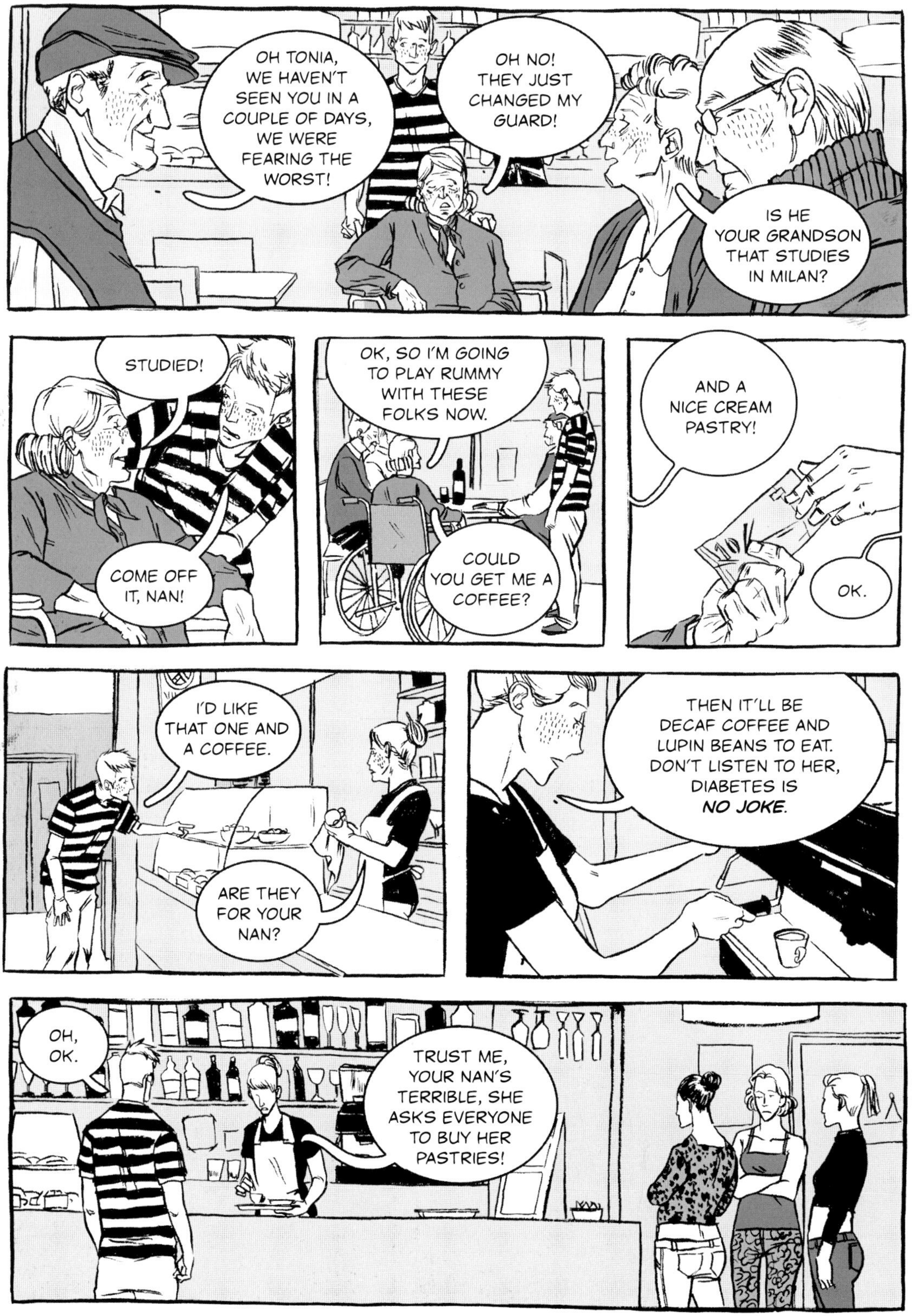
OH TONIA, WE HAVEN'T SEEN YOU IN A COUPLE OF DAYS, WE WERE FEARING THE WORST!
OH NO! THEY JUST CHANGED MY GUARD!
IS HE YOUR GRANDSON THAT STUDIES IN MILAN?
STUDIED!
COME OFF IT, NAN!
OK, SO I'M GOING TO PLAY RUMMY WITH THESE FOLKS NOW.
COULD YOU GET ME A COFFEE?
AND A NICE CREAM PASTRY!
OK.
I'D LIKE THAT ONE AND A COFFEE.
ARE THEY FOR YOUR NAN?
THEN IT'LL BE DECAF COFFEE AND LUPIN BEANS TO EAT. DON'T LISTEN TO HER, DIABETES IS ***NO JOKE***.
OH, OK.
TRUST ME, YOUR NAN'S TERRIBLE, SHE ASKS EVERYONE TO BUY HER PASTRIES!

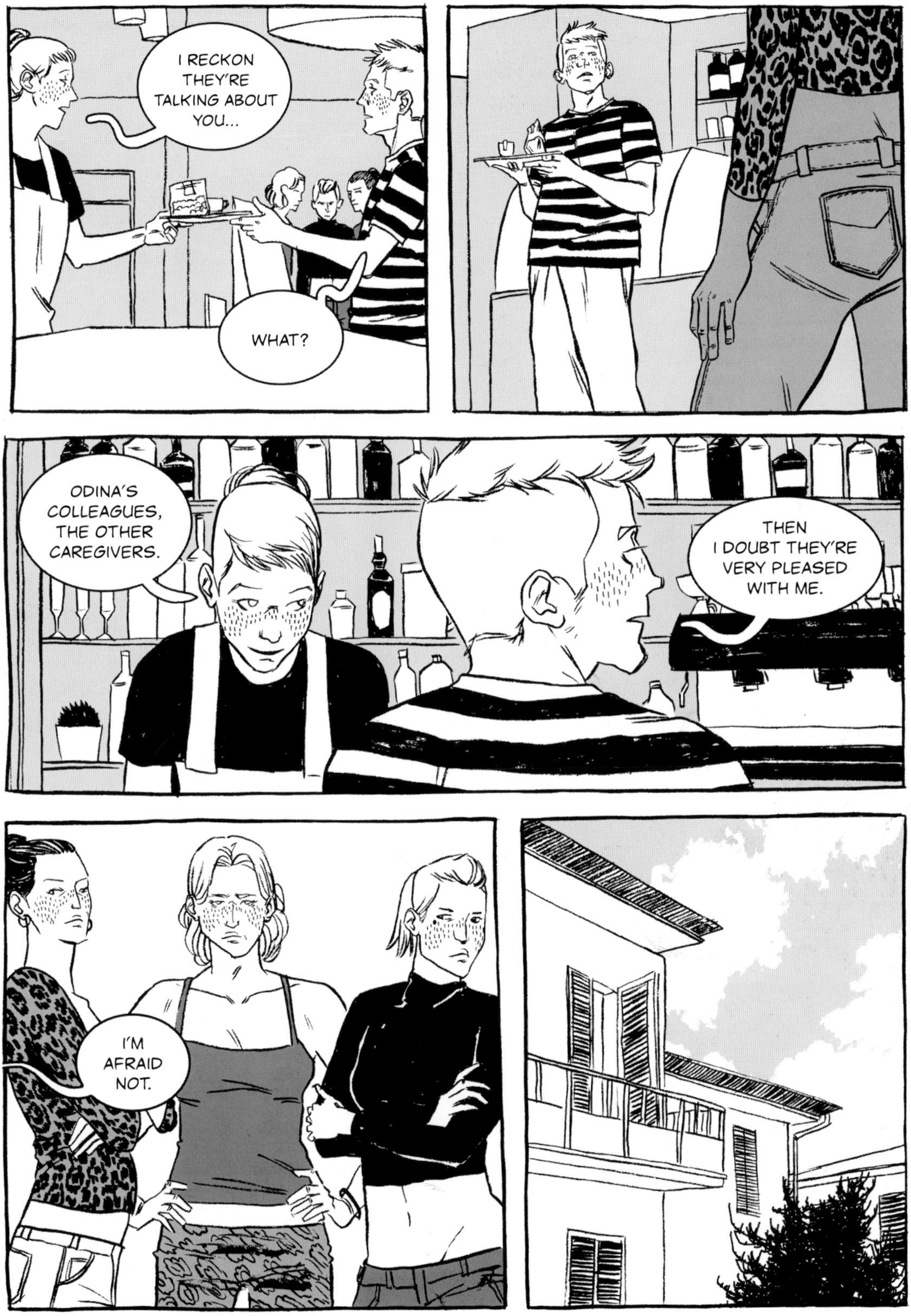
I RECKON THEY'RE TALKING ABOUT YOU...
WHAT?
ODINA'S COLLEAGUES, THE OTHER CAREGIVERS.
THEN I DOUBT THEY'RE VERY PLEASED WITH ME.
I'M AFRAID NOT.

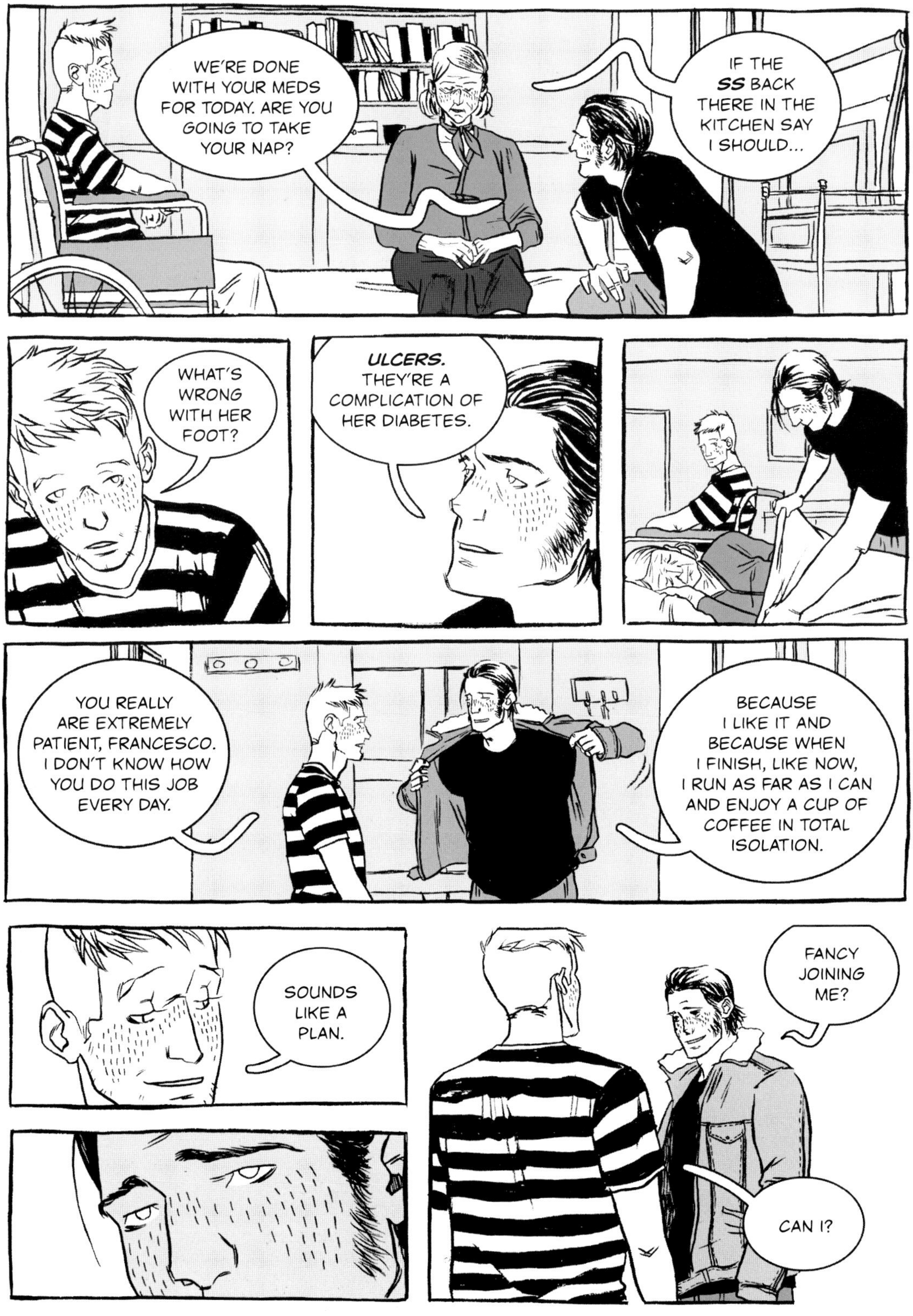
WE'RE DONE WITH YOUR MEDS FOR TODAY. ARE YOU GOING TO TAKE YOUR NAP?
IF THE *SS* BACK THERE IN THE KITCHEN SAY I SHOULD...
WHAT'S WRONG WITH HER FOOT?
ULCERS. THEY'RE A COMPLICATION OF HER DIABETES.
YOU REALLY ARE EXTREMELY PATIENT, FRANCESCO. I DON'T KNOW HOW YOU DO THIS JOB EVERY DAY.
BECAUSE I LIKE IT AND BECAUSE WHEN I FINISH, LIKE NOW, I RUN AS FAR AS I CAN AND ENJOY A CUP OF COFFEE IN TOTAL ISOLATION.
SOUNDS LIKE A PLAN.
FANCY JOINING ME?
CAN I?

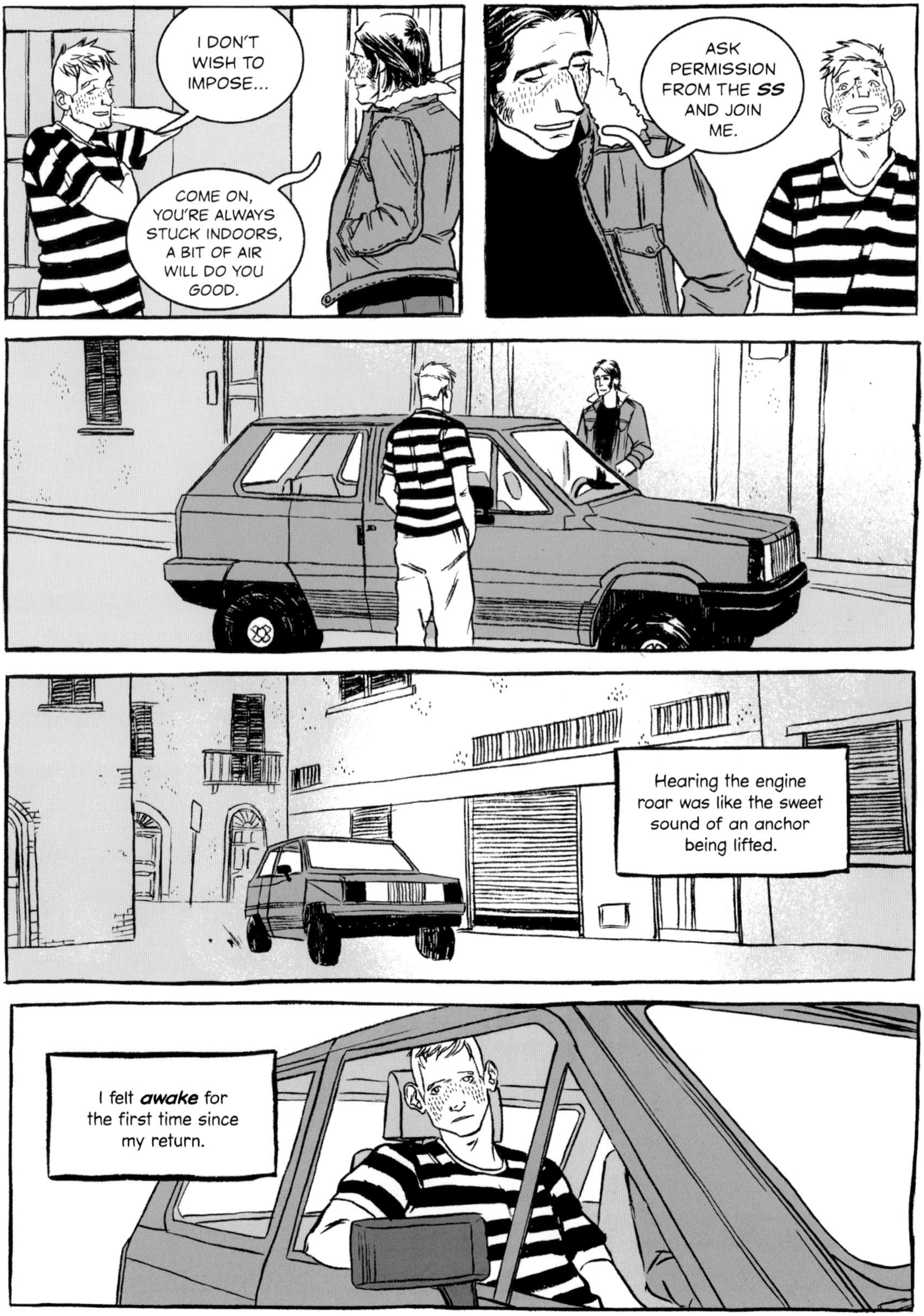

I DON'T WISH TO IMPOSE...
COME ON, YOU'RE ALWAYS STUCK INDOORS, A BIT OF AIR WILL DO YOU GOOD.
ASK PERMISSION FROM THE ***SS*** AND JOIN ME.
Hearing the engine roar was like the sweet sound of an anchor being lifted.
I felt ***awake*** for the first time since my return.

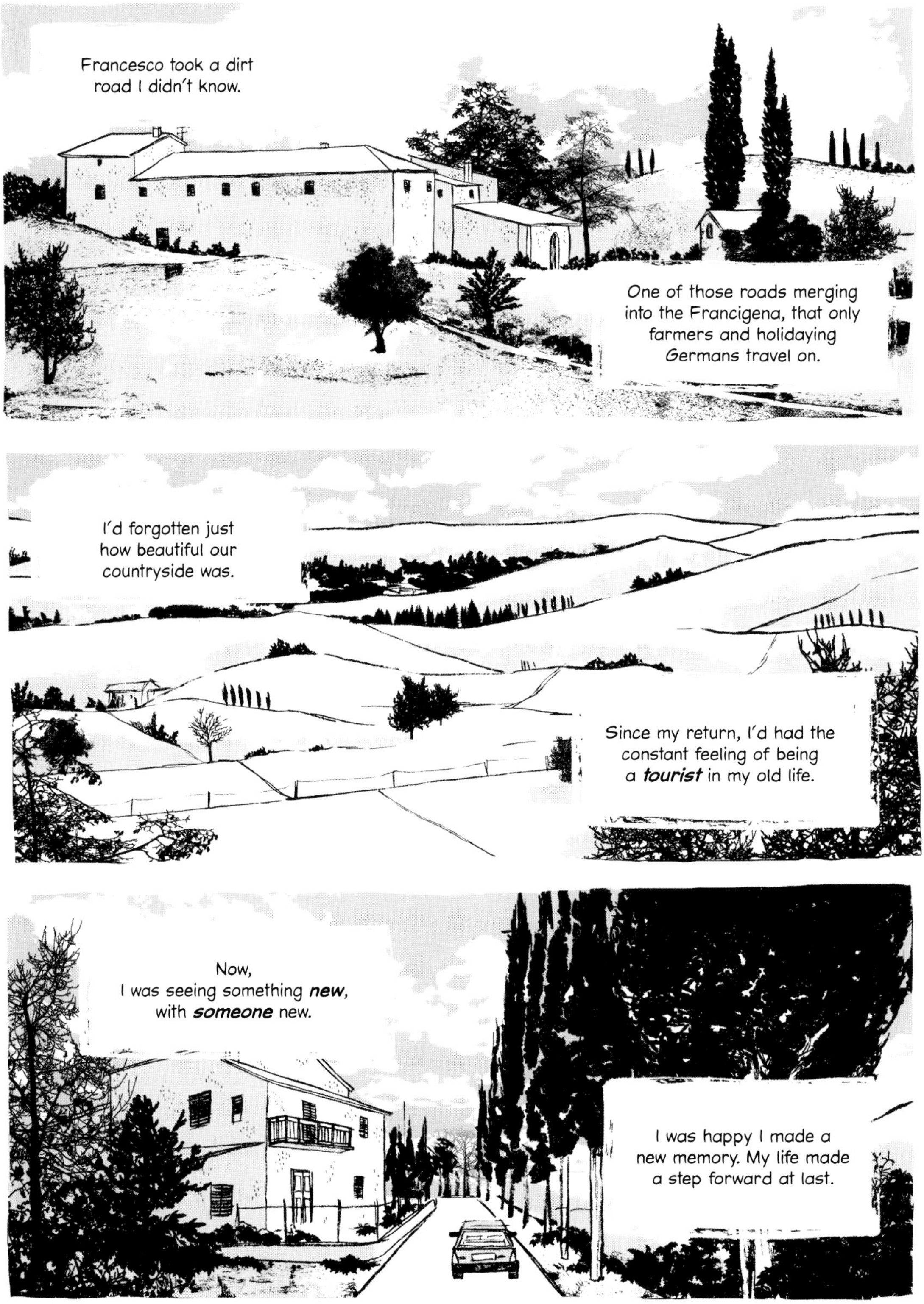
Francesco took a dirt road I didn't know.
One of those roads merging into the Francigena, that only farmers and holidaying Germans travel on.
I'd forgotten just how beautiful our countryside was.
Since my return, I'd had the constant feeling of being a ***tourist*** in my old life.
Now, I was seeing something ***new***, with ***someone*** new.
I was happy I made a new memory. My life made a step forward at last.

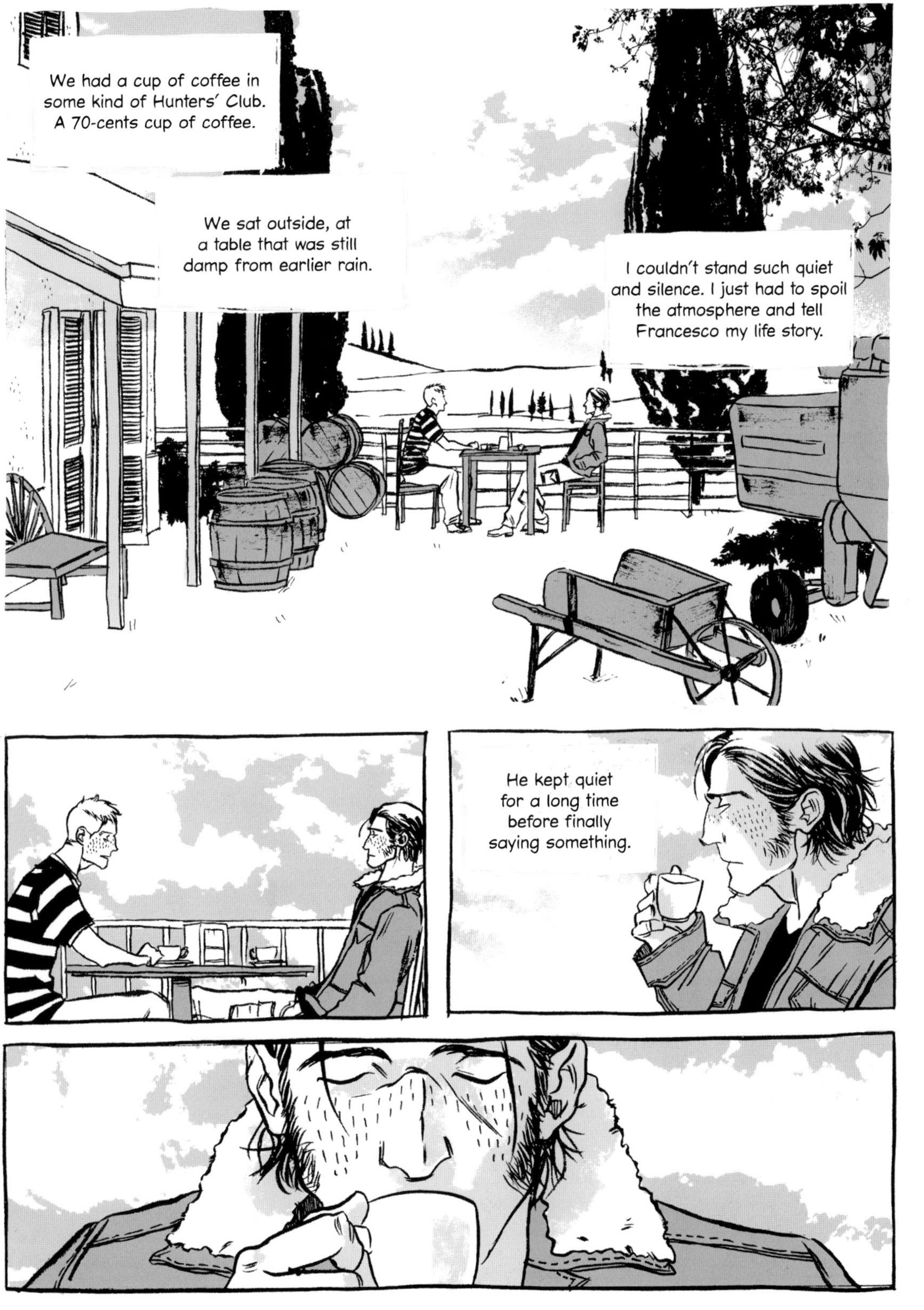
We had a cup of coffee in some kind of Hunters' Club. A 70-cents cup of coffee.
We sat outside, at a table that was still damp from earlier rain.
I couldn't stand such quiet and silence. I just had to spoil the atmosphere and tell Francesco my life story.
He kept quiet for a long time before finally saying something.

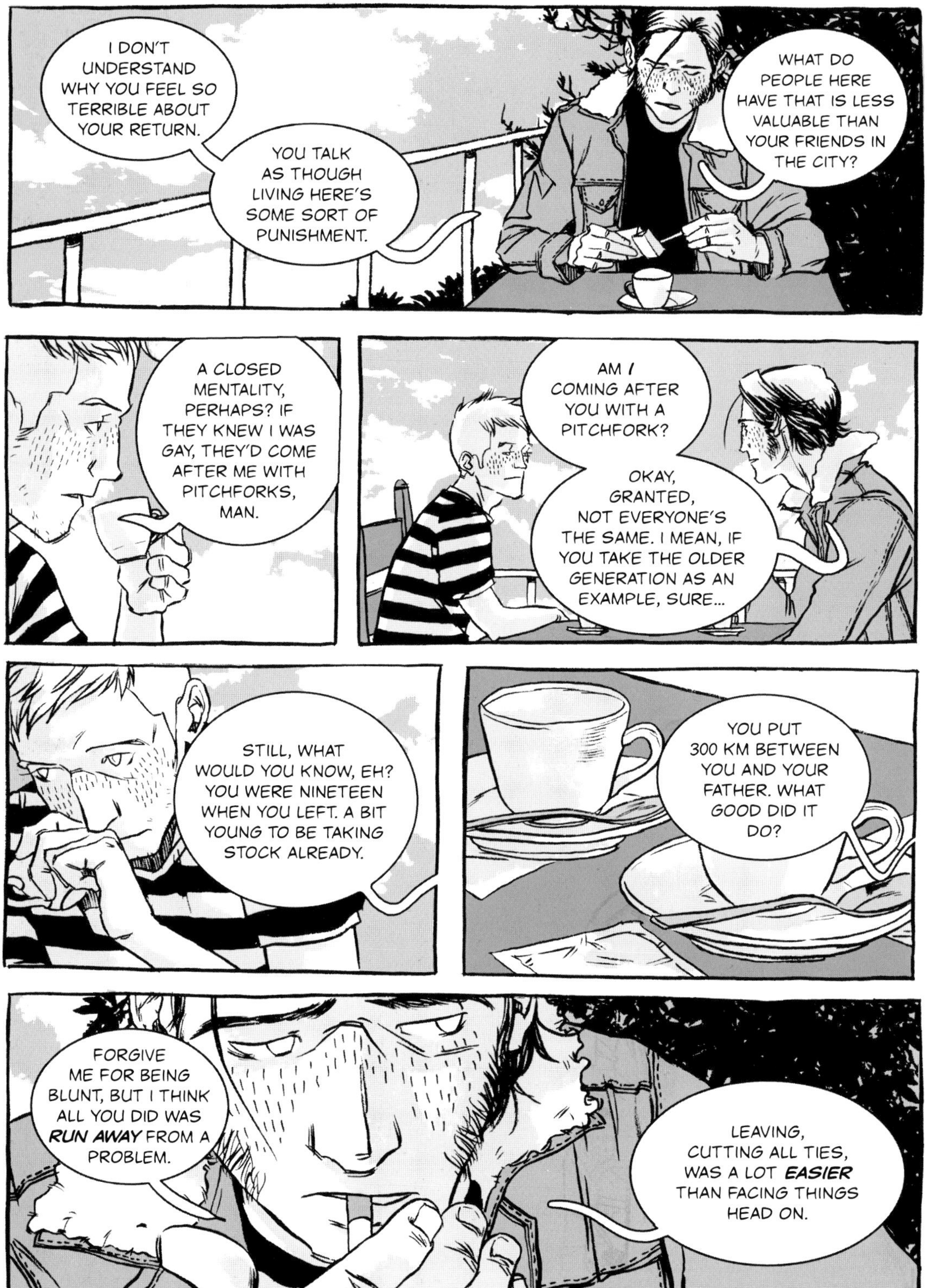
I DON'T UNDERSTAND WHY YOU FEEL SO TERRIBLE ABOUT YOUR RETURN.
YOU TALK AS THOUGH LIVING HERE'S SOME SORT OF PUNISHMENT.
WHAT DO PEOPLE HERE HAVE THAT IS LESS VALUABLE THAN YOUR FRIENDS IN THE CITY?
A CLOSED MENTALITY, PERHAPS? IF THEY KNEW I WAS GAY, THEY'D COME AFTER ME WITH PITCHFORKS, MAN.
AM I COMING AFTER YOU WITH A PITCHFORK?
OKAY, GRANTED, NOT EVERYONE'S THE SAME. I MEAN, IF YOU TAKE THE OLDER GENERATION AS AN EXAMPLE, SURE...
STILL, WHAT WOULD YOU KNOW, EH? YOU WERE NINETEEN WHEN YOU LEFT. A BIT YOUNG TO BE TAKING STOCK ALREADY.
YOU PUT 300 KM BETWEEN YOU AND YOUR FATHER. WHAT GOOD DID IT DO?
FORGIVE ME FOR BEING BLUNT, BUT I THINK ALL YOU DID WAS RUN AWAY FROM A PROBLEM.
LEAVING, CUTTING ALL TIES, WAS A LOT EASIER THAN FACING THINGS HEAD ON.

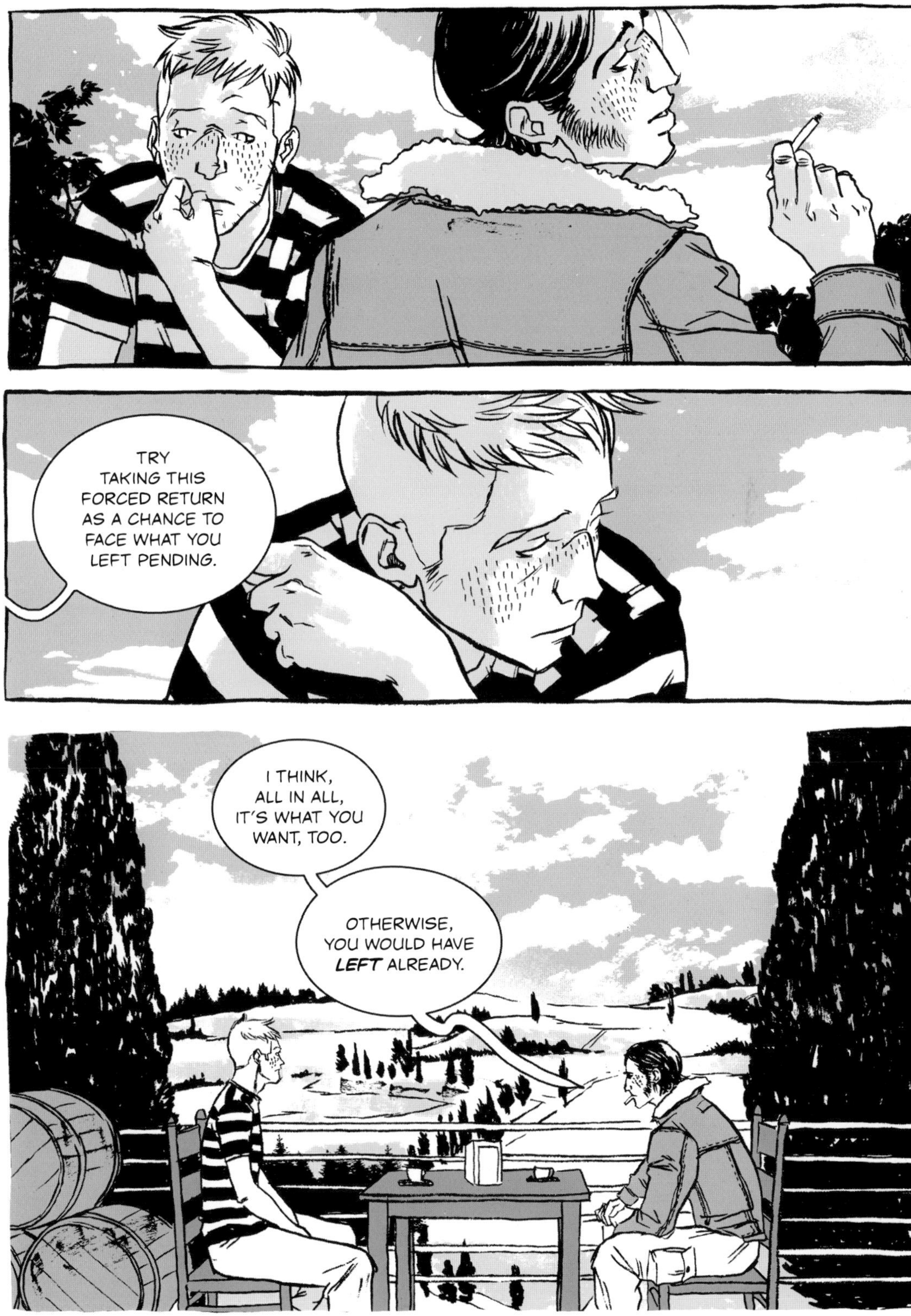
TRY TAKING THIS FORCED RETURN AS A CHANCE TO FACE WHAT YOU LEFT PENDING.
I THINK, ALL IN ALL, IT'S WHAT YOU WANT, TOO.
OTHERWISE, YOU WOULD HAVE *LEFT* ALREADY.

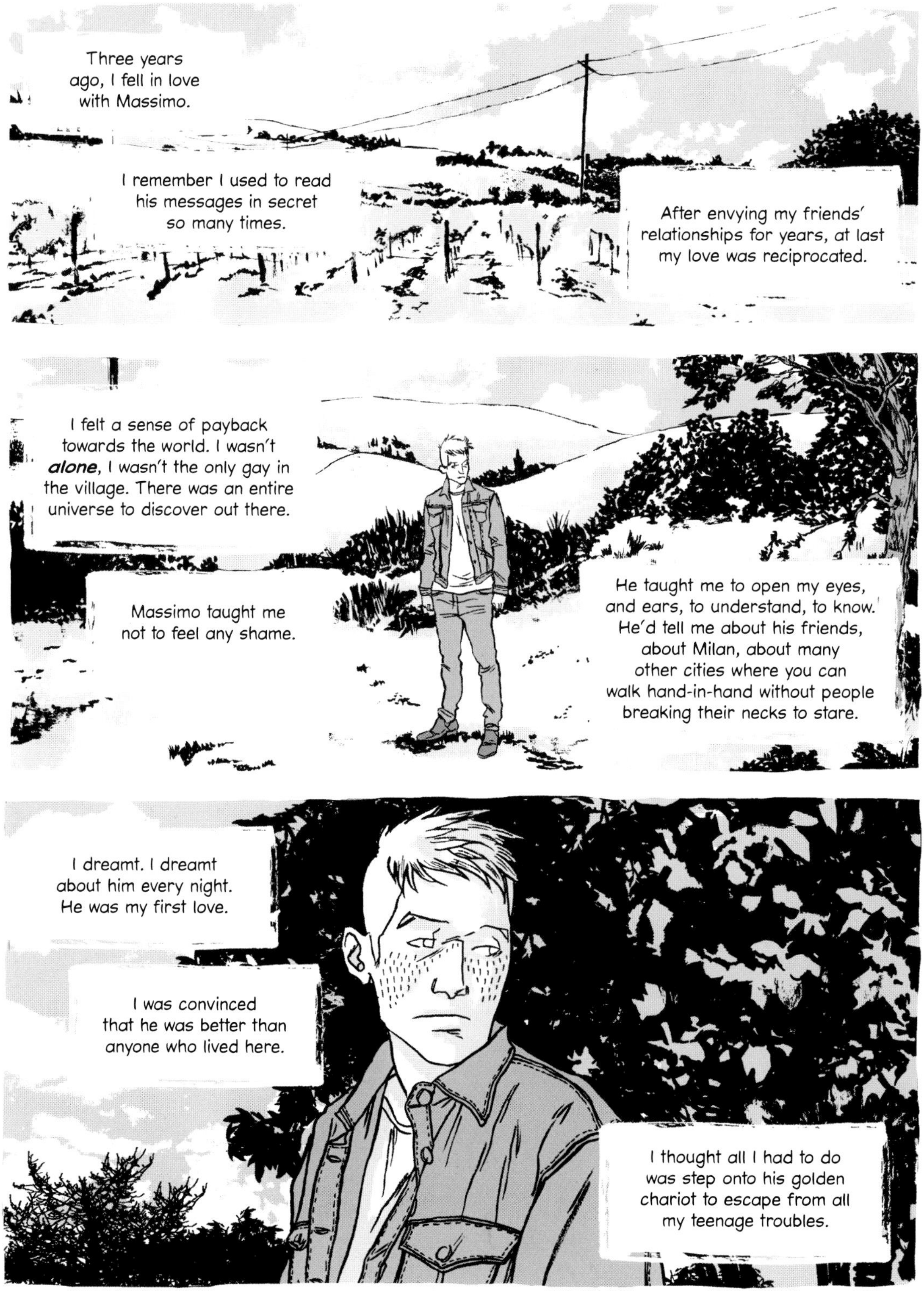
Three years ago, I fell in love with Massimo.
I remember I used to read his messages in secret so many times.
After envying my friends' relationships for years, at last my love was reciprocated.
I felt a sense of payback towards the world. I wasn't ***alone***, I wasn't the only gay in the village. There was an entire universe to discover out there.
Massimo taught me not to feel any shame.
He taught me to open my eyes, and ears, to understand, to know. He'd tell me about his friends, about Milan, about many other cities where you can walk hand-in-hand without people breaking their necks to stare.
I dreamt. I dreamt about him every night. He was my first love.
I was convinced that he was better than anyone who lived here.
I thought all I had to do was step onto his golden chariot to escape from all my teenage troubles.

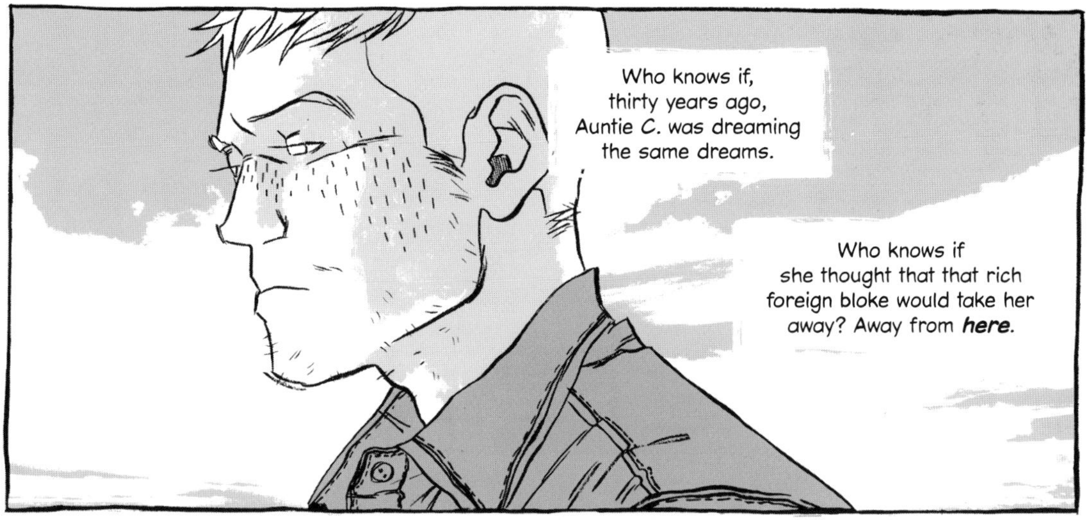
Who knows if, thirty years ago, Auntie C. was dreaming the same dreams.
Who knows if she thought that that rich foreign bloke would take her away? Away from ***here.***

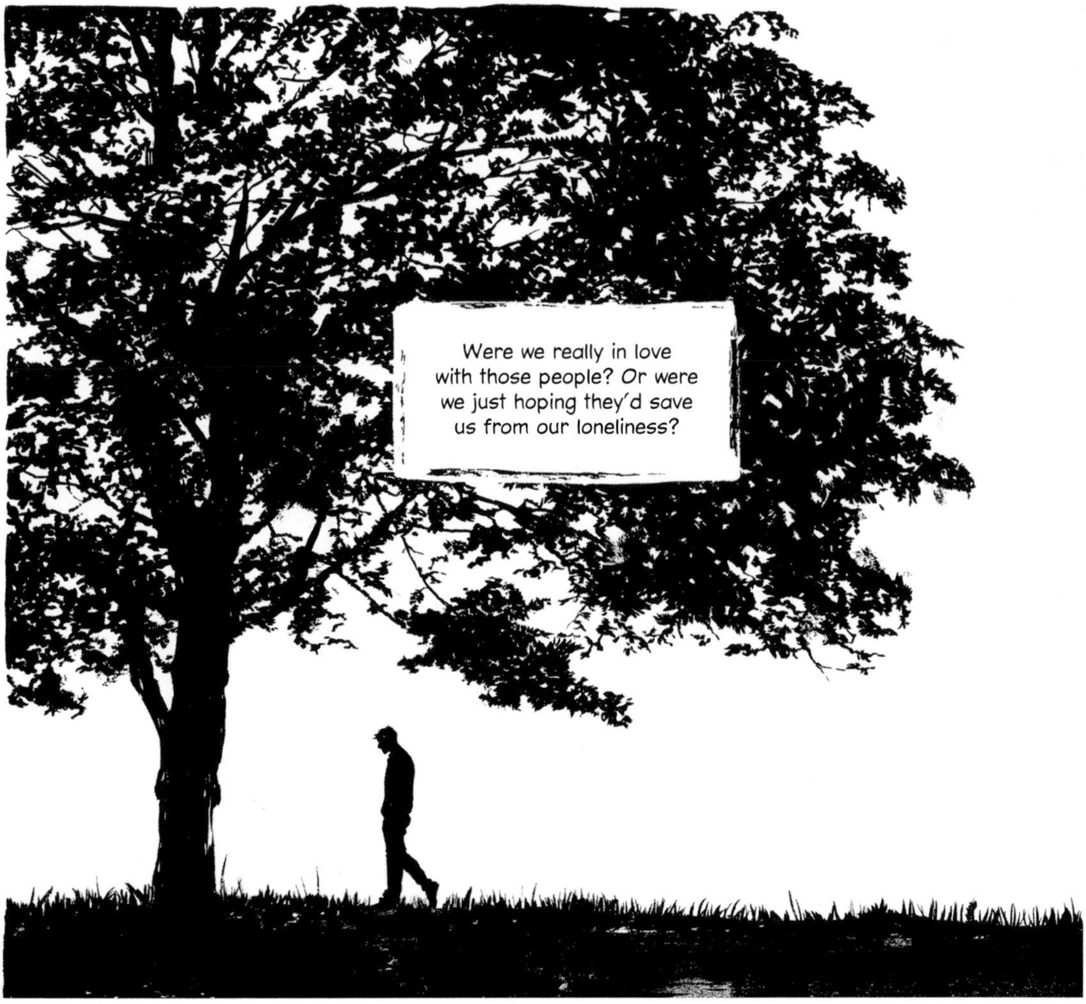
Were we really in love with those people? Or were we just hoping they'd save us from our loneliness?

The more I try to think, the less I remember my last argument with my father.

I remember that I waited till I graduated to tell him about Massimo. My bags were packed.

I didn't give him time to understand nor did I fight to be accepted. We *argued*. I *left*.

I was both cause and effect. Laying it all on him is not fair.

Still, he must have found out I'm back...

...Why isn't he here looking for me?

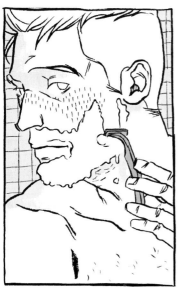

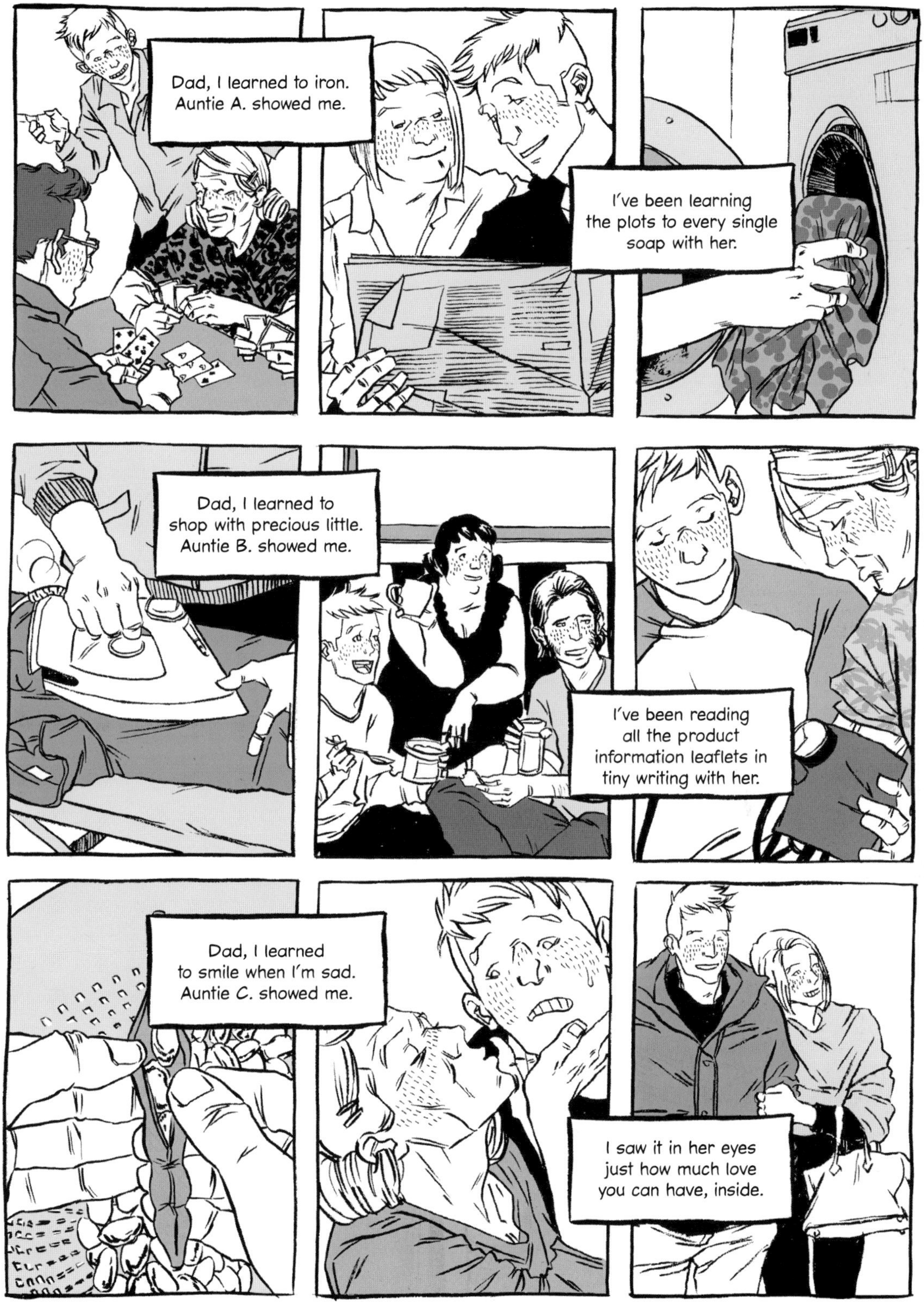

Dad, I learned to iron. Auntie A. showed me.
I've been learning the plots to every single soap with her.
Dad, I learned to shop with precious little. Auntie B. showed me.
I've been reading all the product information leaflets in tiny writing with her.
Dad, I learned to smile when I'm sad. Auntie C. showed me.
I saw it in her eyes just how much love you can have, inside.

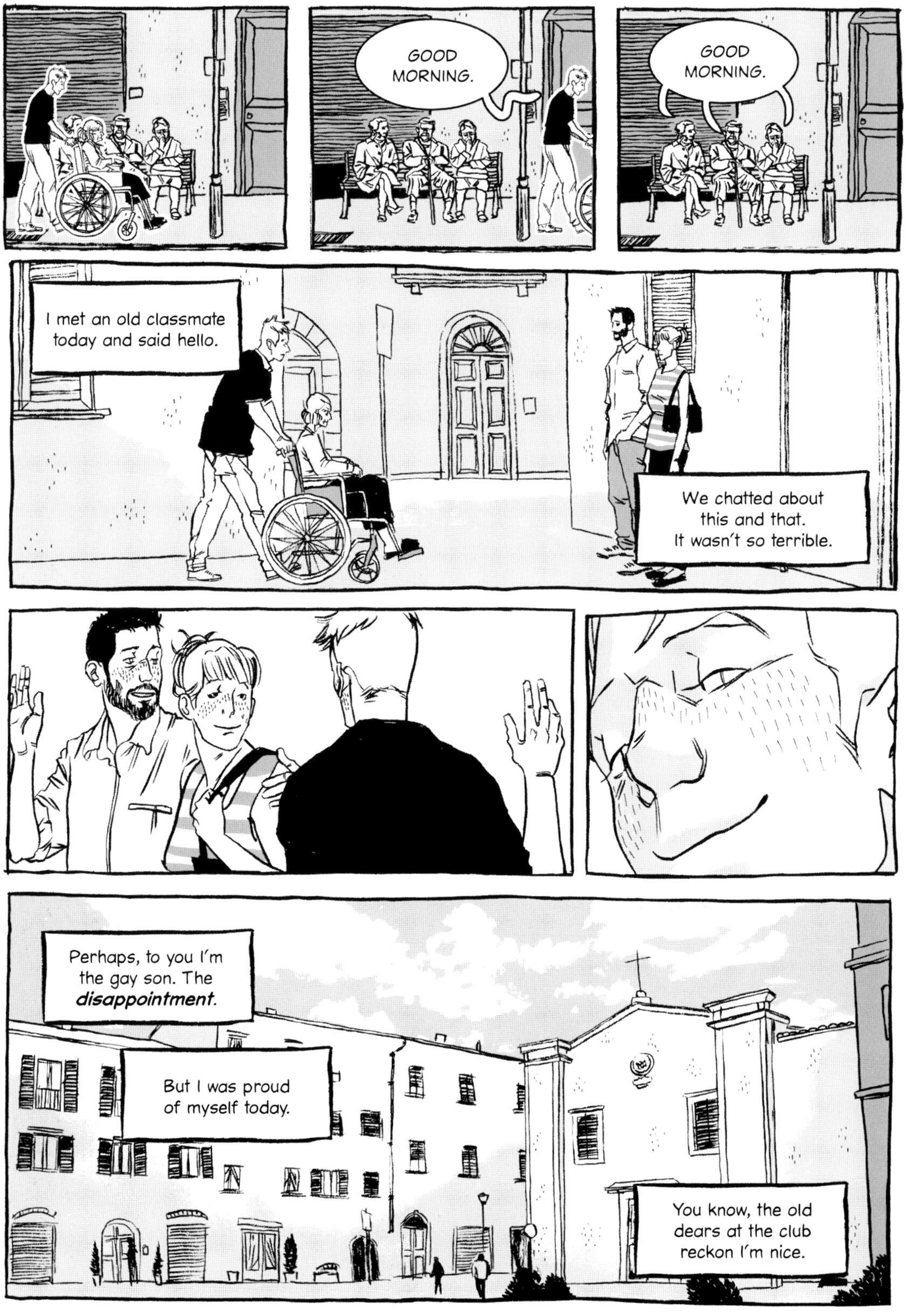
GOOD MORNING.
GOOD MORNING.
I met an old classmate today and said hello.
We chatted about this and that. It wasn't so terrible.
Perhaps, to you I'm the gay son. The ***disappointment***.
But I was proud of myself today.
You know, the old dears at the club reckon I'm nice.

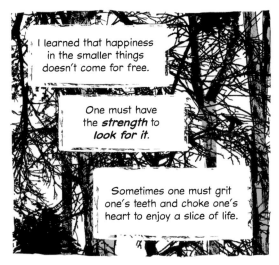

I learned that happiness in the smaller things doesn't come for free.

One must have the **strength** to **look for it**.

Sometimes one must grit one's teeth and choke one's heart to enjoy a slice of life.

I know I have no job, no pension scheme.

I know I'm moving in **slow motion** in the world.

But Francesco took me mushroom hunting on Saturday.

We said nothing almost the entire time.

And I stopped thinking about you and about tomorrow.

I'm slowly starting to breathe again.

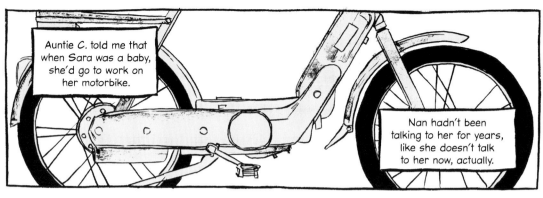

Auntie C. told me that when Sara was a baby, she'd go to work on her motorbike.

Nan hadn't been talking to her for years, like she doesn't talk to her now, actually.

But that morning she had to go God knows where in the next town.

So she forced herself to ask Auntie C. for a lift.

Auntie C. let her on and went downhill at great speed on purpose.

Nan gritted her teeth, trying not to scream, you know, not to give her the satisfaction.

Then she caved in and screamed **blue murder** at her to get her to slow down.

She **spoke** to her.

Auntie C. enjoyed that small victory.

She even reckoned Nan had fun.

Did you know about this, Dad?

Let's not end up this way.

I don't know if I'll have the guts to call you first...

...I just hope that, sooner or later, however we get there, we'll also take a ride on that same motorbike.

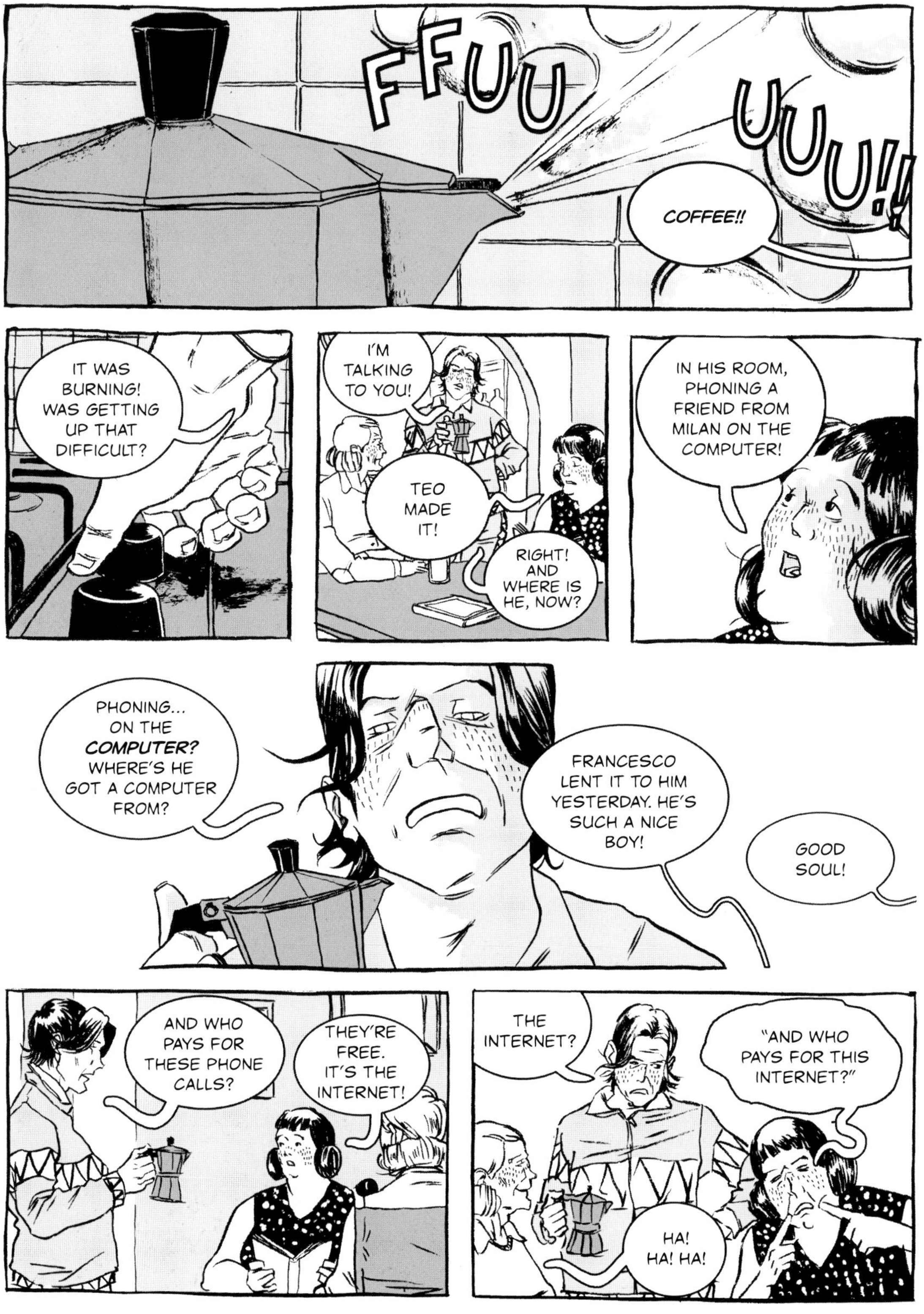
FFUUUUU!!
COFFEE!!
IT WAS BURNING! WAS GETTING UP THAT DIFFICULT?
I'M TALKING TO YOU!
TEO MADE IT!
RIGHT! AND WHERE IS HE, NOW?
IN HIS ROOM, PHONING A FRIEND FROM MILAN ON THE COMPUTER!
PHONING... ON THE **COMPUTER?** WHERE'S HE GOT A COMPUTER FROM?
FRANCESCO LENT IT TO HIM YESTERDAY. HE'S SUCH A NICE BOY!
GOOD SOUL!
AND WHO PAYS FOR THESE PHONE CALLS?
THEY'RE FREE. IT'S THE INTERNET!
THE INTERNET?
"AND WHO PAYS FOR THIS INTERNET?"
HA! HA! HA!

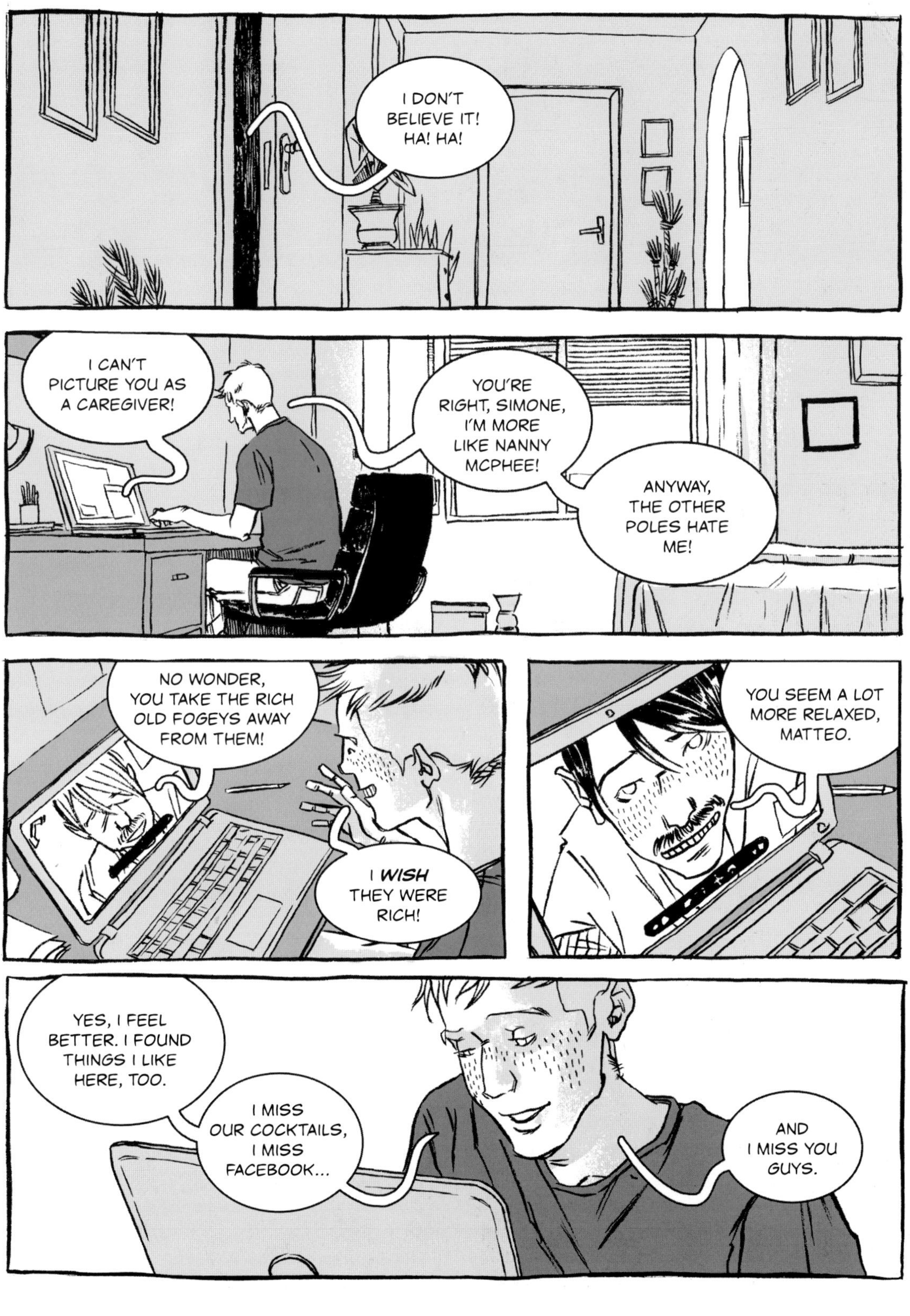
I DON'T BELIEVE IT! HA! HA!
I CAN'T PICTURE YOU AS A CAREGIVER!
YOU'RE RIGHT, SIMONE, I'M MORE LIKE NANNY MCPHEE!
ANYWAY, THE OTHER POLES HATE ME!
NO WONDER, YOU TAKE THE RICH OLD FOGEYS AWAY FROM THEM!
I *WISH* THEY WERE RICH!
YOU SEEM A LOT MORE RELAXED, MATTEO.
YES, I FEEL BETTER. I FOUND THINGS I LIKE HERE, TOO.
I MISS OUR COCKTAILS, I MISS FACEBOOK...
AND I MISS YOU GUYS.

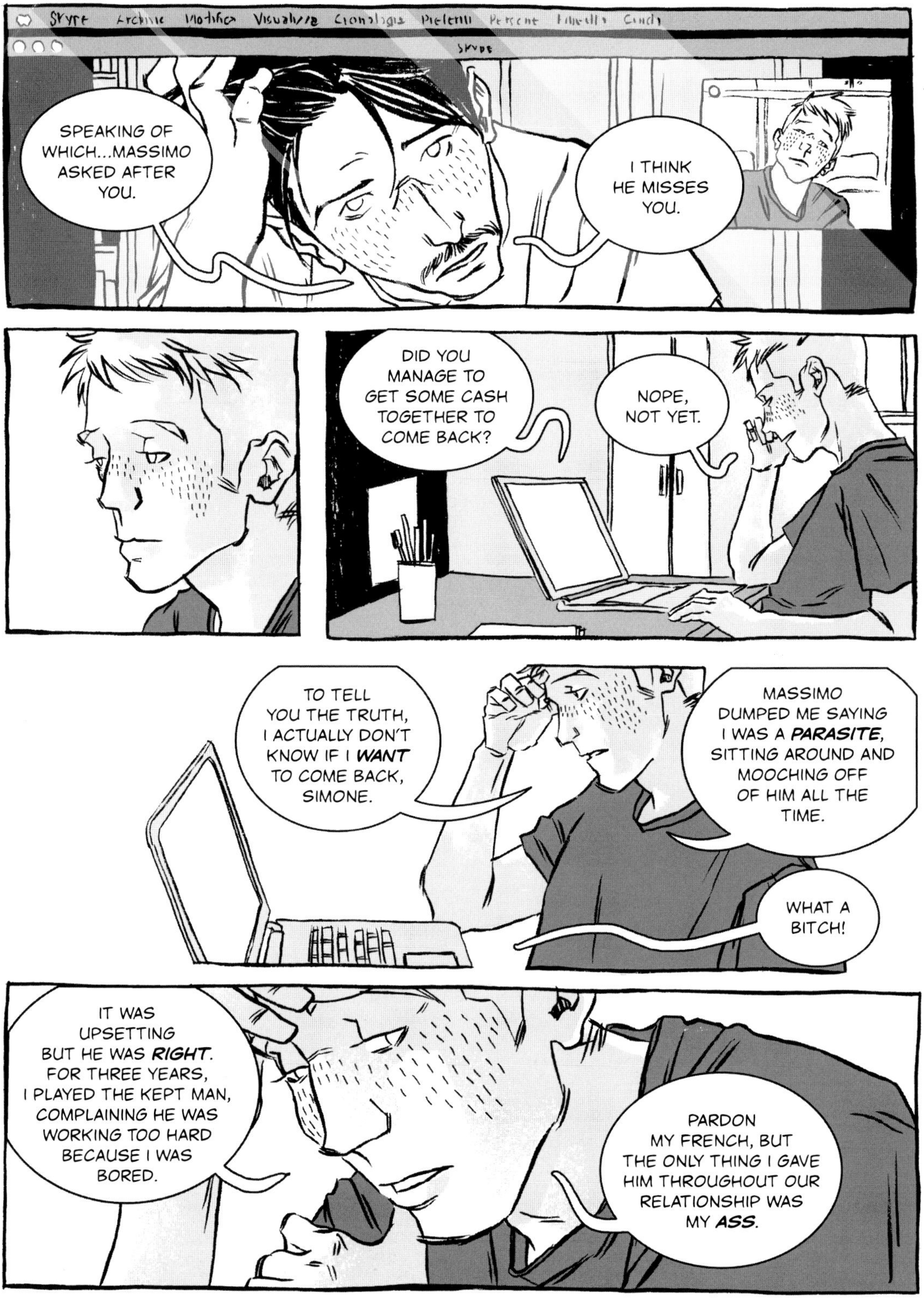
SKYPE
SPEAKING OF WHICH...MASSIMO ASKED AFTER YOU.
I THINK HE MISSES YOU.
DID YOU MANAGE TO GET SOME CASH TOGETHER TO COME BACK?
NOPE, NOT YET.
TO TELL YOU THE TRUTH, I ACTUALLY DON'T KNOW IF I *WANT* TO COME BACK, SIMONE.
MASSIMO DUMPED ME SAYING I WAS A *PARASITE*, SITTING AROUND AND MOOCHING OFF OF HIM ALL THE TIME.
WHAT A BITCH!
IT WAS UPSETTING BUT HE WAS *RIGHT*. FOR THREE YEARS, I PLAYED THE KEPT MAN, COMPLAINING HE WAS WORKING TOO HARD BECAUSE I WAS BORED.
PARDON MY FRENCH, BUT THE ONLY THING I GAVE HIM THROUGHOUT OUR RELATIONSHIP WAS MY *ASS*.

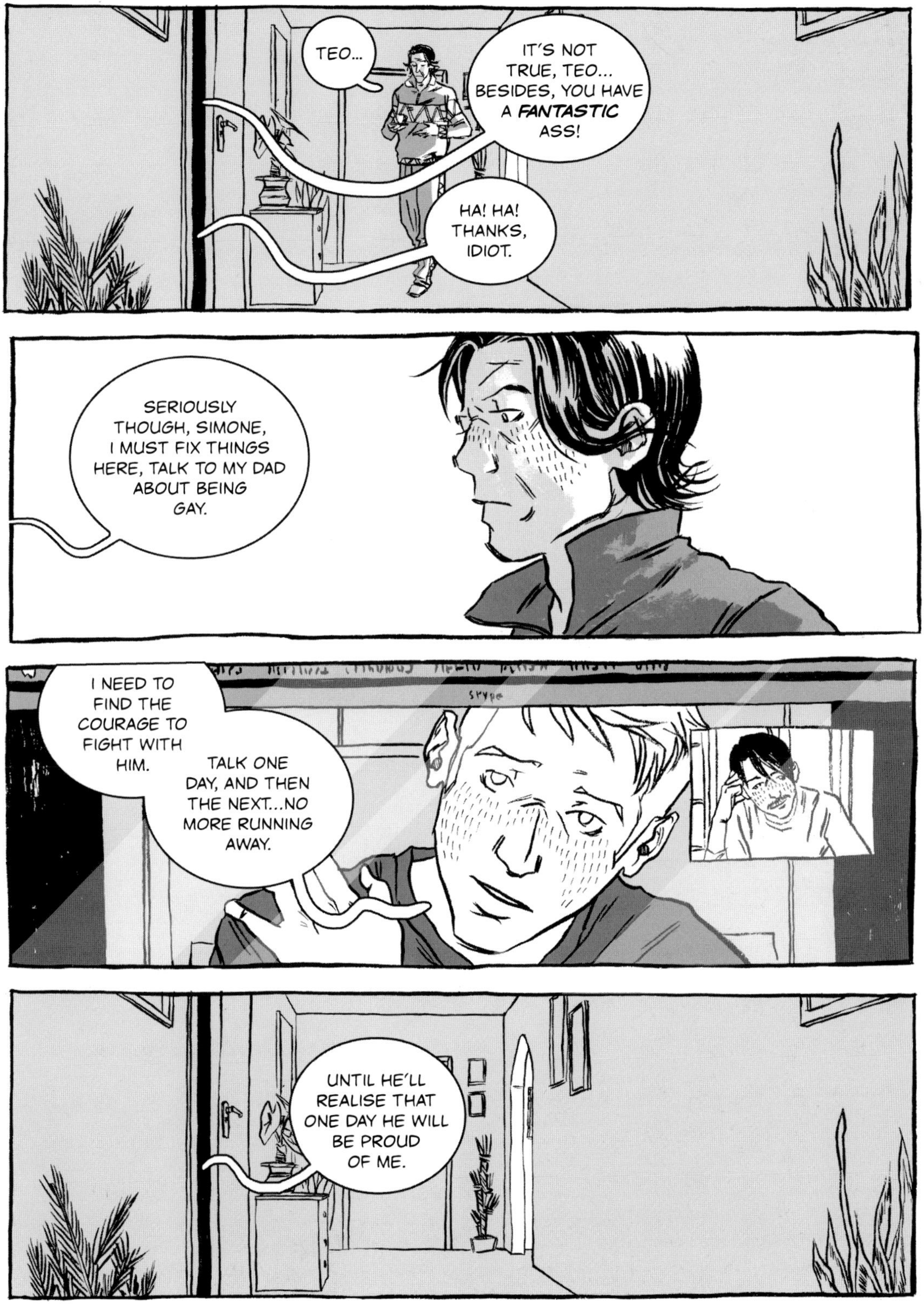
TEO...
IT'S NOT TRUE, TEO... BESIDES, YOU HAVE A ***FANTASTIC*** ASS!
HA! HA! THANKS, IDIOT.
SERIOUSLY THOUGH, SIMONE, I MUST FIX THINGS HERE, TALK TO MY DAD ABOUT BEING GAY.
I NEED TO FIND THE COURAGE TO FIGHT WITH HIM.
TALK ONE DAY, AND THEN THE NEXT...NO MORE RUNNING AWAY.
UNTIL HE'LL REALISE THAT ONE DAY HE WILL BE PROUD OF ME.

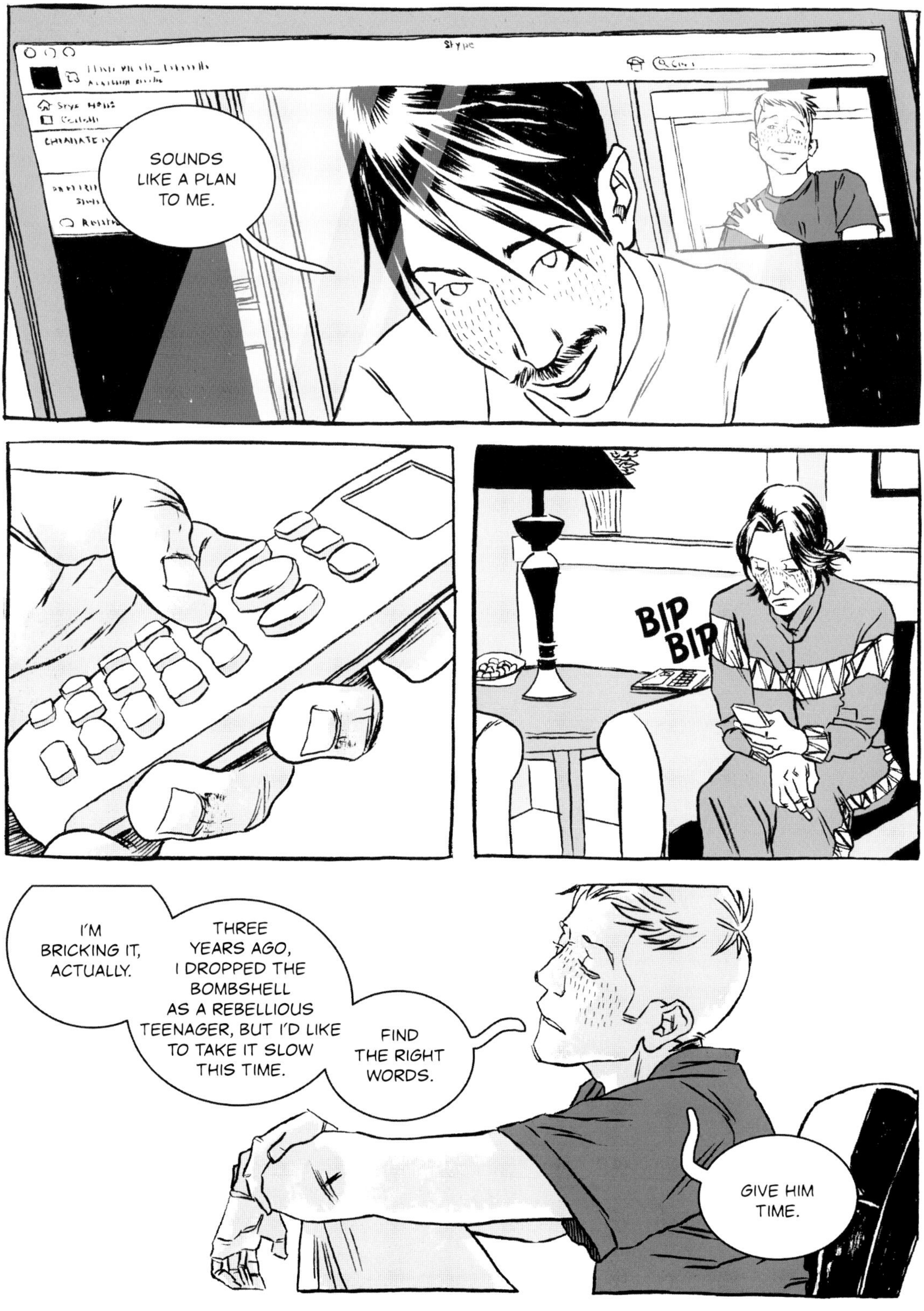
SOUNDS LIKE A PLAN TO ME.
BIP BIP
I'M BRICKING IT, ACTUALLY.
THREE YEARS AGO, I DROPPED THE BOMBSHELL AS A REBELLIOUS TEENAGER, BUT I'D LIKE TO TAKE IT SLOW THIS TIME.
FIND THE RIGHT WORDS.
GIVE HIM TIME.

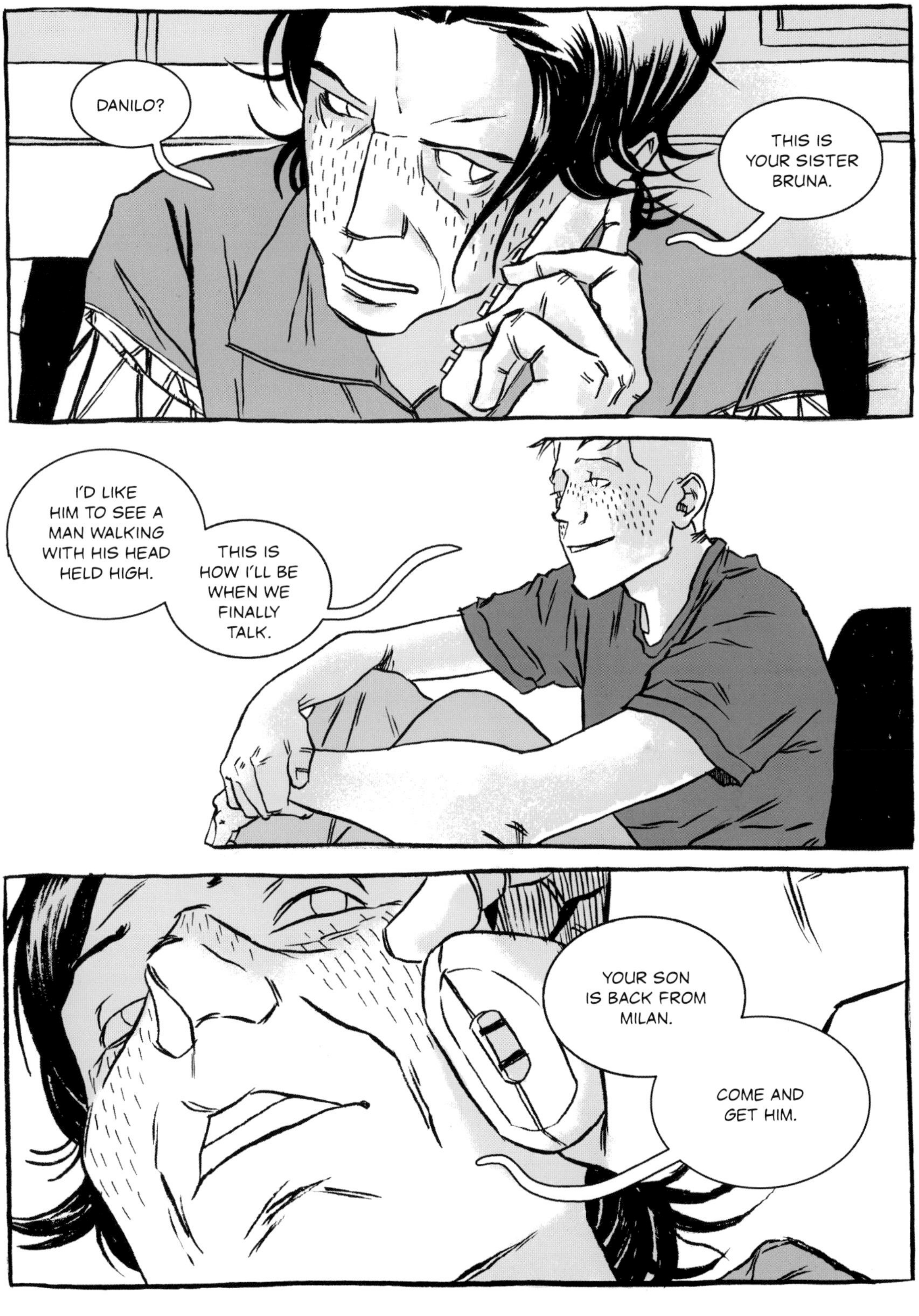
DANILO?
THIS IS YOUR SISTER BRUNA.
I'D LIKE HIM TO SEE A MAN WALKING WITH HIS HEAD HELD HIGH.
THIS IS HOW I'LL BE WHEN WE FINALLY TALK.
YOUR SON IS BACK FROM MILAN.
COME AND GET HIM.

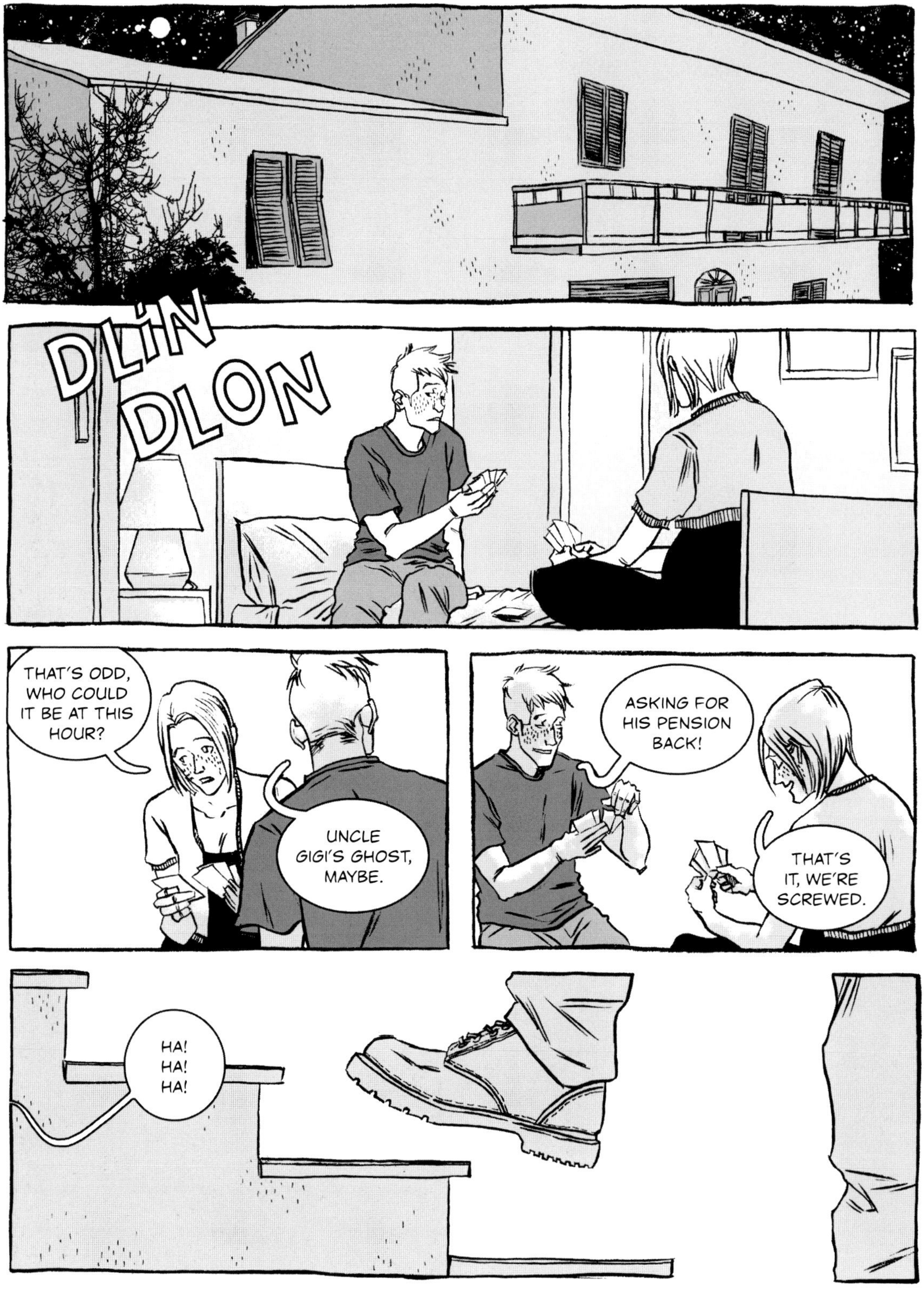
DLIN DLON
THAT'S ODD, WHO COULD IT BE AT THIS HOUR?
UNCLE GIGI'S GHOST, MAYBE.
ASKING FOR HIS PENSION BACK!
THAT'S IT, WE'RE SCREWED.
HA! HA! HA!

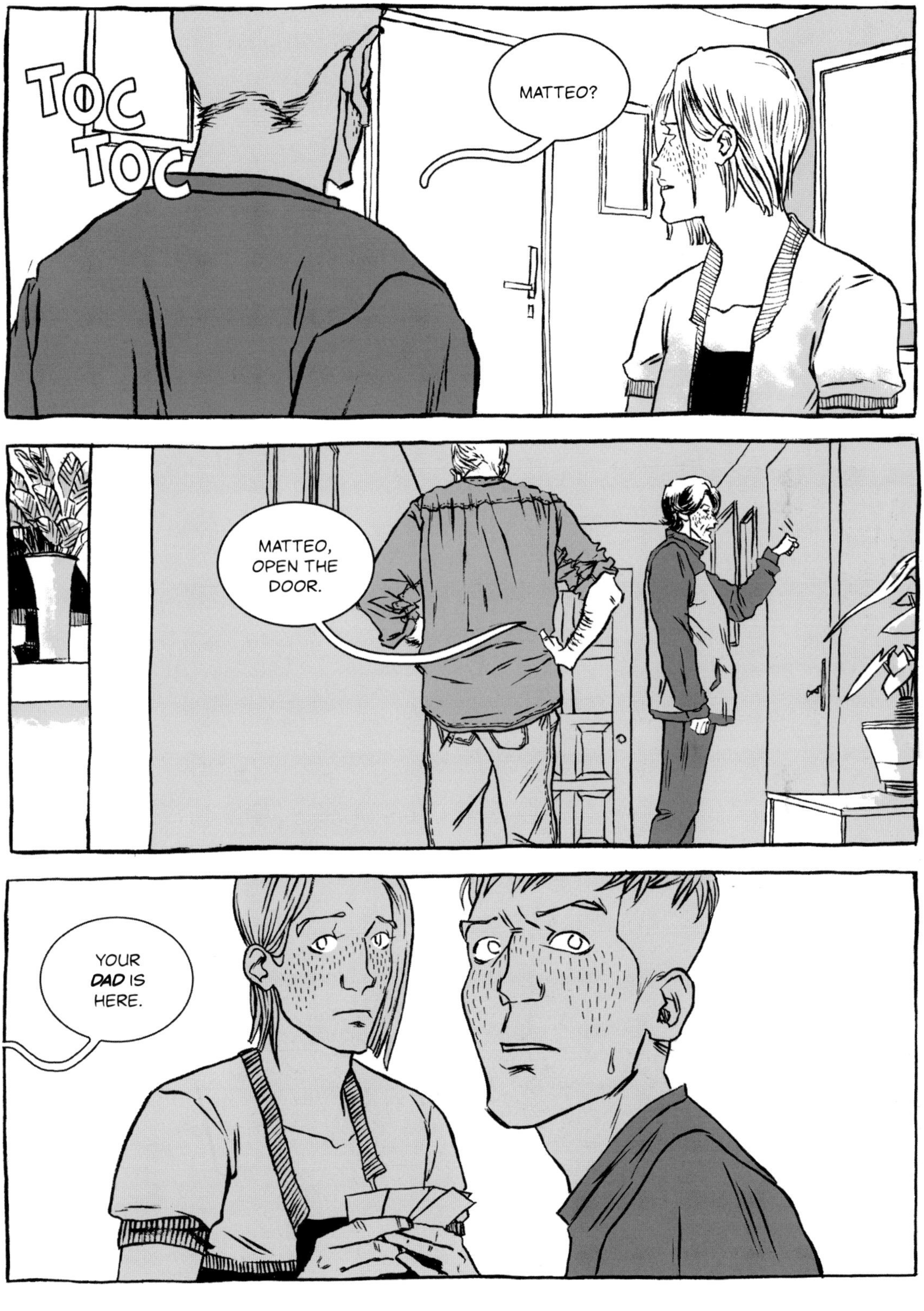
TOC TOC
MATTEO?
MATTEO, OPEN THE DOOR.
YOUR DAD IS HERE.

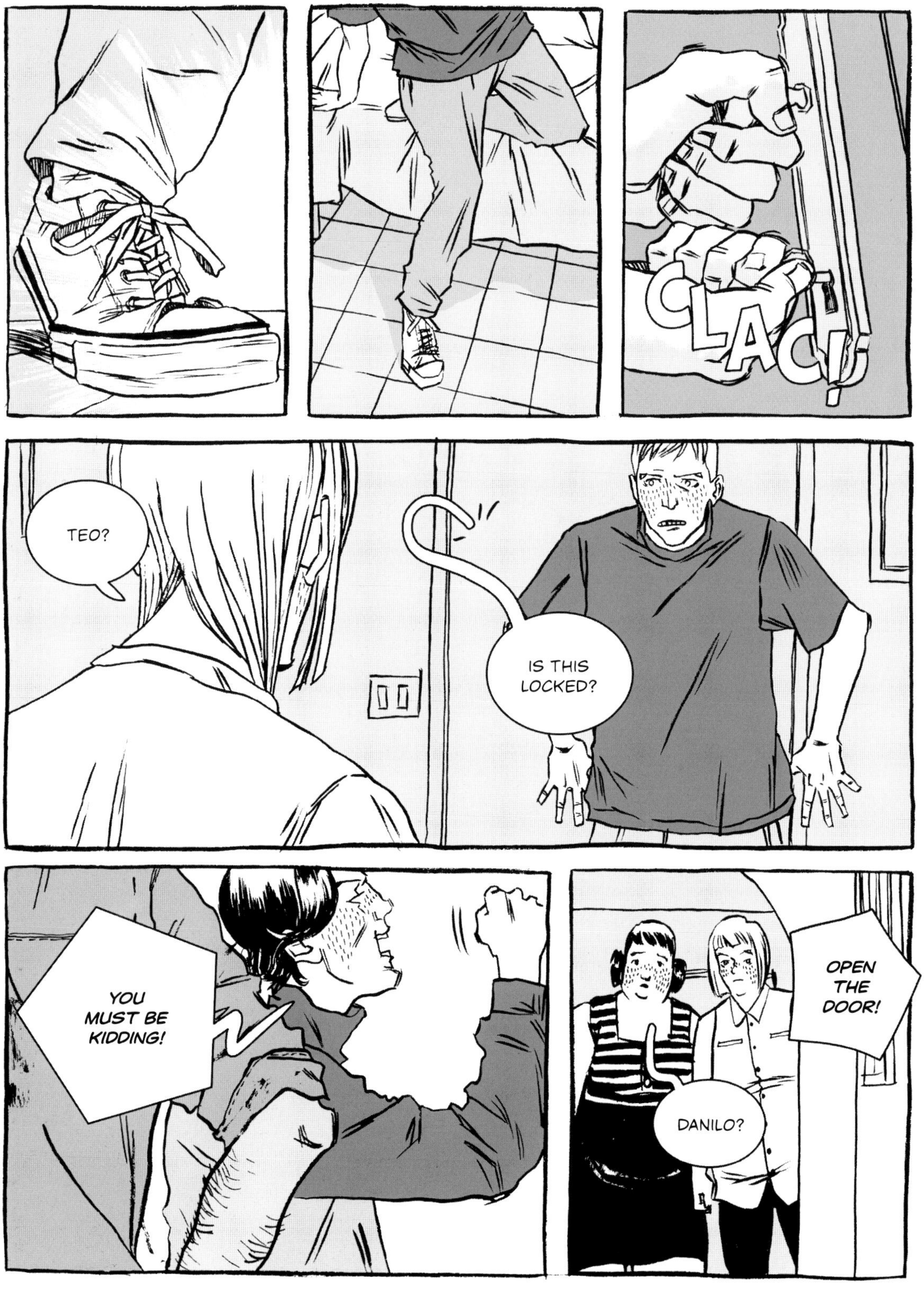
CLAC!
TEO?
IS THIS LOCKED?
YOU MUST BE KIDDING!
OPEN THE DOOR!
DANILO?

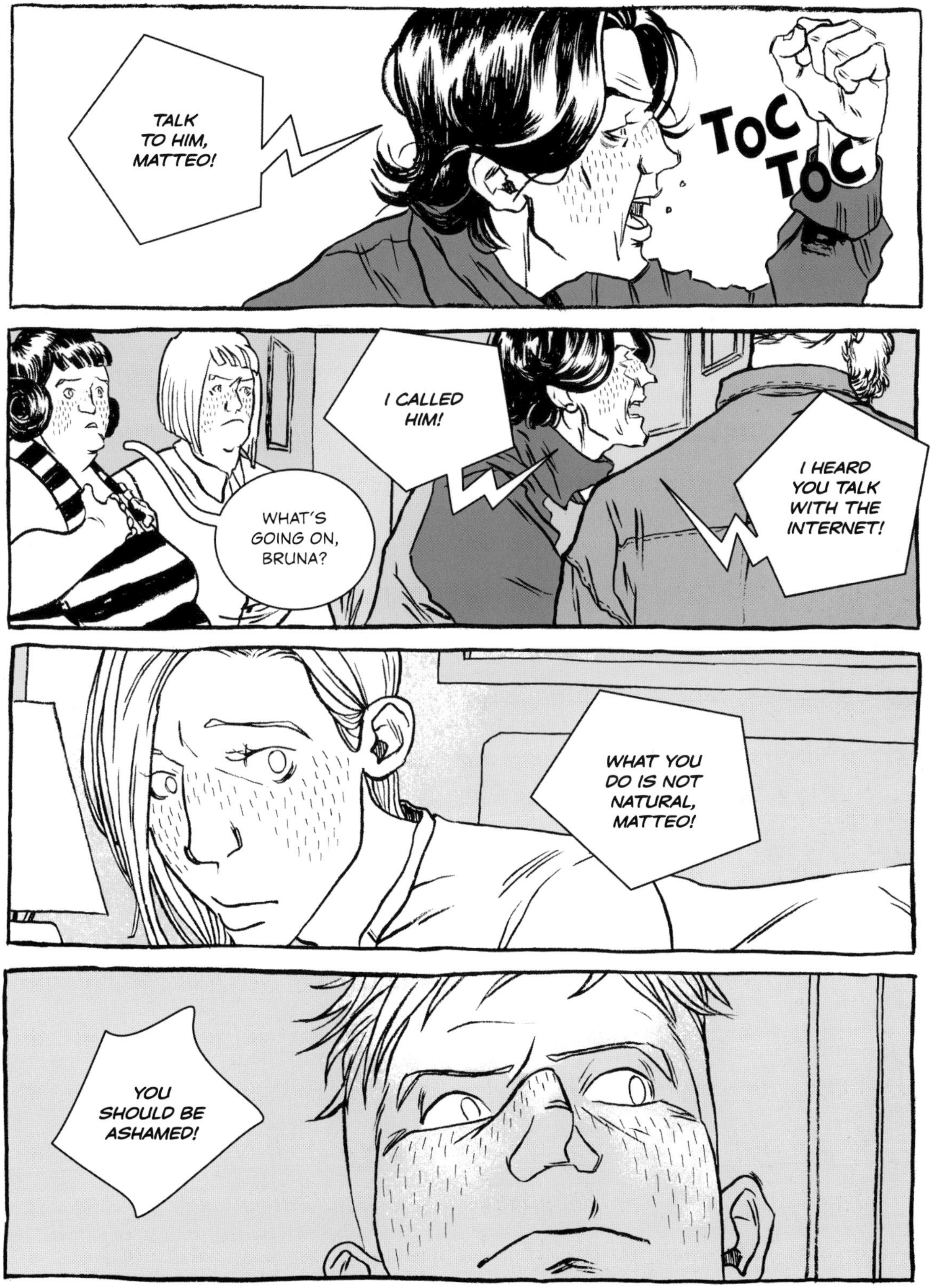
TALK TO HIM, MATTEO!
TOC TOC
I CALLED HIM!
WHAT'S GOING ON, BRUNA?
I HEARD YOU TALK WITH THE INTERNET!
WHAT YOU DO IS NOT NATURAL, MATTEO!
YOU SHOULD BE ASHAMED!

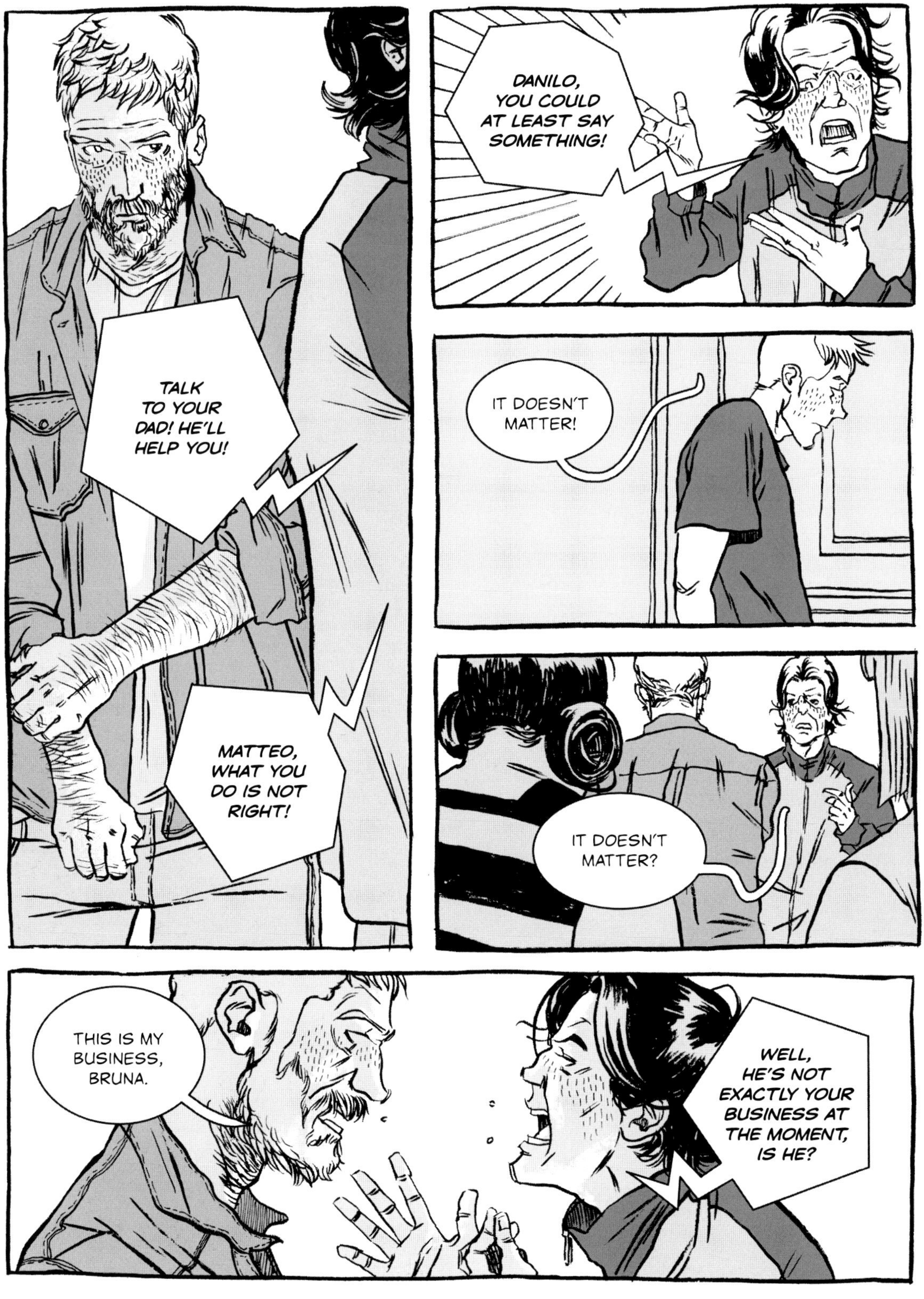
TALK TO YOUR DAD! HE'LL HELP YOU!
MATTEO, WHAT YOU DO IS NOT RIGHT!
DANILO, YOU COULD AT LEAST SAY SOMETHING!
IT DOESN'T MATTER!
IT DOESN'T MATTER?
THIS IS MY BUSINESS, BRUNA.
WELL, HE'S NOT EXACTLY YOUR BUSINESS AT THE MOMENT, IS HE?

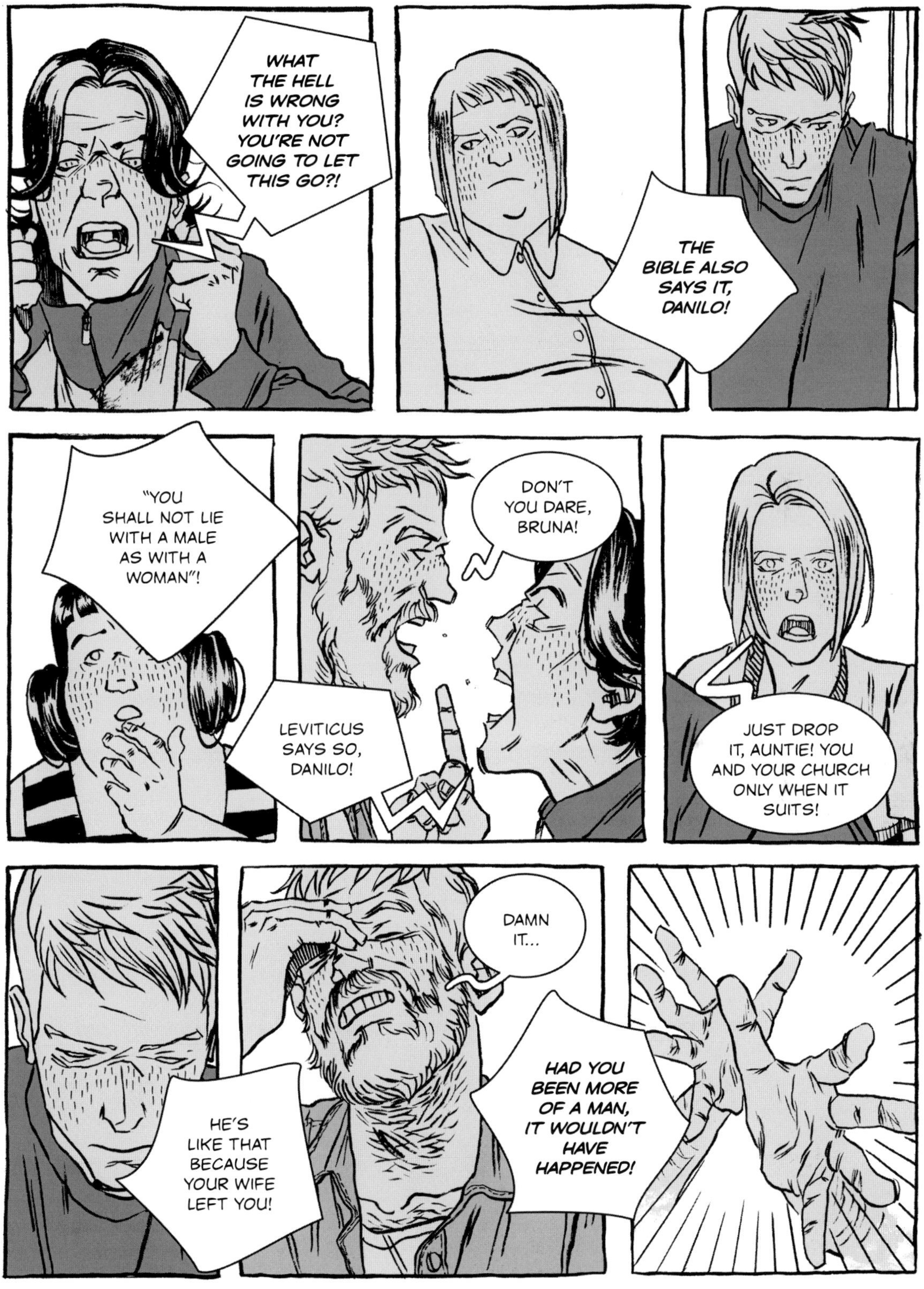
WHAT THE HELL IS WRONG WITH YOU? YOU'RE NOT GOING TO LET THIS GO?!
THE BIBLE ALSO SAYS IT, DANILO!
"YOU SHALL NOT LIE WITH A MALE AS WITH A WOMAN"!
LEVITICUS SAYS SO, DANILO!
DON'T YOU DARE, BRUNA!
JUST DROP IT, AUNTIE! YOU AND YOUR CHURCH ONLY WHEN IT SUITS!
HE'S LIKE THAT BECAUSE YOUR WIFE LEFT YOU!
DAMN IT...
HAD YOU BEEN MORE OF A MAN, IT WOULDN'T HAVE HAPPENED!

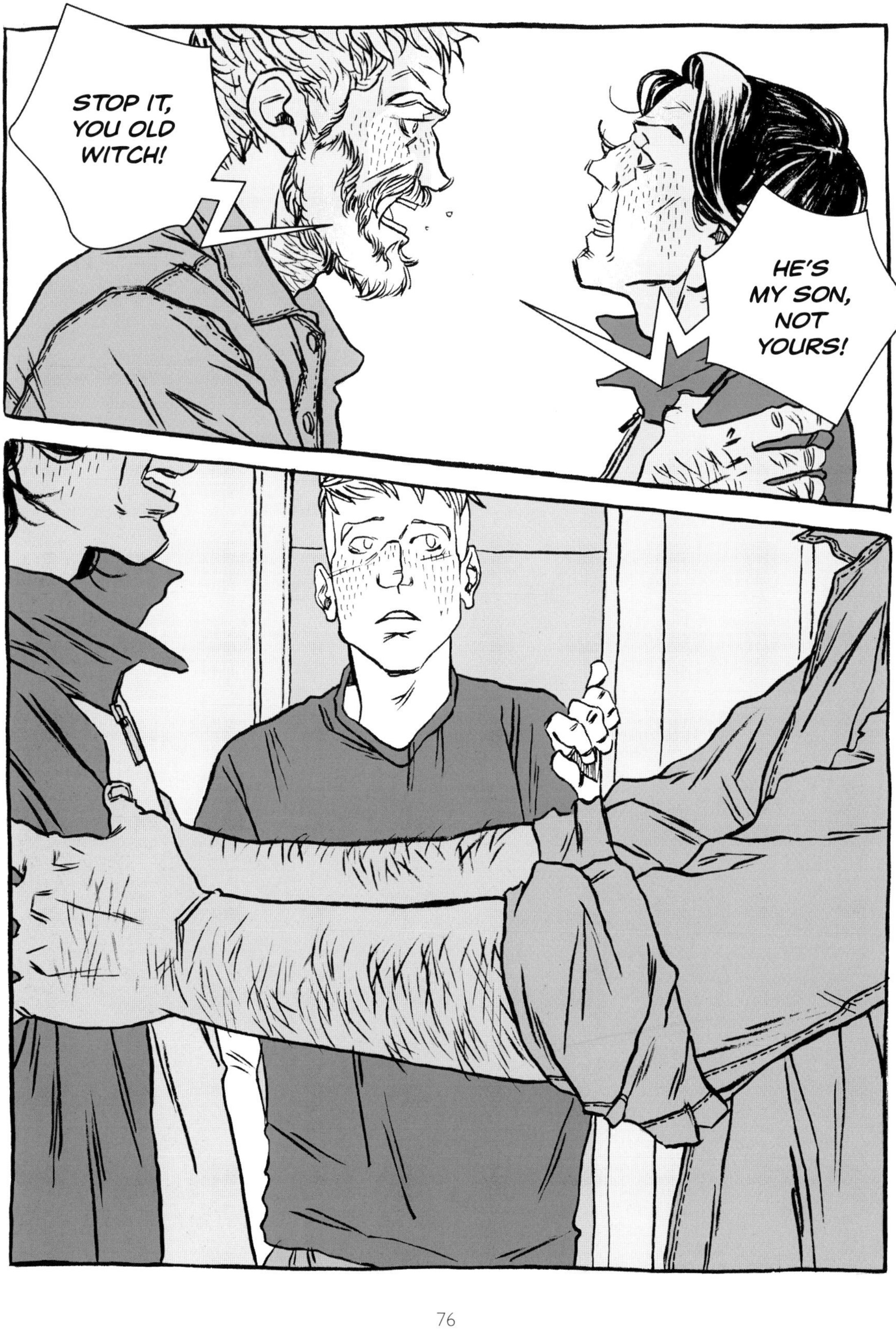
STOP IT, YOU OLD WITCH!
HE'S MY SON, NOT YOURS!

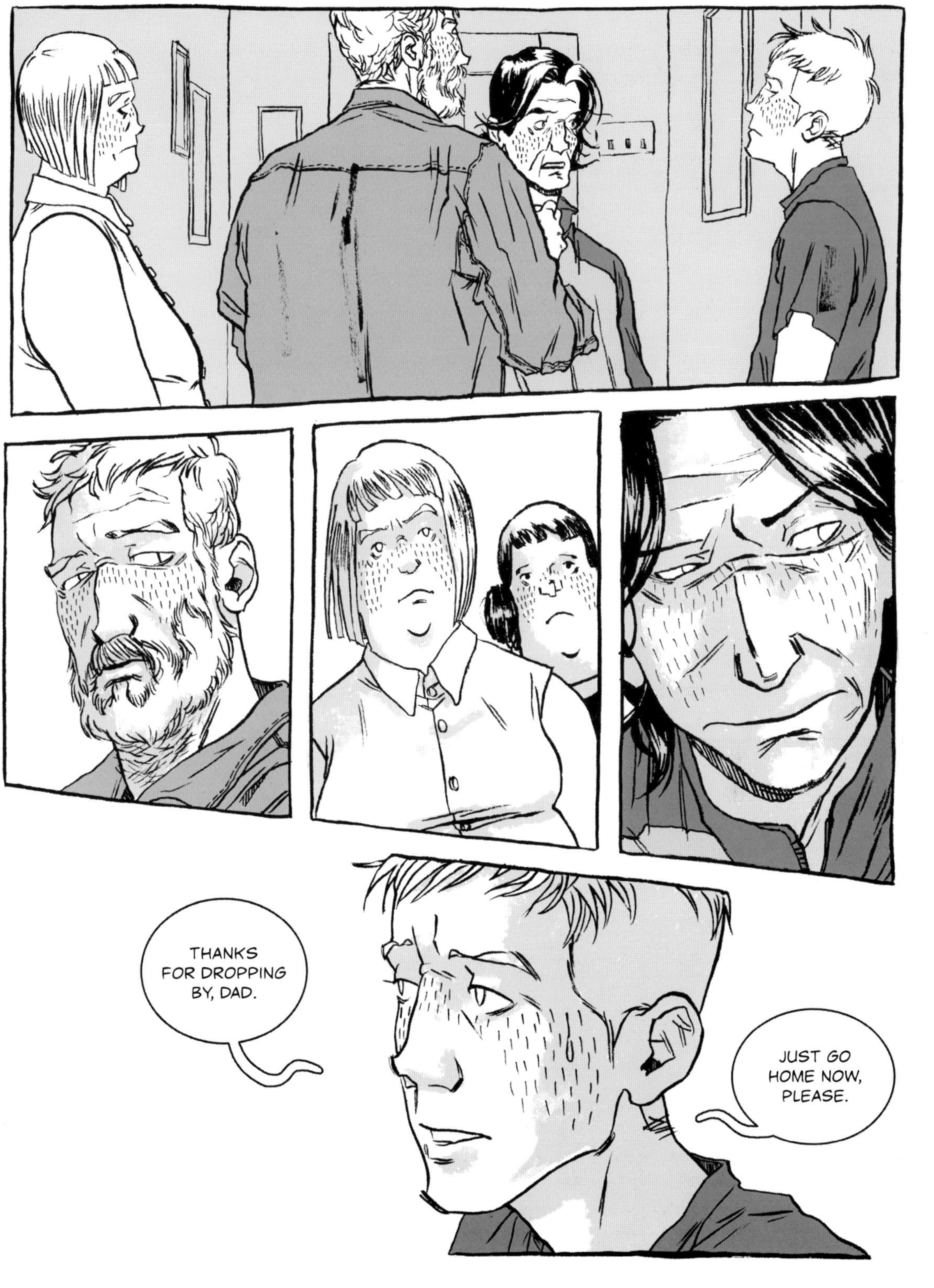
THANKS FOR DROPPING BY, DAD.
JUST GO HOME NOW, PLEASE.

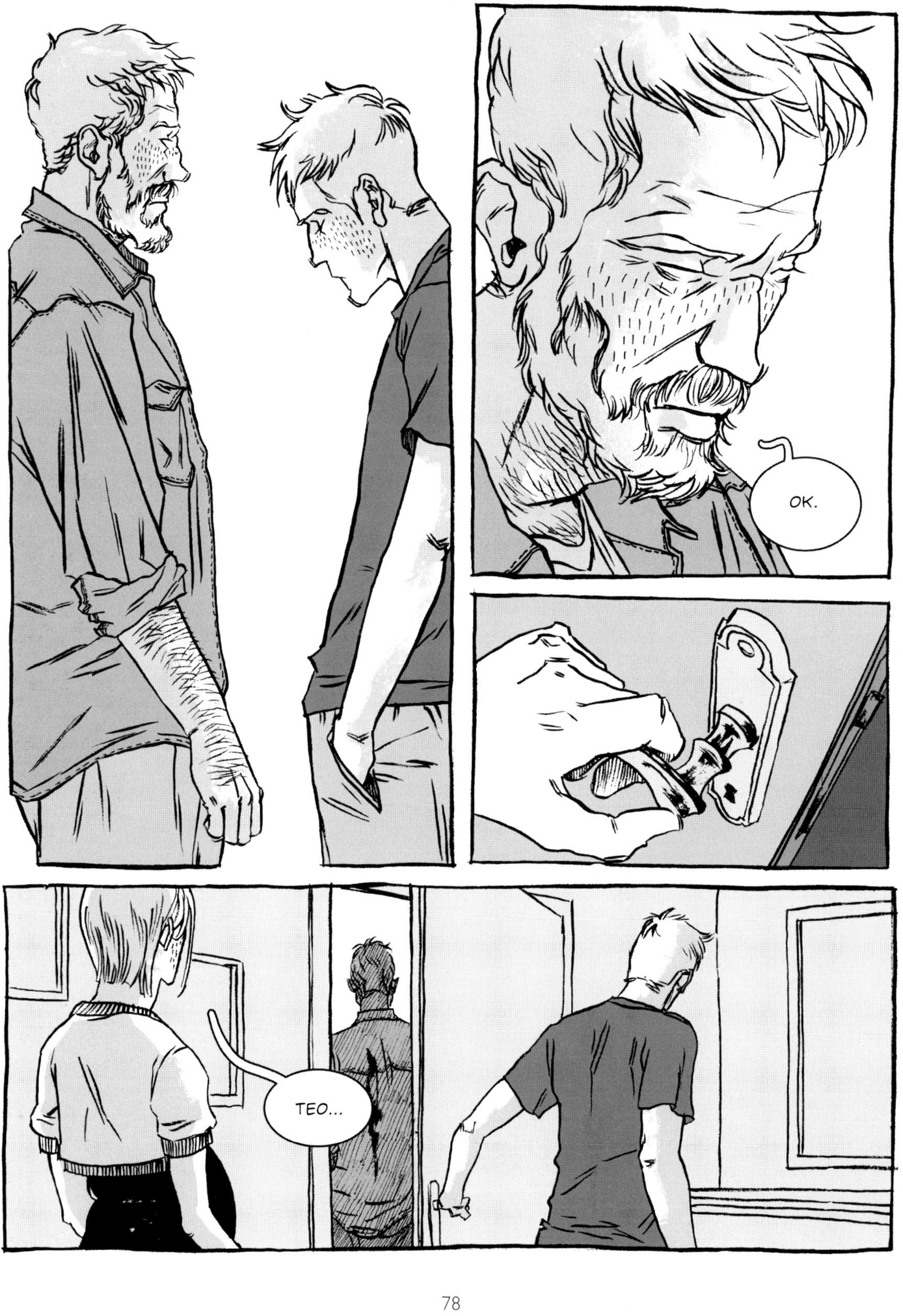
OK.
TEO...

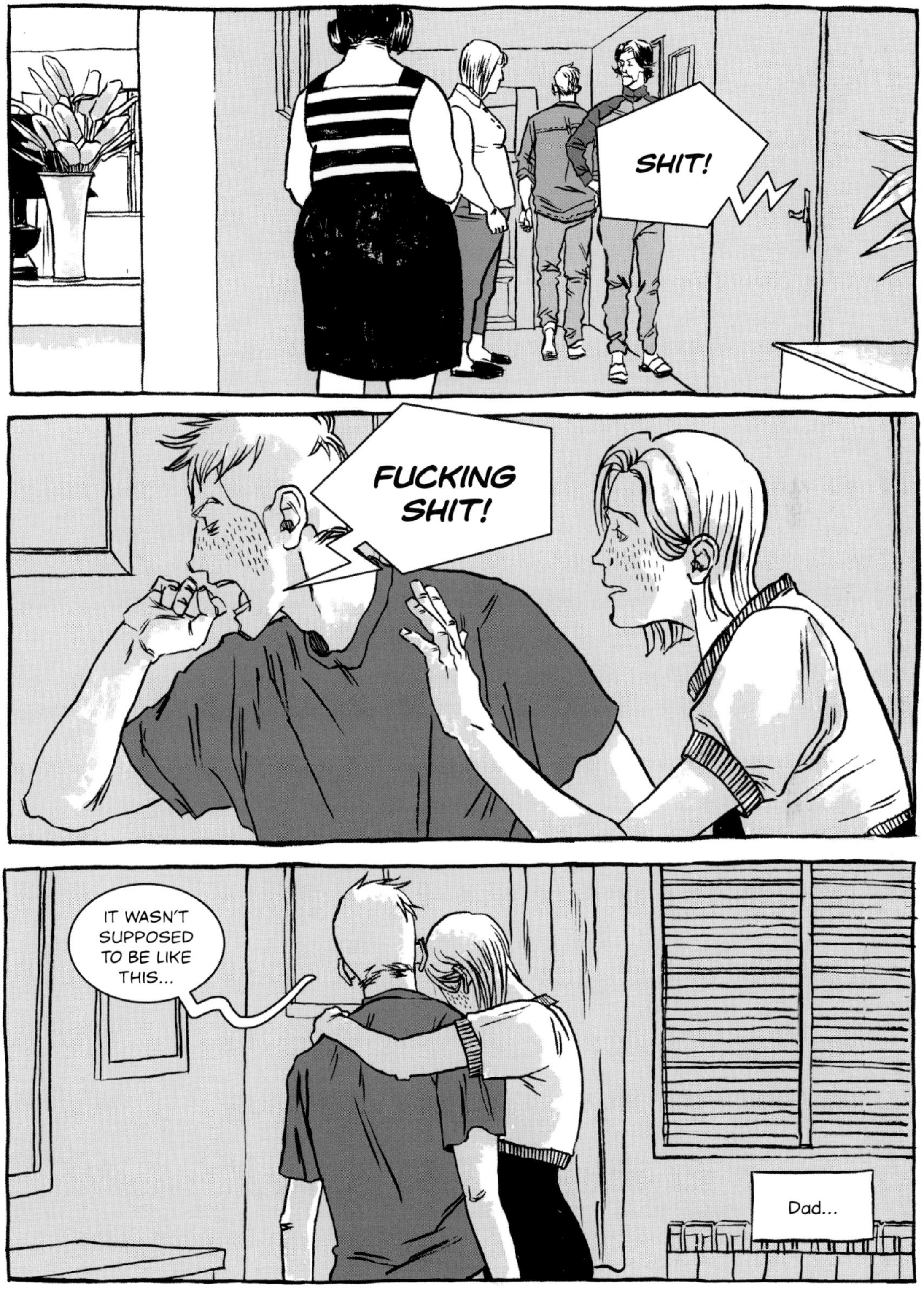
SHIT!
FUCKING SHIT!
IT WASN'T SUPPOSED TO BE LIKE THIS...
Dad...

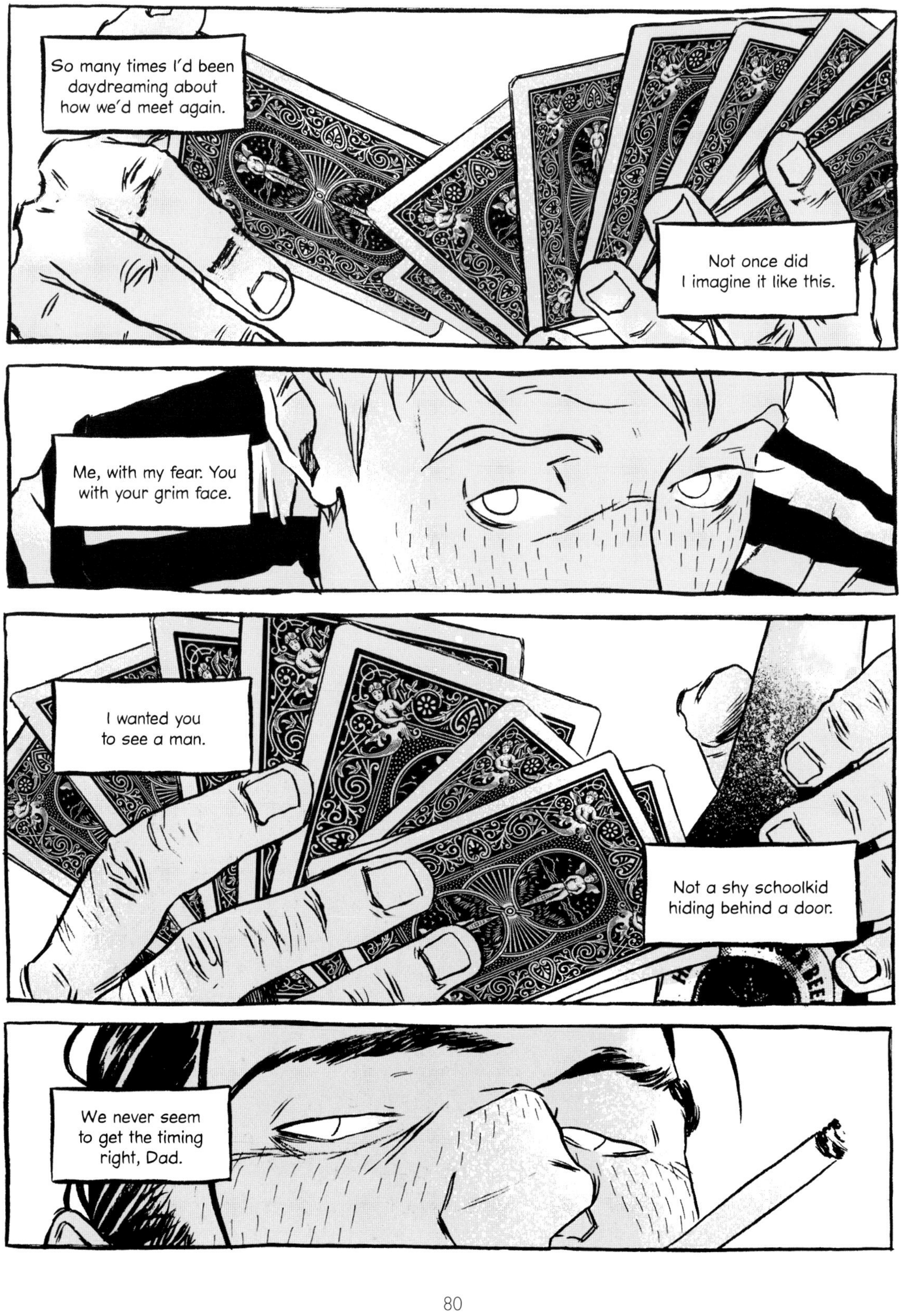
So many times I'd been daydreaming about how we'd meet again.
Not once did I imagine it like this.
Me, with my fear. You with your grim face.
I wanted you to see a man.
Not a shy schoolkid hiding behind a door.
We never seem to get the timing right, Dad.

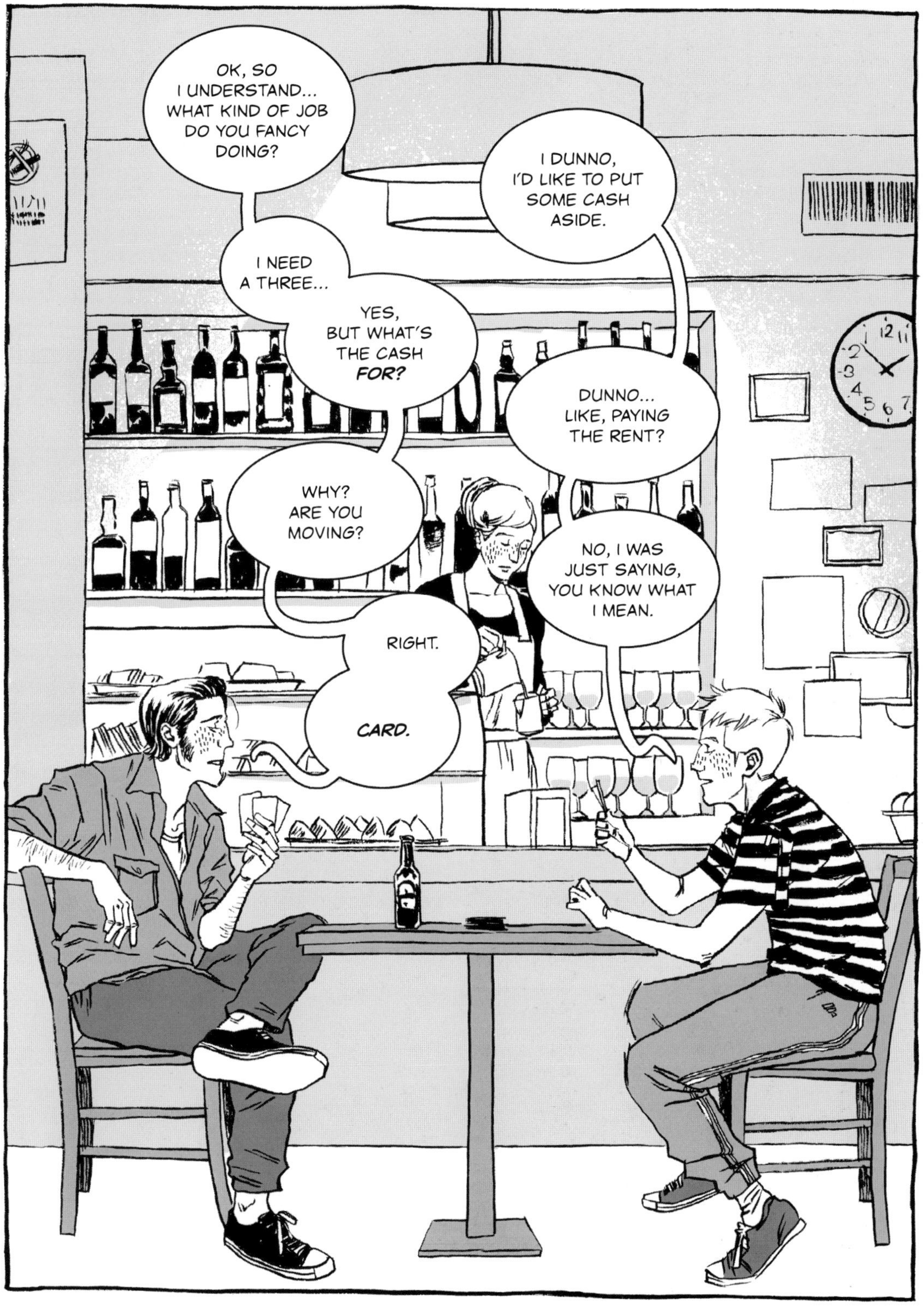
OK, SO I UNDERSTAND... WHAT KIND OF JOB DO YOU FANCY DOING?
I DUNNO, I'D LIKE TO PUT SOME CASH ASIDE.
I NEED A THREE...
YES, BUT WHAT'S THE CASH **FOR?**
DUNNO... LIKE, PAYING THE RENT?
WHY? ARE YOU MOVING?
NO, I WAS JUST SAYING, YOU KNOW WHAT I MEAN.
RIGHT.
CARD.

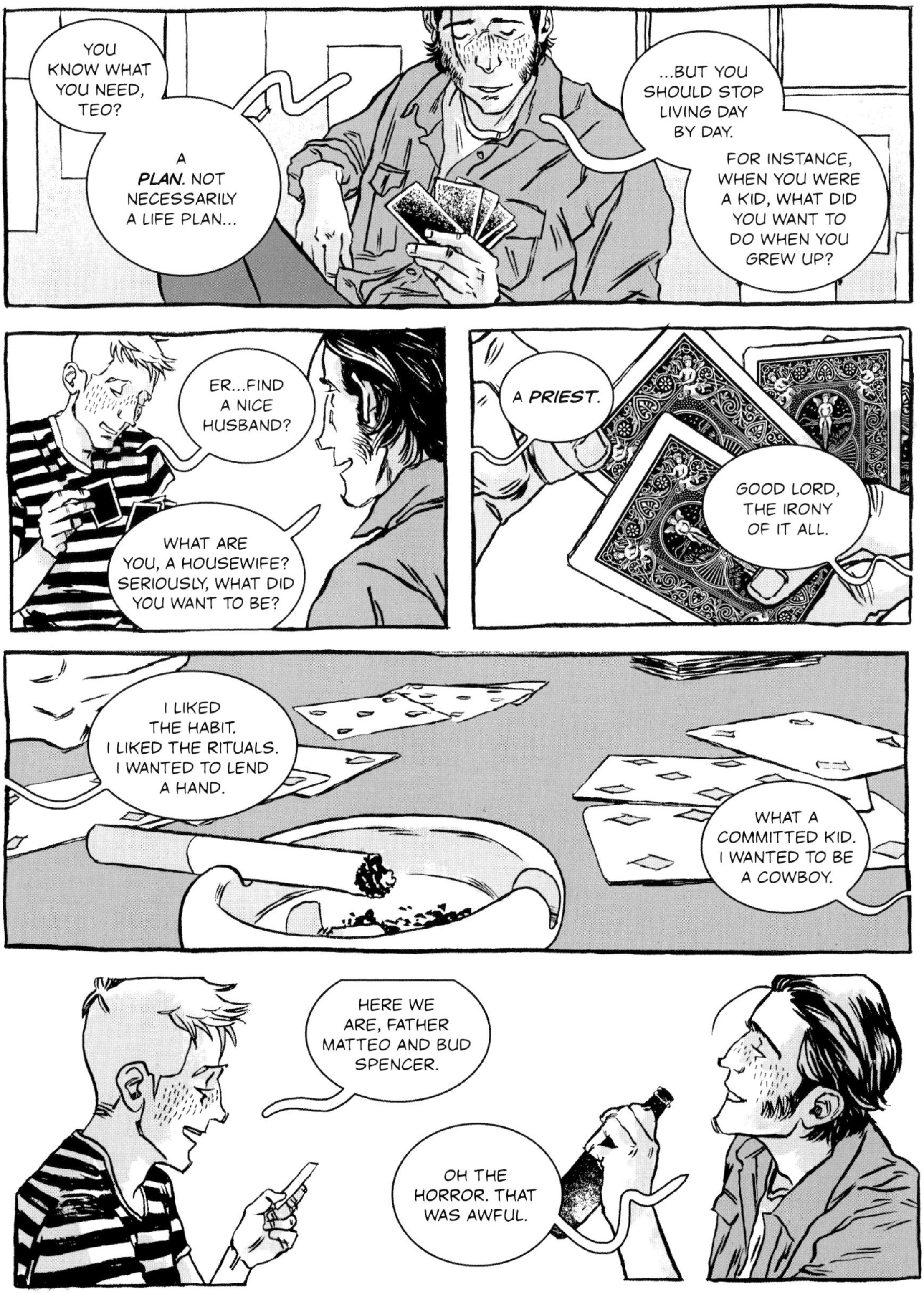
YOU KNOW WHAT YOU NEED, TEO?
A PLAN. NOT NECESSARILY A LIFE PLAN...
...BUT YOU SHOULD STOP LIVING DAY BY DAY.
FOR INSTANCE, WHEN YOU WERE A KID, WHAT DID YOU WANT TO DO WHEN YOU GREW UP?
ER...FIND A NICE HUSBAND?
WHAT ARE YOU, A HOUSEWIFE? SERIOUSLY, WHAT DID YOU WANT TO BE?
A PRIEST.
GOOD LORD, THE IRONY OF IT ALL.
I LIKED THE HABIT. I LIKED THE RITUALS. I WANTED TO LEND A HAND.
WHAT A COMMITTED KID. I WANTED TO BE A COWBOY.
HERE WE ARE, FATHER MATTEO AND BUD SPENCER.
OH THE HORROR. THAT WAS AWFUL.

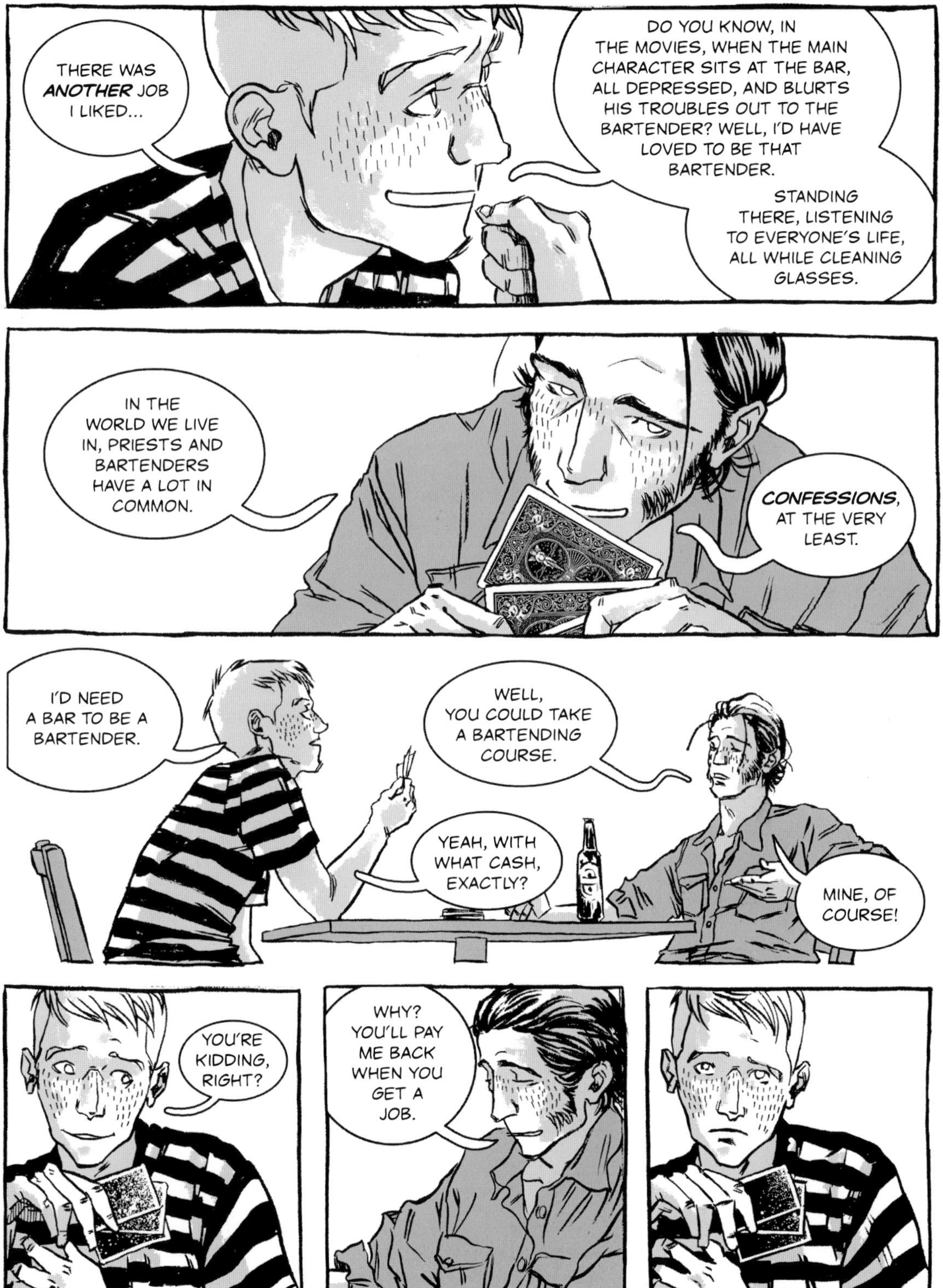
THERE WAS ANOTHER JOB I LIKED...
DO YOU KNOW, IN THE MOVIES, WHEN THE MAIN CHARACTER SITS AT THE BAR, ALL DEPRESSED, AND BLURTS HIS TROUBLES OUT TO THE BARTENDER? WELL, I'D HAVE LOVED TO BE THAT BARTENDER.
STANDING THERE, LISTENING TO EVERYONE'S LIFE, ALL WHILE CLEANING GLASSES.
IN THE WORLD WE LIVE IN, PRIESTS AND BARTENDERS HAVE A LOT IN COMMON.
CONFESSIONS, AT THE VERY LEAST.
I'D NEED A BAR TO BE A BARTENDER.
WELL, YOU COULD TAKE A BARTENDING COURSE.
YEAH, WITH WHAT CASH, EXACTLY?
MINE, OF COURSE!
YOU'RE KIDDING, RIGHT?
WHY? YOU'LL PAY ME BACK WHEN YOU GET A JOB.

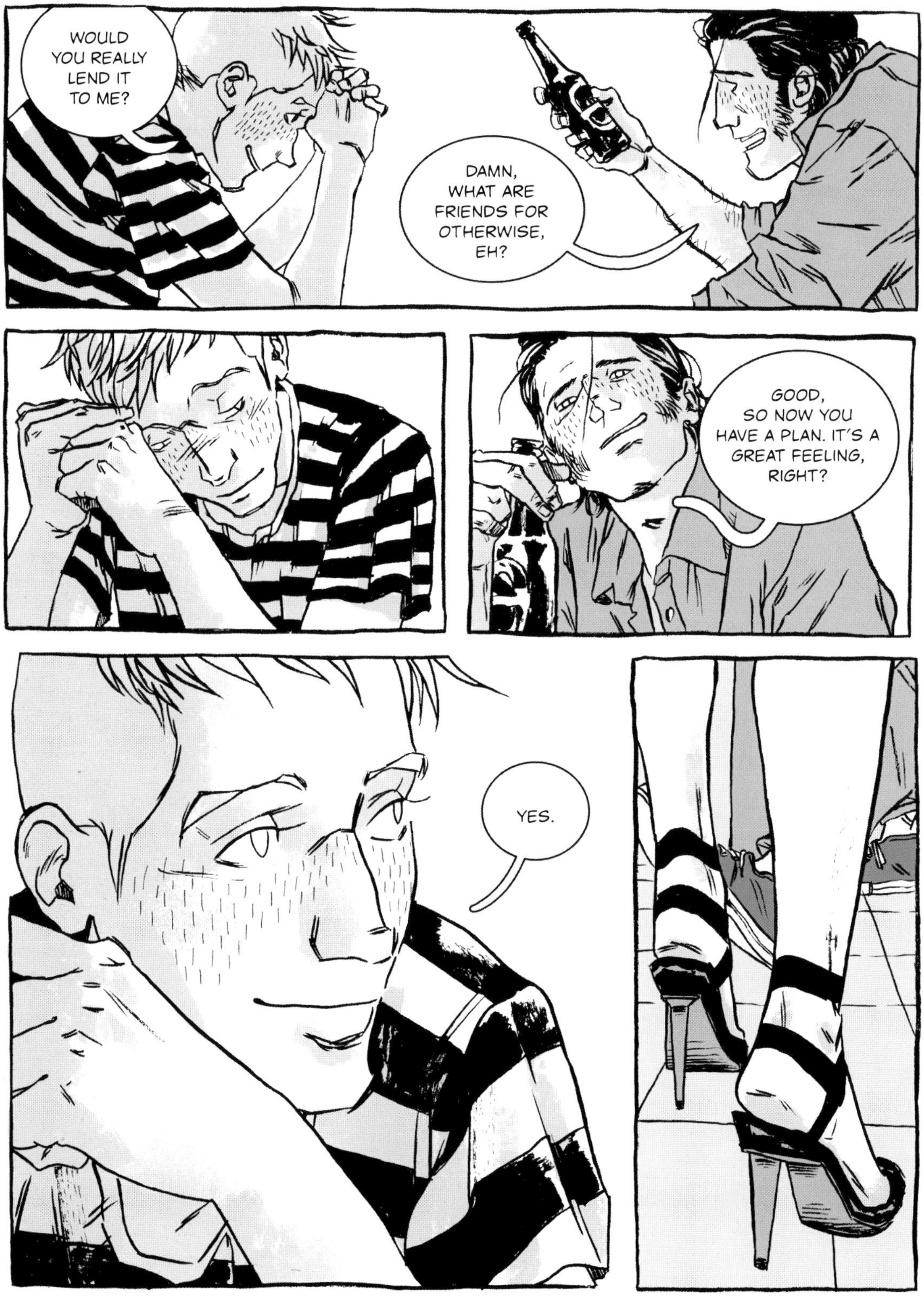
WOULD YOU REALLY LEND IT TO ME?
DAMN, WHAT ARE FRIENDS FOR OTHERWISE, EH?
GOOD, SO NOW YOU HAVE A PLAN. IT'S A GREAT FEELING, RIGHT?
YES.

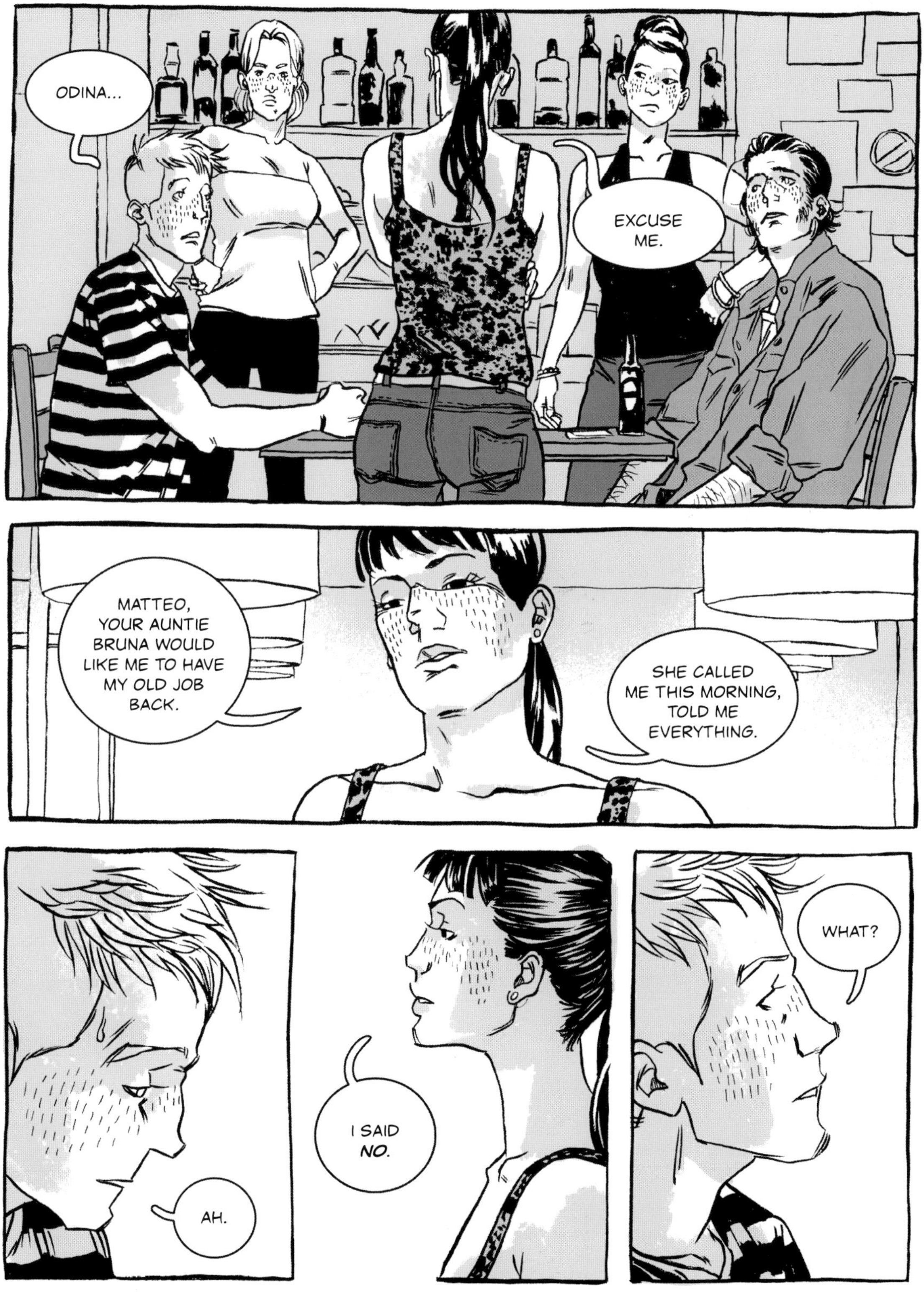
ODINA...
EXCUSE ME.
MATTEO, YOUR AUNTIE BRUNA WOULD LIKE ME TO HAVE MY OLD JOB BACK.
SHE CALLED ME THIS MORNING, TOLD ME EVERYTHING.
AH.
I SAID NO.
WHAT?

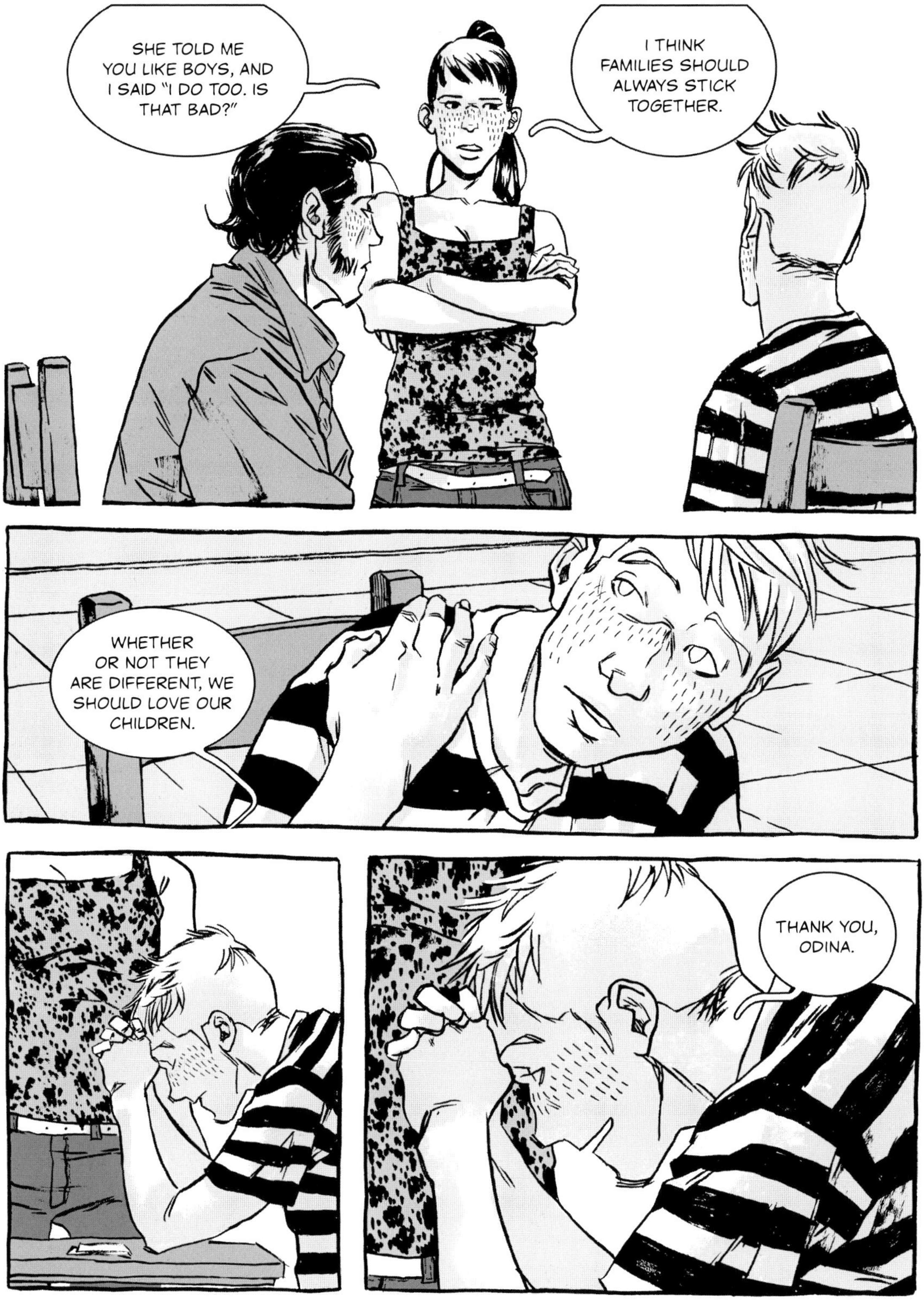
SHE TOLD ME YOU LIKE BOYS, AND I SAID "I DO TOO. IS THAT BAD?"
I THINK FAMILIES SHOULD ALWAYS STICK TOGETHER.
WHETHER OR NOT THEY ARE DIFFERENT, WE SHOULD LOVE OUR CHILDREN.
THANK YOU, ODINA.

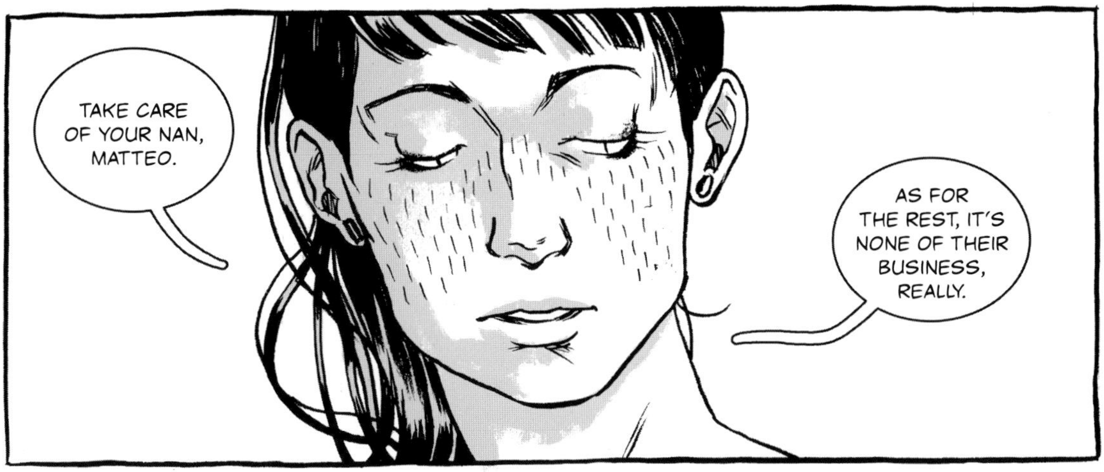
TAKE CARE OF YOUR NAN, MATTEO.
AS FOR THE REST, IT'S NONE OF THEIR BUSINESS, REALLY.

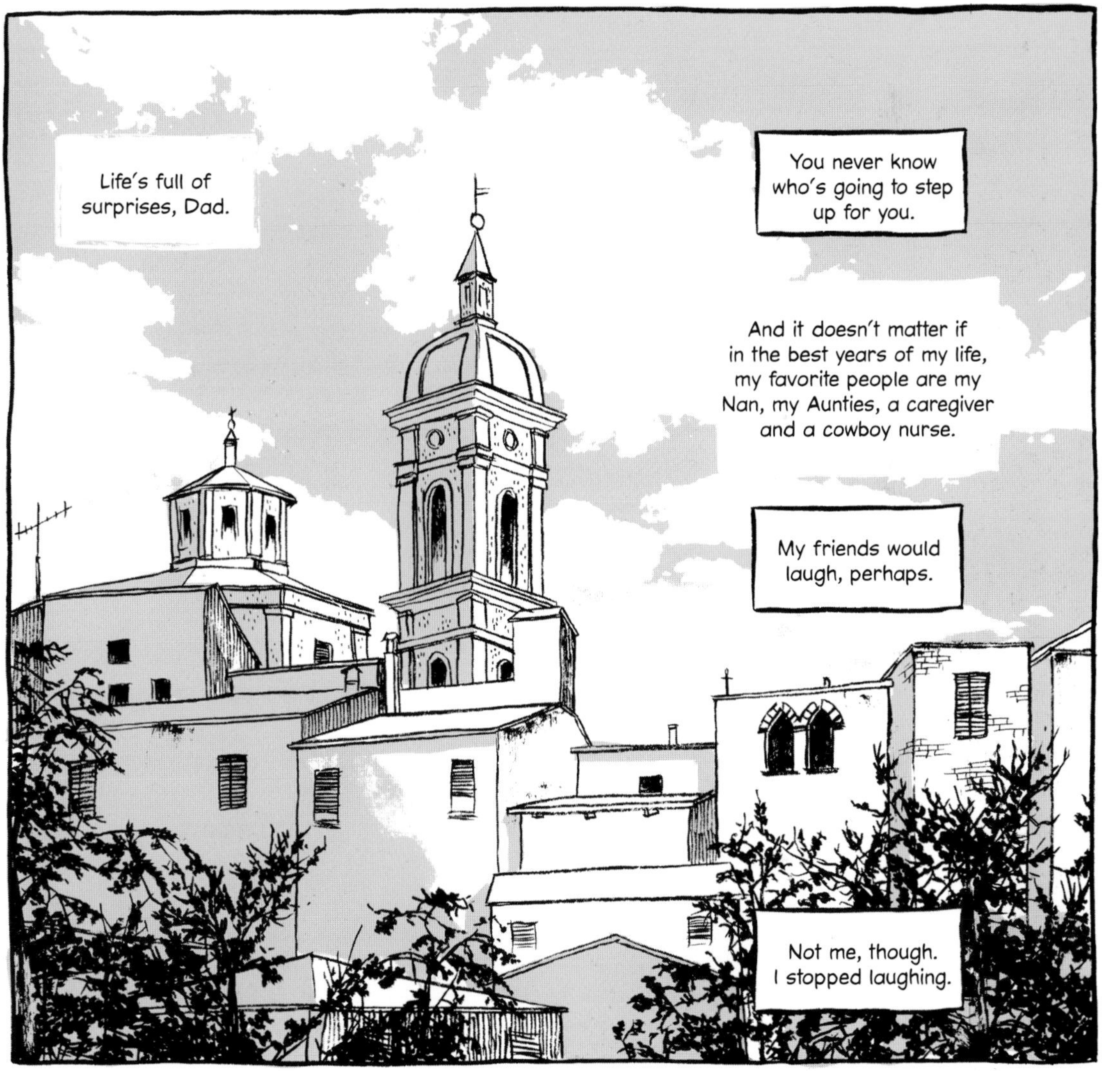
Life's full of surprises, Dad.
You never know who's going to step up for you.
And it doesn't matter if in the best years of my life, my favorite people are my Nan, my Aunties, a caregiver and a cowboy nurse.
My friends would laugh, perhaps.
Not me, though. I stopped laughing.

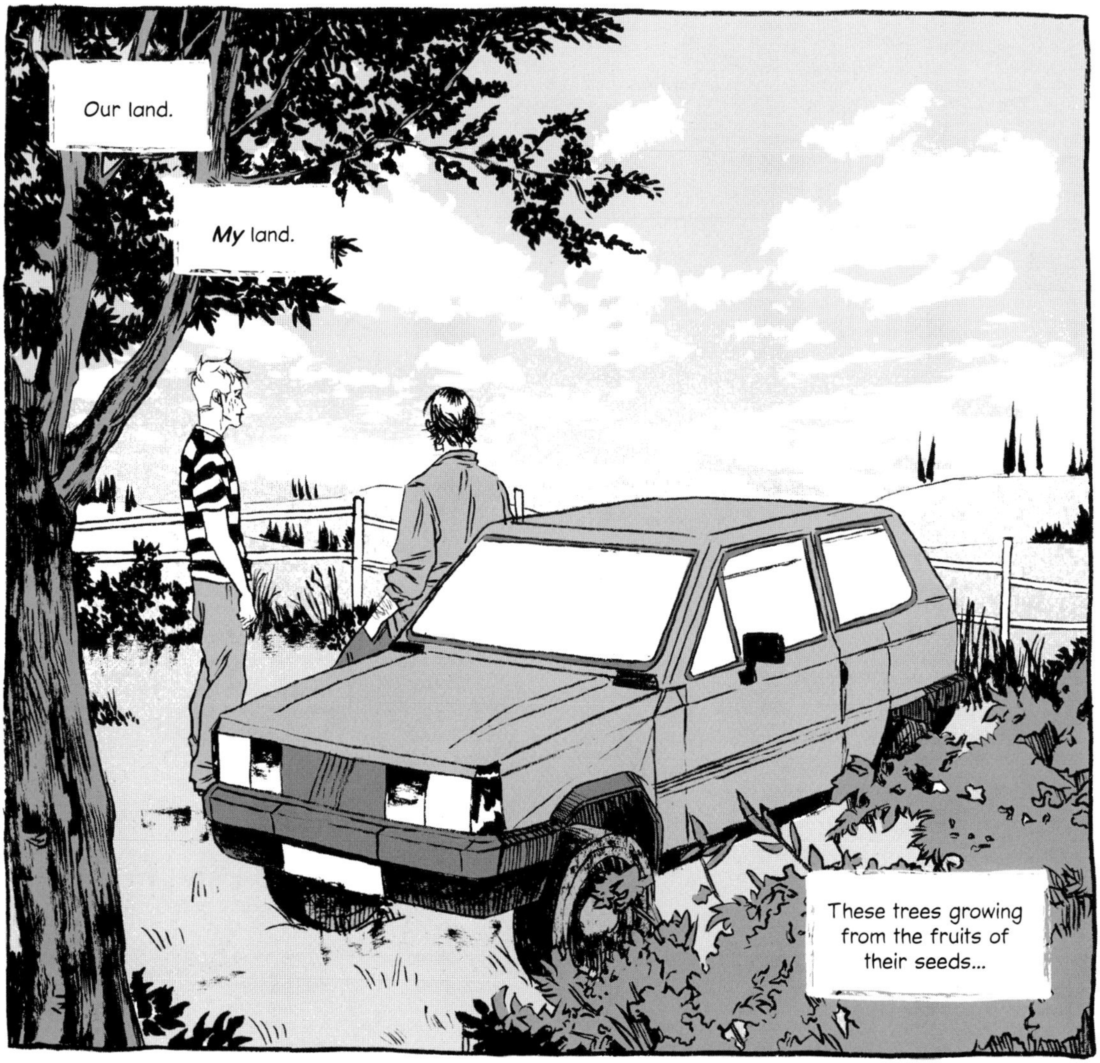
Our land.
My land.
These trees growing from the fruits of their seeds...

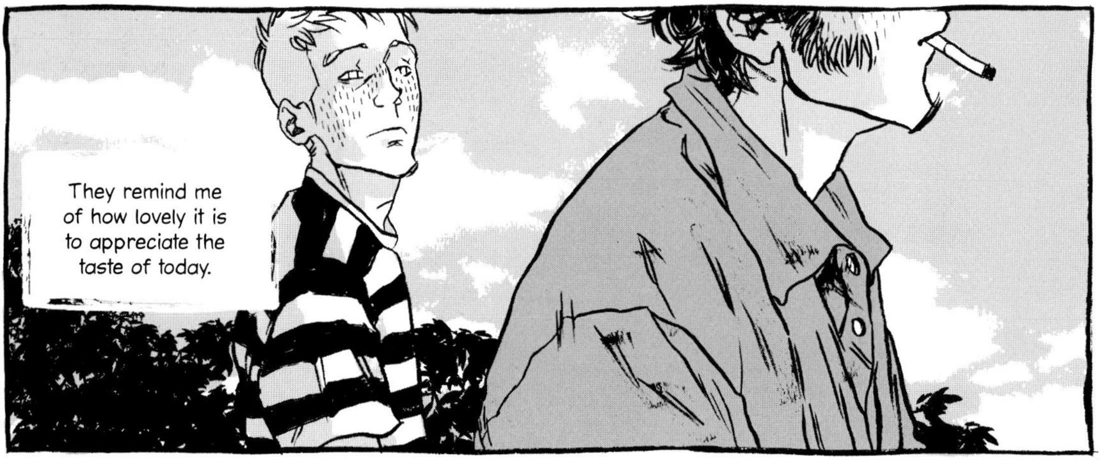
They remind me of how lovely it is to appreciate the taste of today.

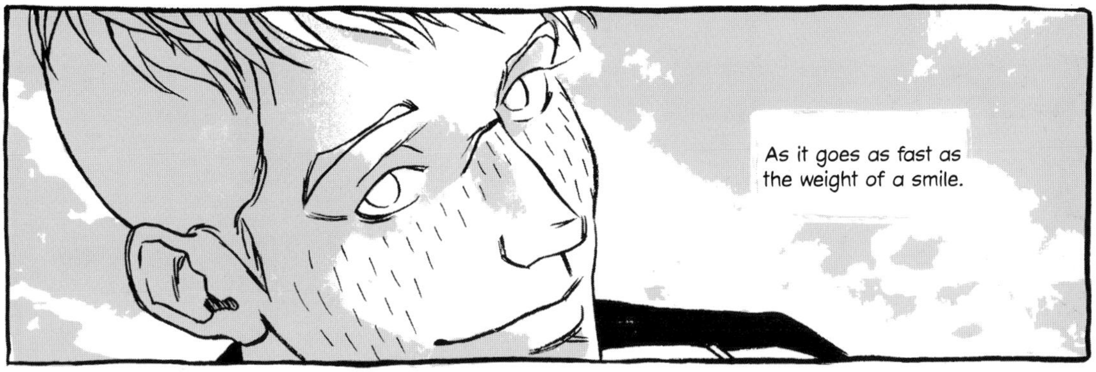
As it goes as fast as the weight of a smile.

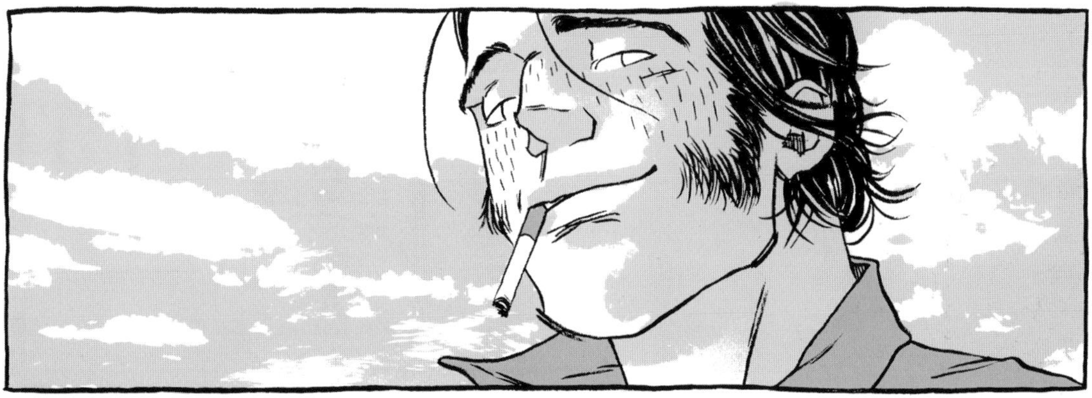

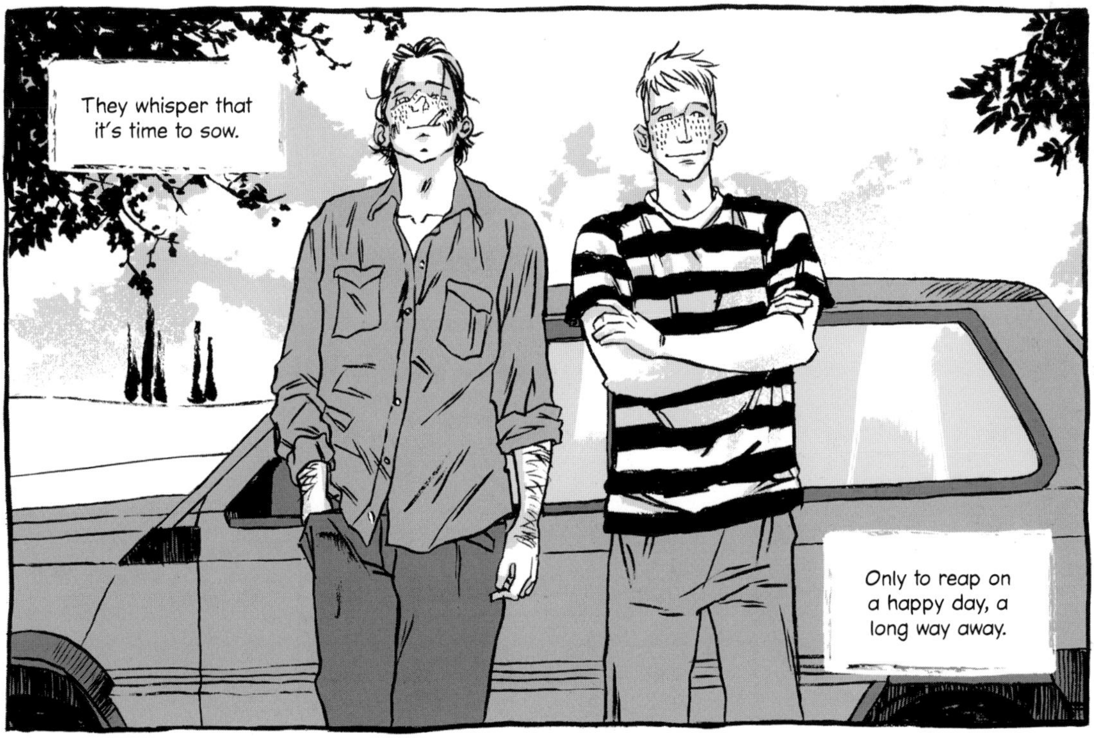
They whisper that it's time to sow.
Only to reap on a happy day, a long way away.

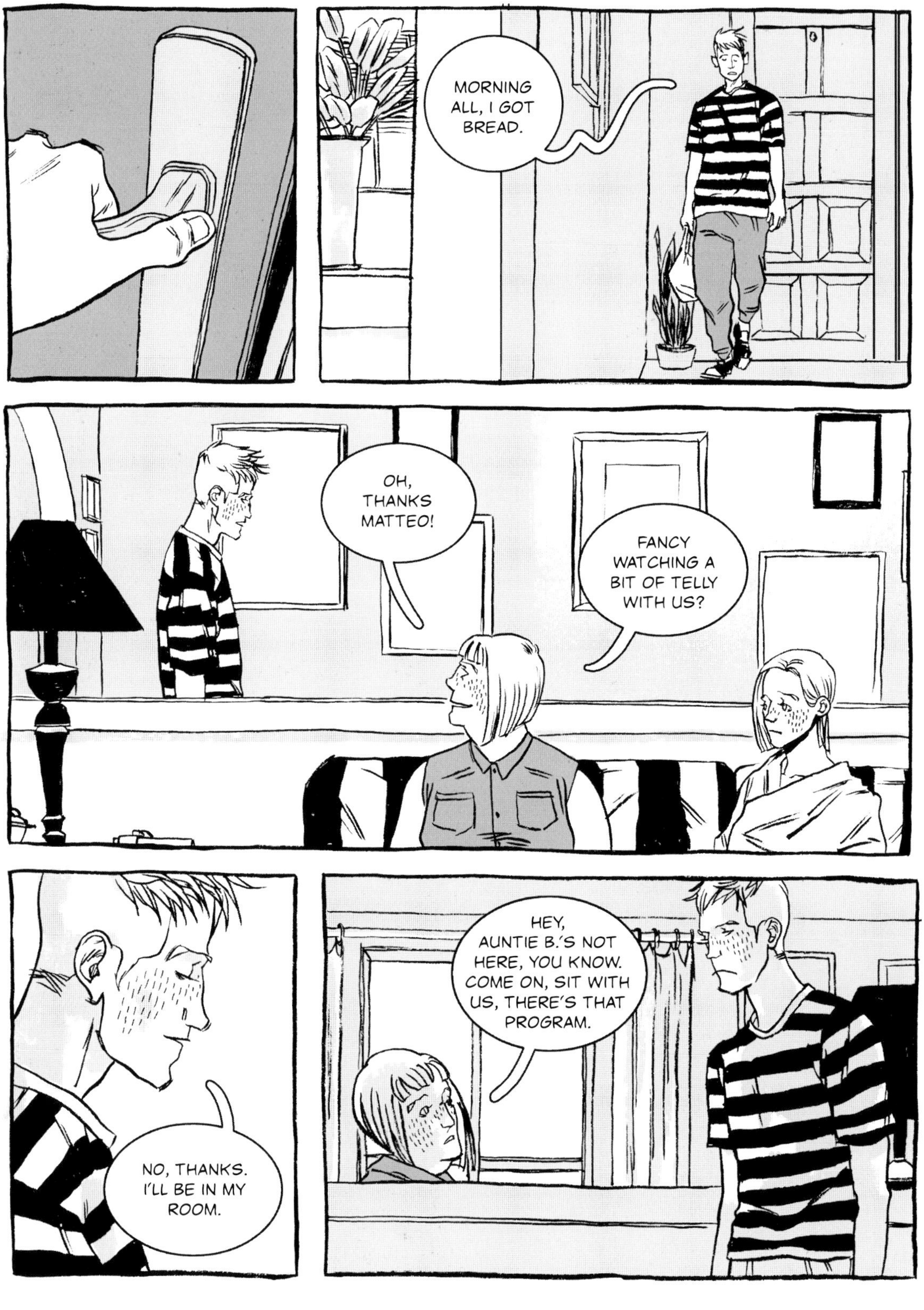
MORNING ALL, I GOT BREAD.
OH, THANKS MATTEO!
FANCY WATCHING A BIT OF TELLY WITH US?
NO, THANKS. I'LL BE IN MY ROOM.
HEY, AUNTIE B.'S NOT HERE, YOU KNOW. COME ON, SIT WITH US, THERE'S THAT PROGRAM.

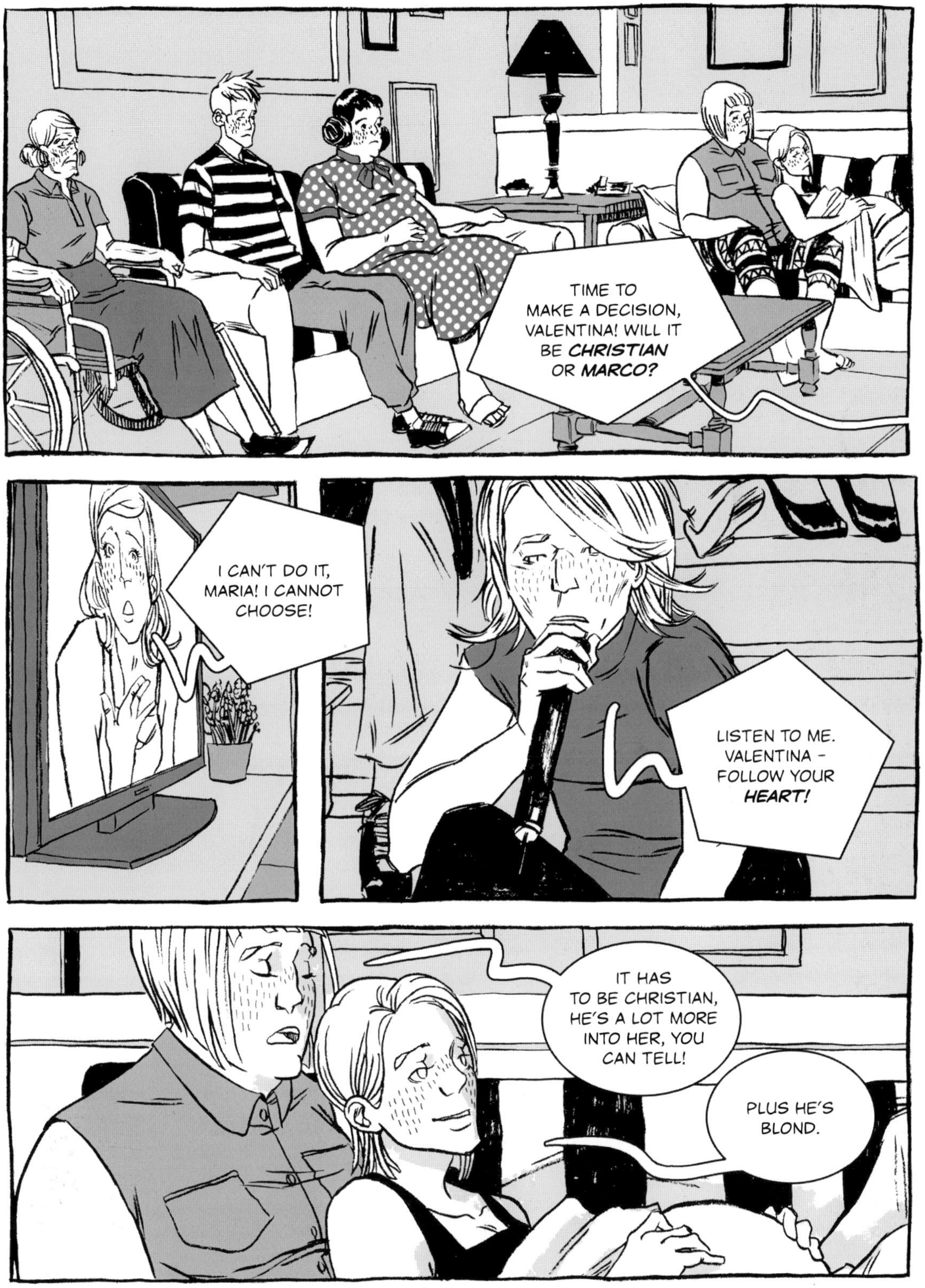
TIME TO MAKE A DECISION, VALENTINA! WILL IT BE **CHRISTIAN** OR **MARCO?**
I CAN'T DO IT, MARIA! I CANNOT CHOOSE!
LISTEN TO ME. VALENTINA - FOLLOW YOUR **HEART!**
IT HAS TO BE CHRISTIAN, HE'S A LOT MORE INTO HER, YOU CAN TELL!
PLUS HE'S BLOND.

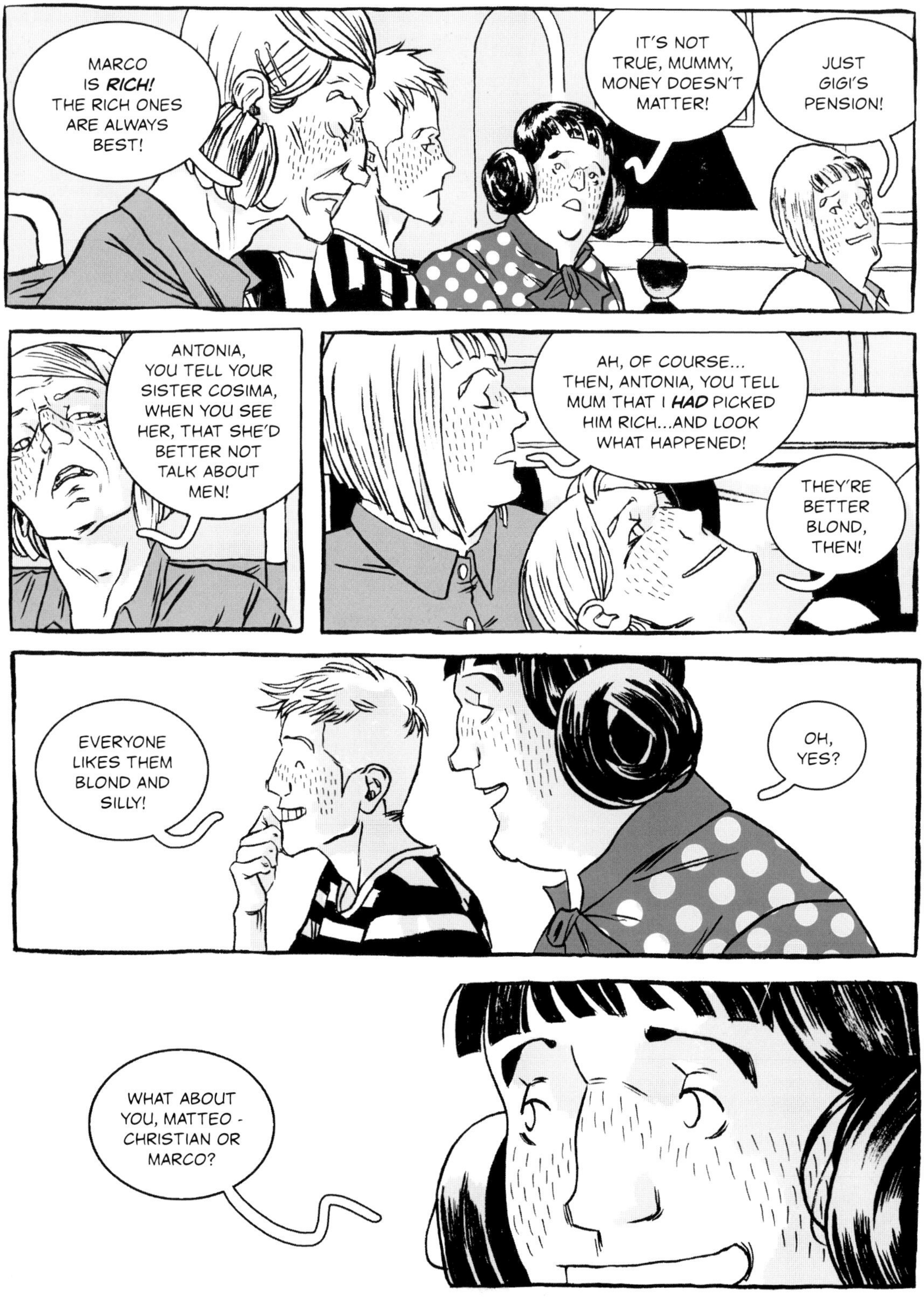
MARCO IS RICH! THE RICH ONES ARE ALWAYS BEST!
IT'S NOT TRUE, MUMMY, MONEY DOESN'T MATTER!
JUST GIGI'S PENSION!
ANTONIA, YOU TELL YOUR SISTER COSIMA, WHEN YOU SEE HER, THAT SHE'D BETTER NOT TALK ABOUT MEN!
AH, OF COURSE... THEN, ANTONIA, YOU TELL MUM THAT I HAD PICKED HIM RICH...AND LOOK WHAT HAPPENED!
THEY'RE BETTER BLOND, THEN!
EVERYONE LIKES THEM BLOND AND SILLY!
OH, YES?
WHAT ABOUT YOU, MATTEO - CHRISTIAN OR MARCO?

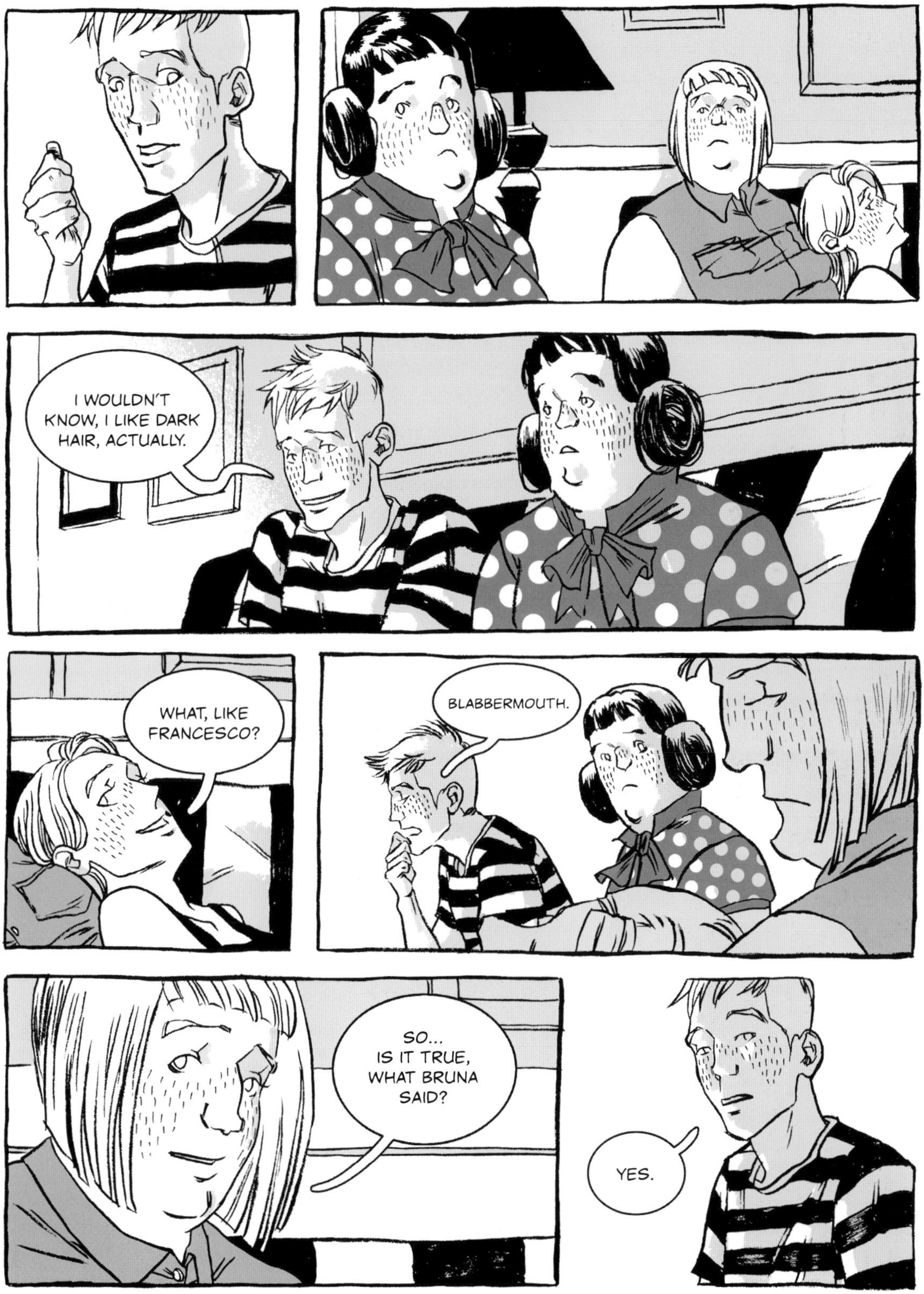
I WOULDN'T KNOW, I LIKE DARK HAIR, ACTUALLY.
WHAT, LIKE FRANCESCO?
BLABBERMOUTH.
SO... IS IT TRUE, WHAT BRUNA SAID?
YES.

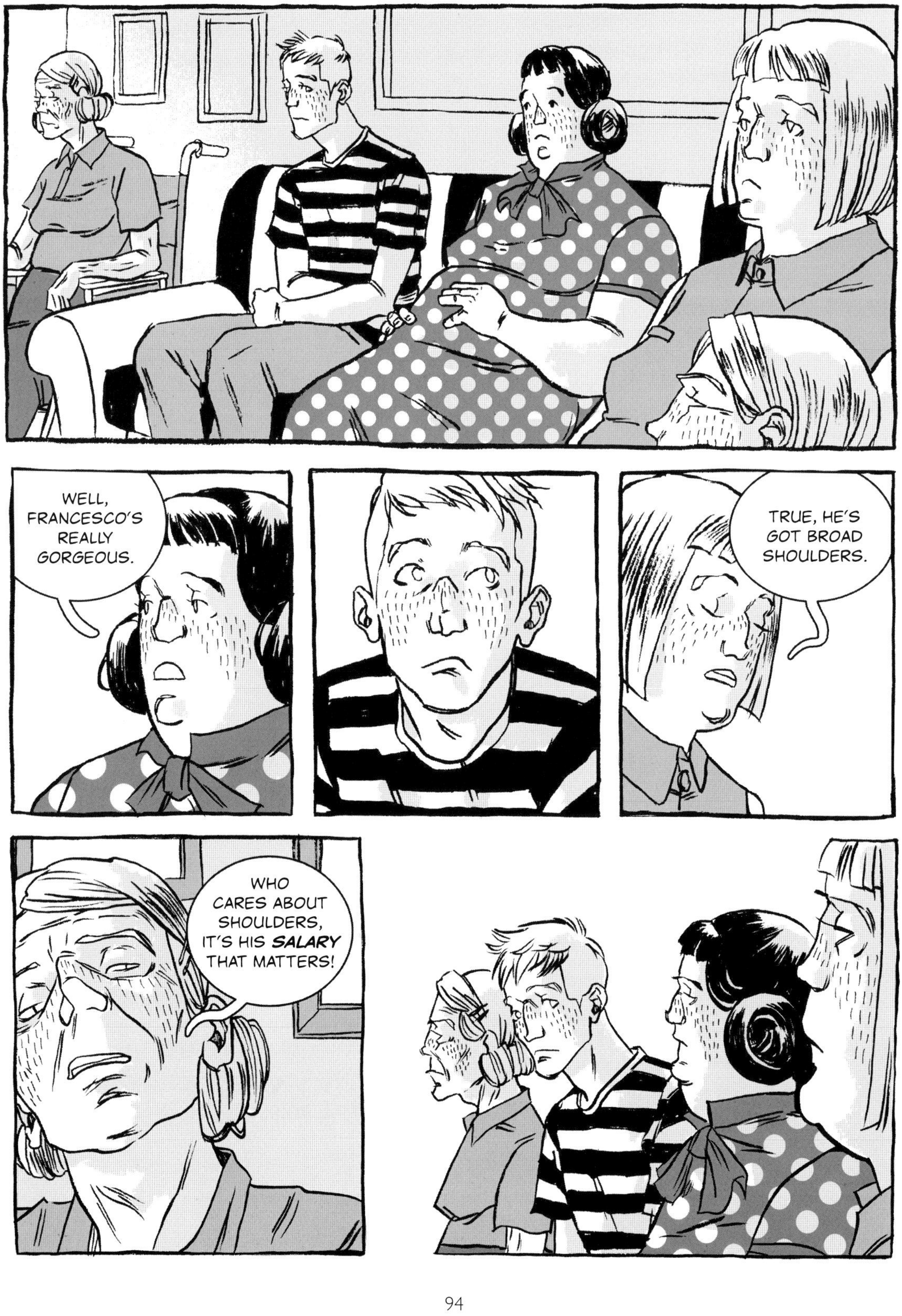
WELL, FRANCESCO'S REALLY GORGEOUS.
TRUE, HE'S GOT BROAD SHOULDERS.
WHO CARES ABOUT SHOULDERS, IT'S HIS **SALARY** THAT MATTERS!

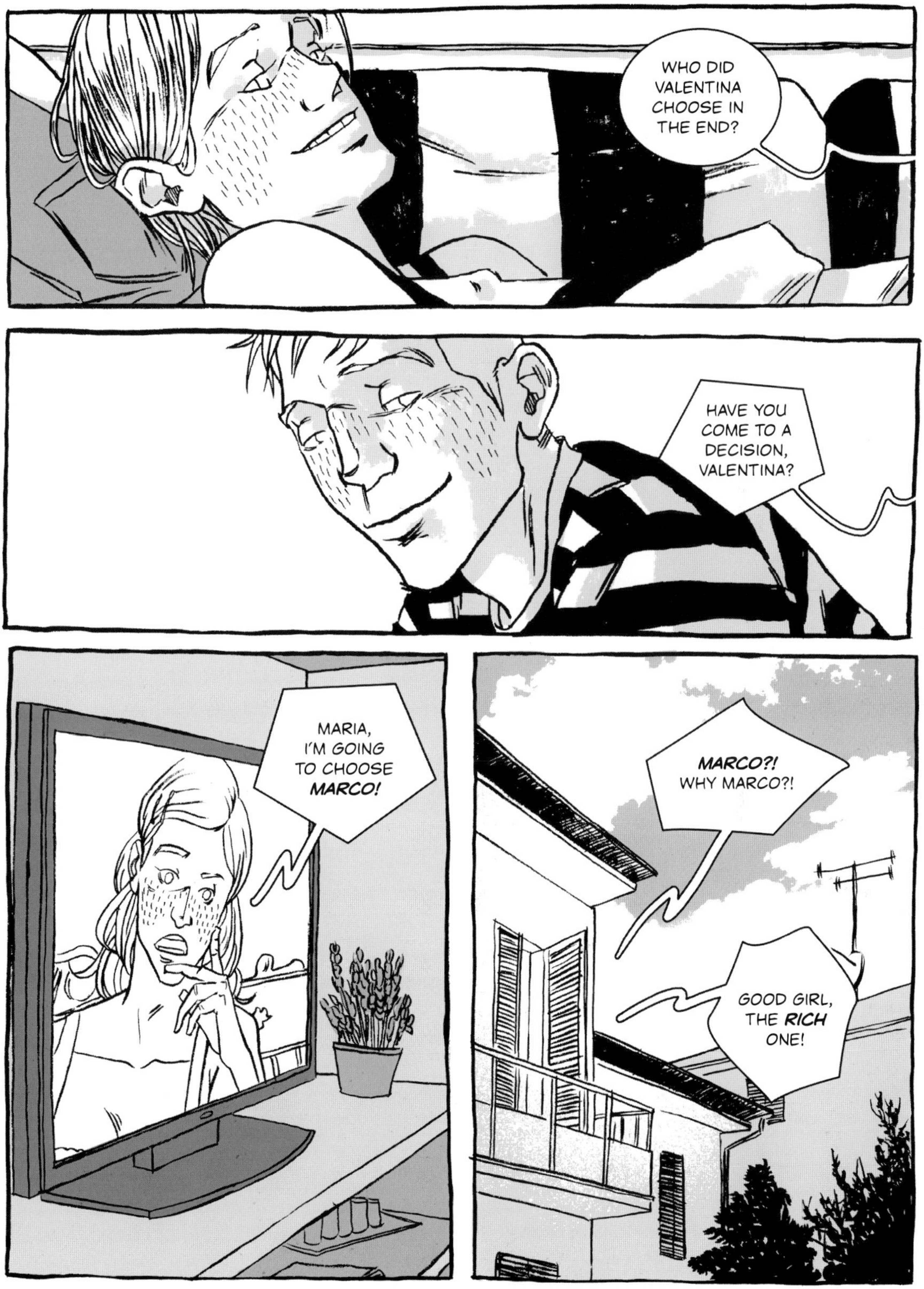
WHO DID VALENTINA CHOOSE IN THE END?
HAVE YOU COME TO A DECISION, VALENTINA?
MARIA, I'M GOING TO CHOOSE ***MARCO!***
MARCO?! WHY MARCO?!
GOOD GIRL, THE ***RICH*** ONE!

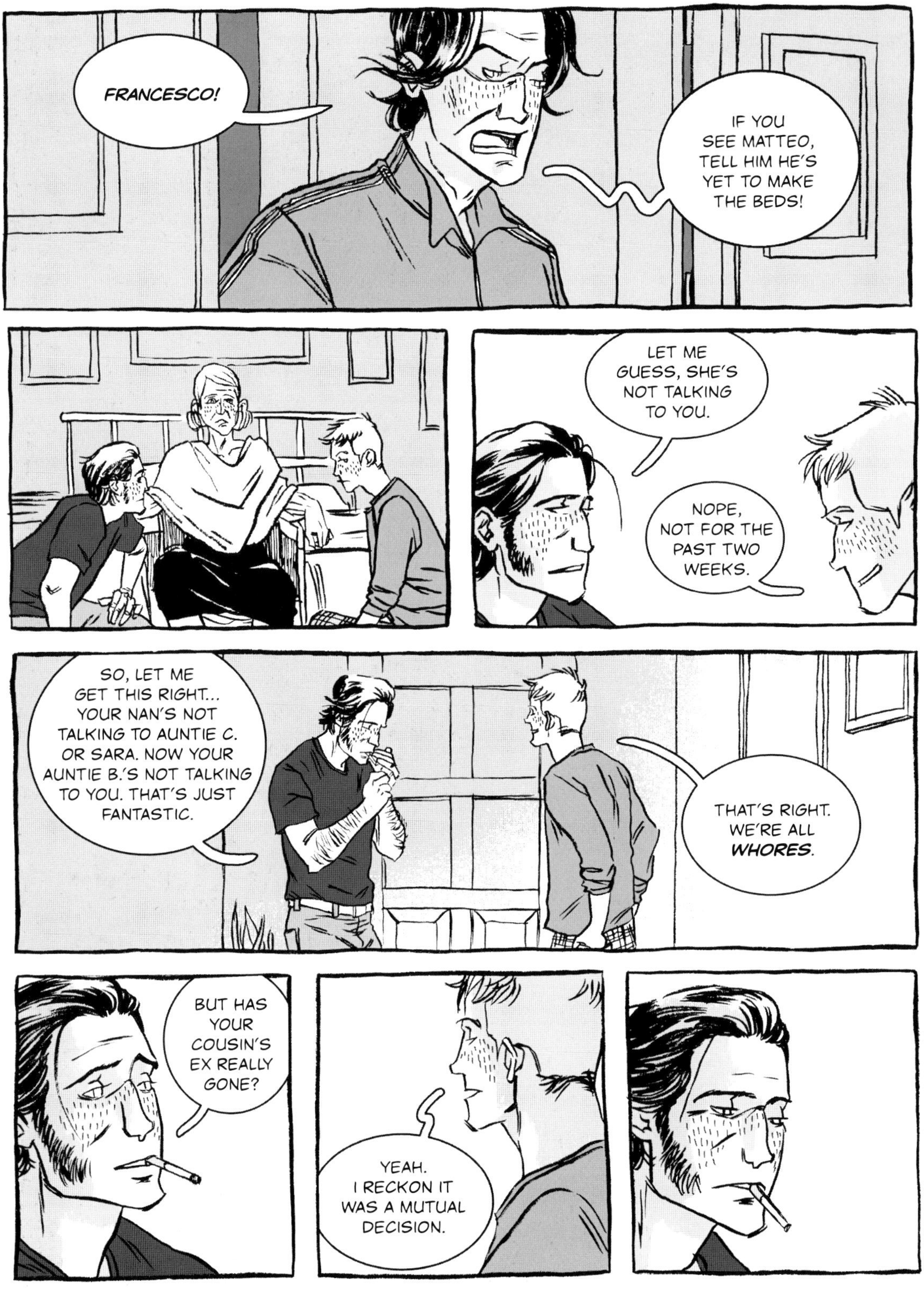
FRANCESCO!
IF YOU SEE MATTEO, TELL HIM HE'S YET TO MAKE THE BEDS!
LET ME GUESS, SHE'S NOT TALKING TO YOU.
NOPE, NOT FOR THE PAST TWO WEEKS.
SO, LET ME GET THIS RIGHT... YOUR NAN'S NOT TALKING TO AUNTIE C. OR SARA. NOW YOUR AUNTIE B.'S NOT TALKING TO YOU. THAT'S JUST FANTASTIC.
THAT'S RIGHT. WE'RE ALL *WHORES*.
BUT HAS YOUR COUSIN'S EX REALLY GONE?
YEAH. I RECKON IT WAS A MUTUAL DECISION.

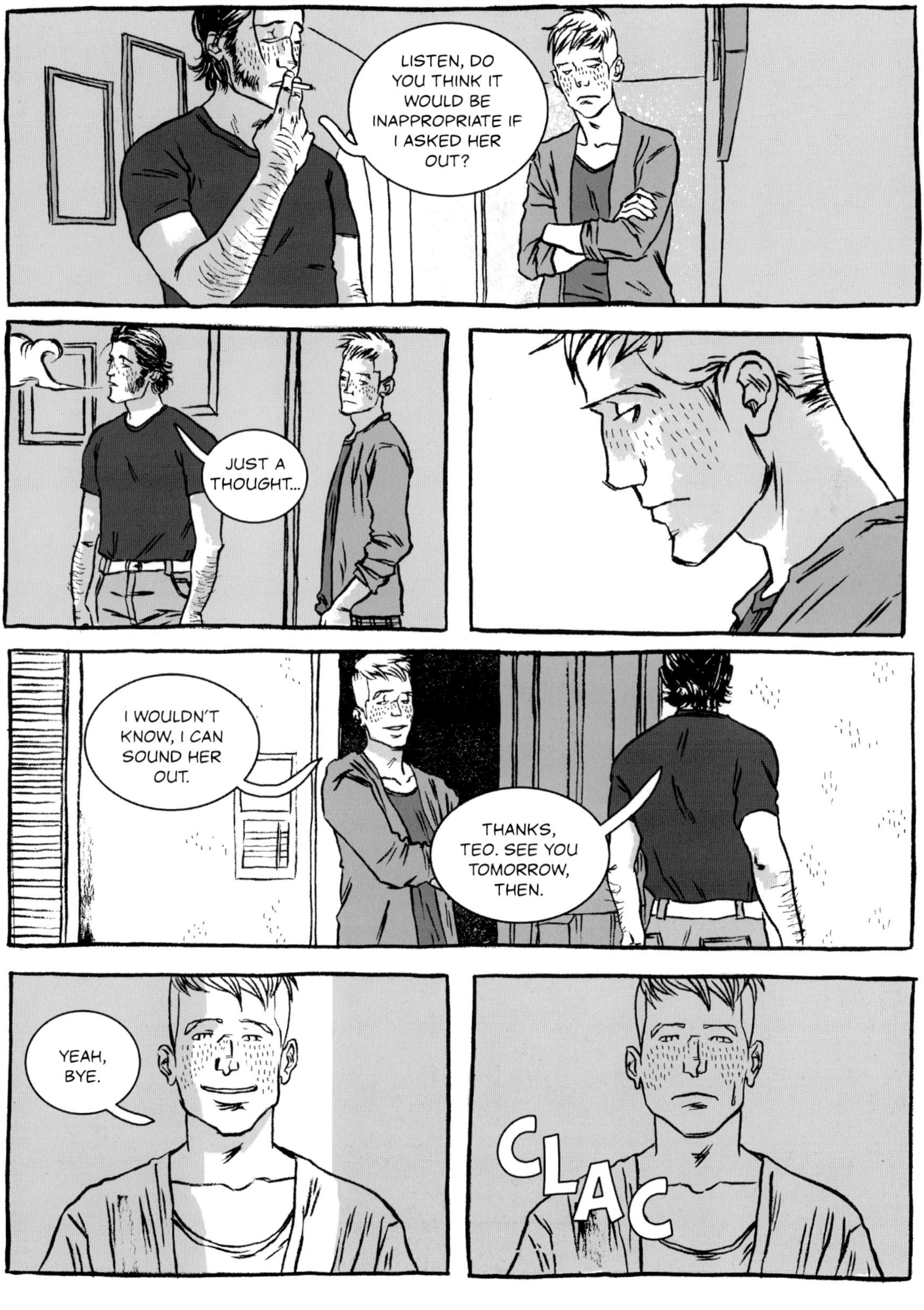
LISTEN, DO YOU THINK IT WOULD BE INAPPROPRIATE IF I ASKED HER OUT?
JUST A THOUGHT...
I WOULDN'T KNOW, I CAN SOUND HER OUT.
THANKS, TEO. SEE YOU TOMORROW, THEN.
YEAH, BYE.
CLAC

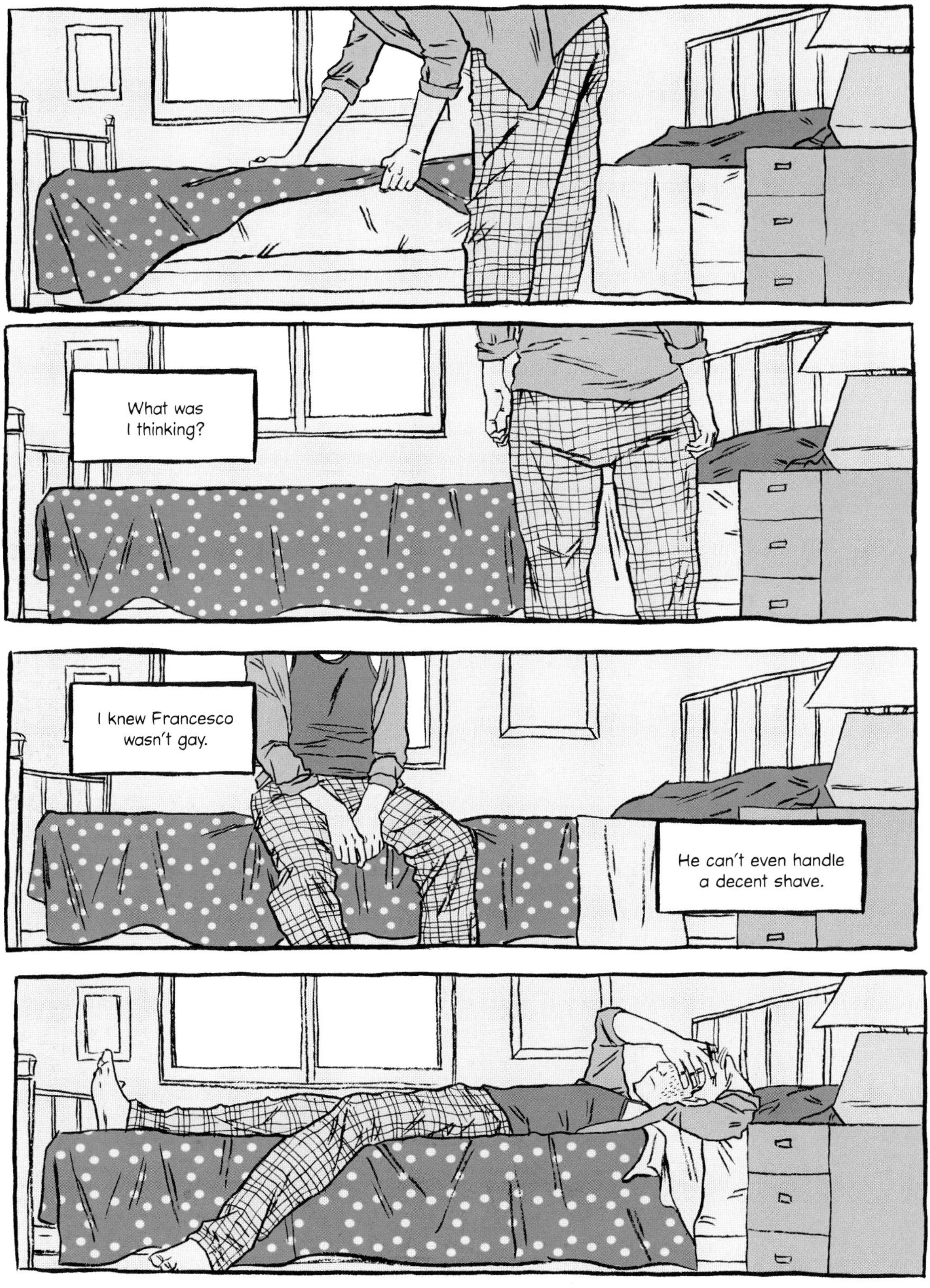
What was I thinking?
I knew Francesco wasn't gay.
He can't even handle a decent shave.

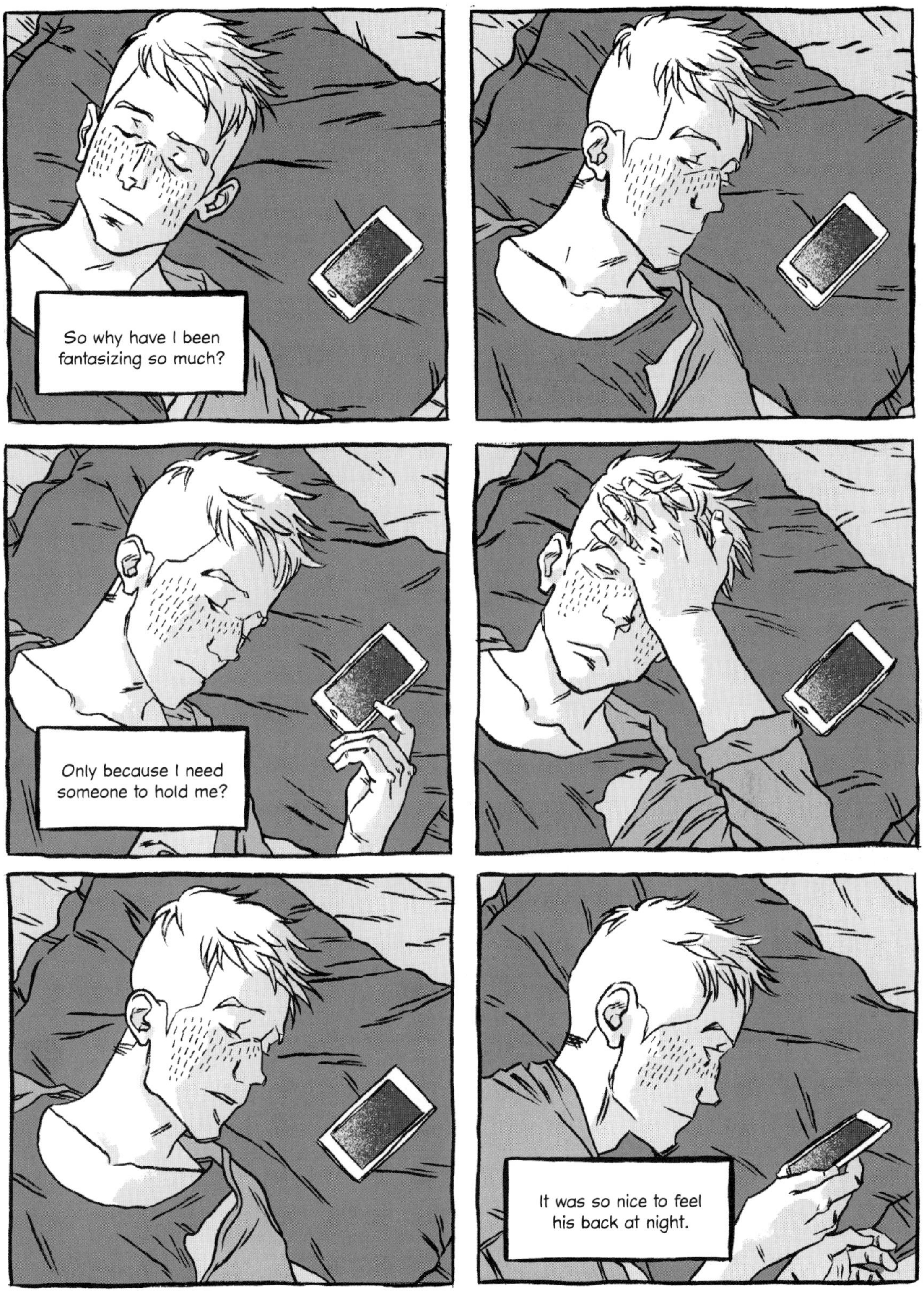
So why have I been fantasizing so much?
Only because I need someone to hold me?
It was so nice to feel his back at night.

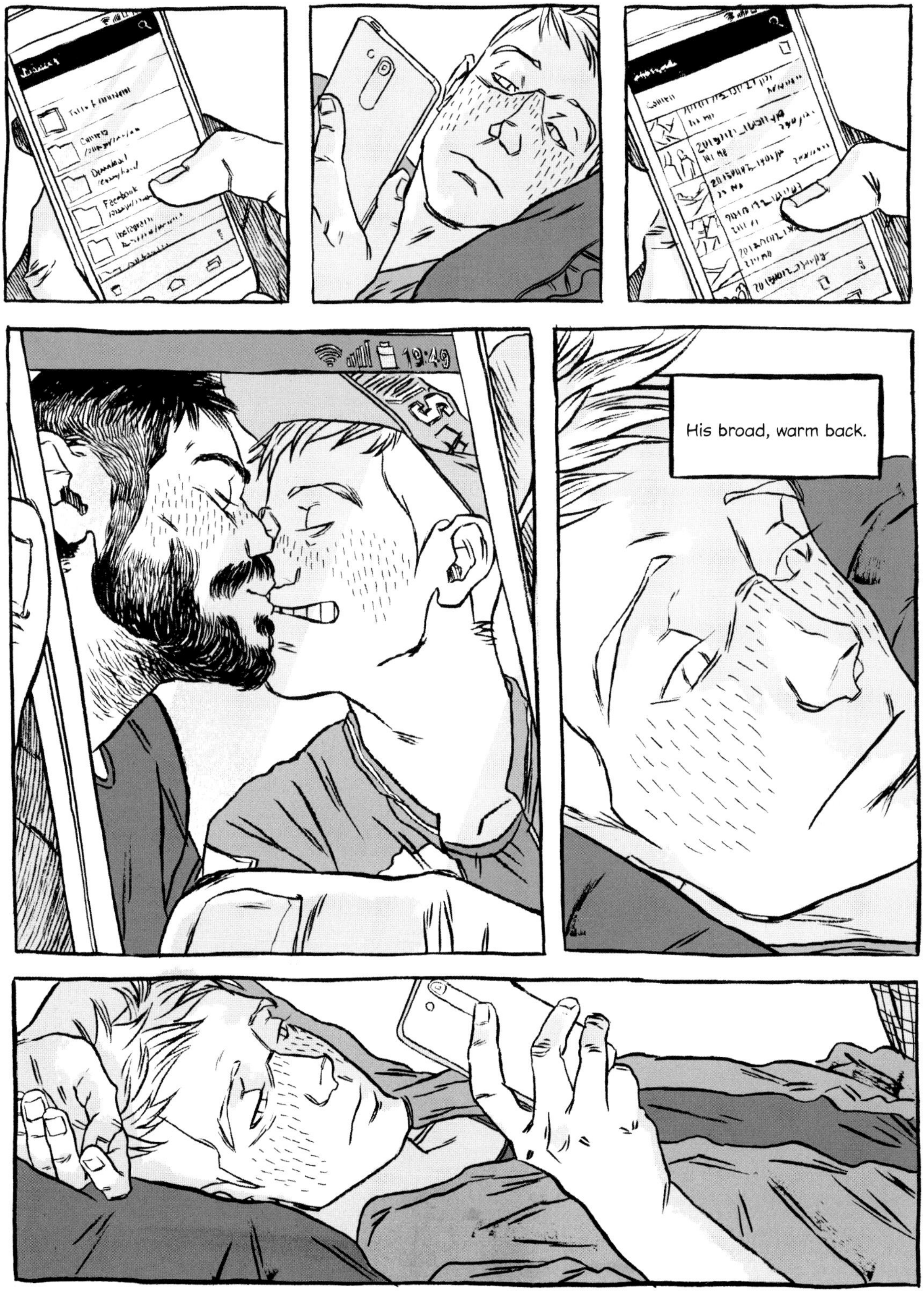
19:49
His broad, warm back.

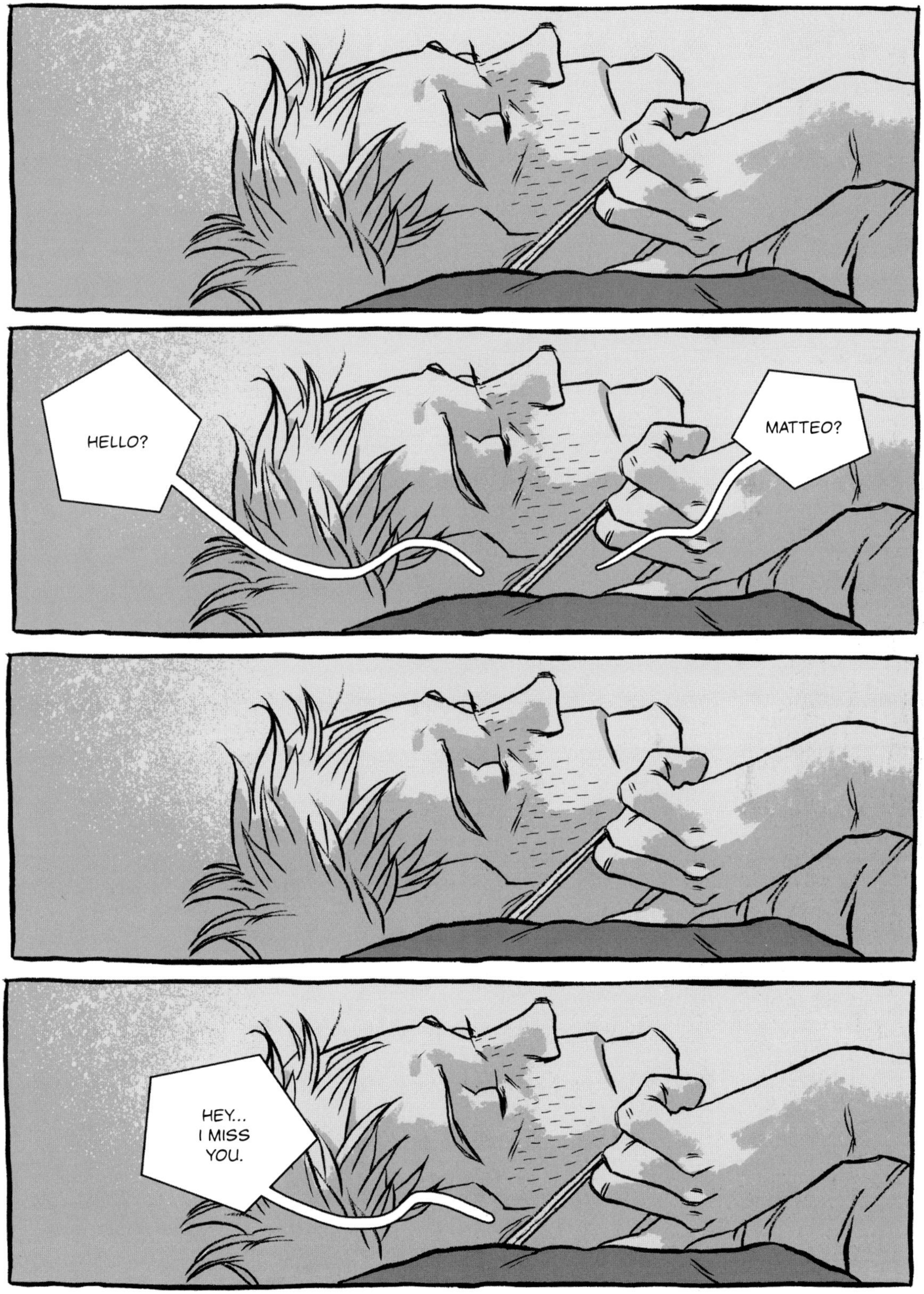
HELLO?
MATTEO?
HEY... I MISS YOU.

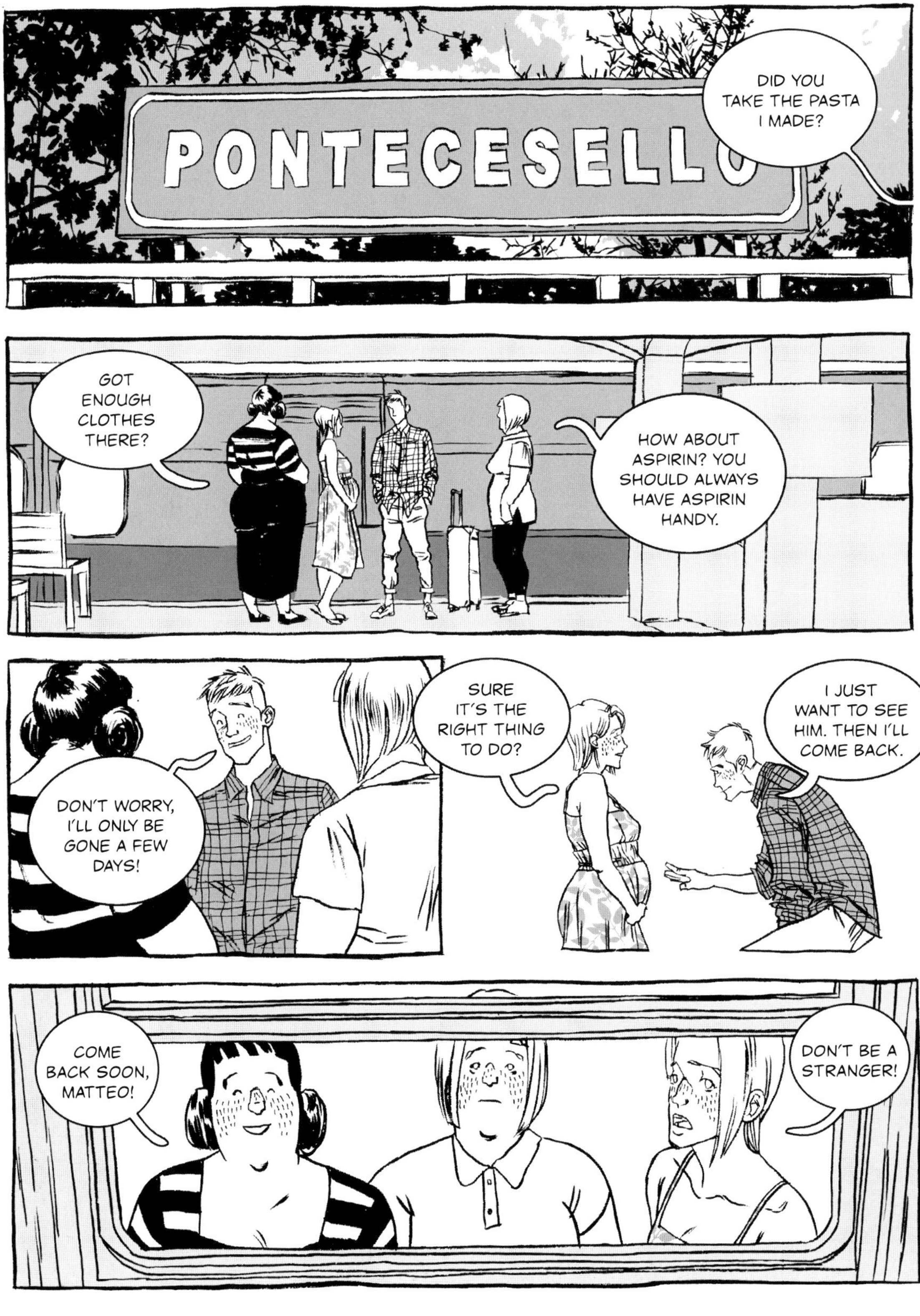
PONTECESELLO
DID YOU TAKE THE PASTA I MADE?
GOT ENOUGH CLOTHES THERE?
HOW ABOUT ASPIRIN? YOU SHOULD ALWAYS HAVE ASPIRIN HANDY.
DON'T WORRY, I'LL ONLY BE GONE A FEW DAYS!
SURE IT'S THE RIGHT THING TO DO?
I JUST WANT TO SEE HIM. THEN I'LL COME BACK.
COME BACK SOON, MATTEO!
DON'T BE A STRANGER!

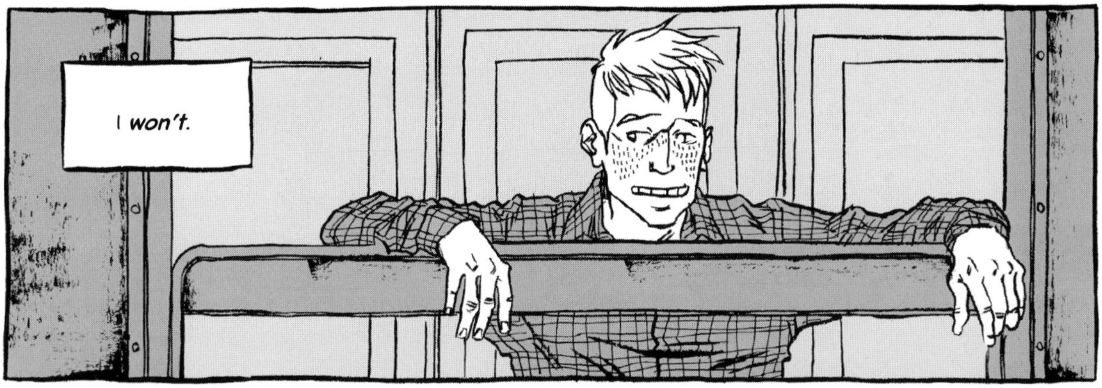
I *won't*.

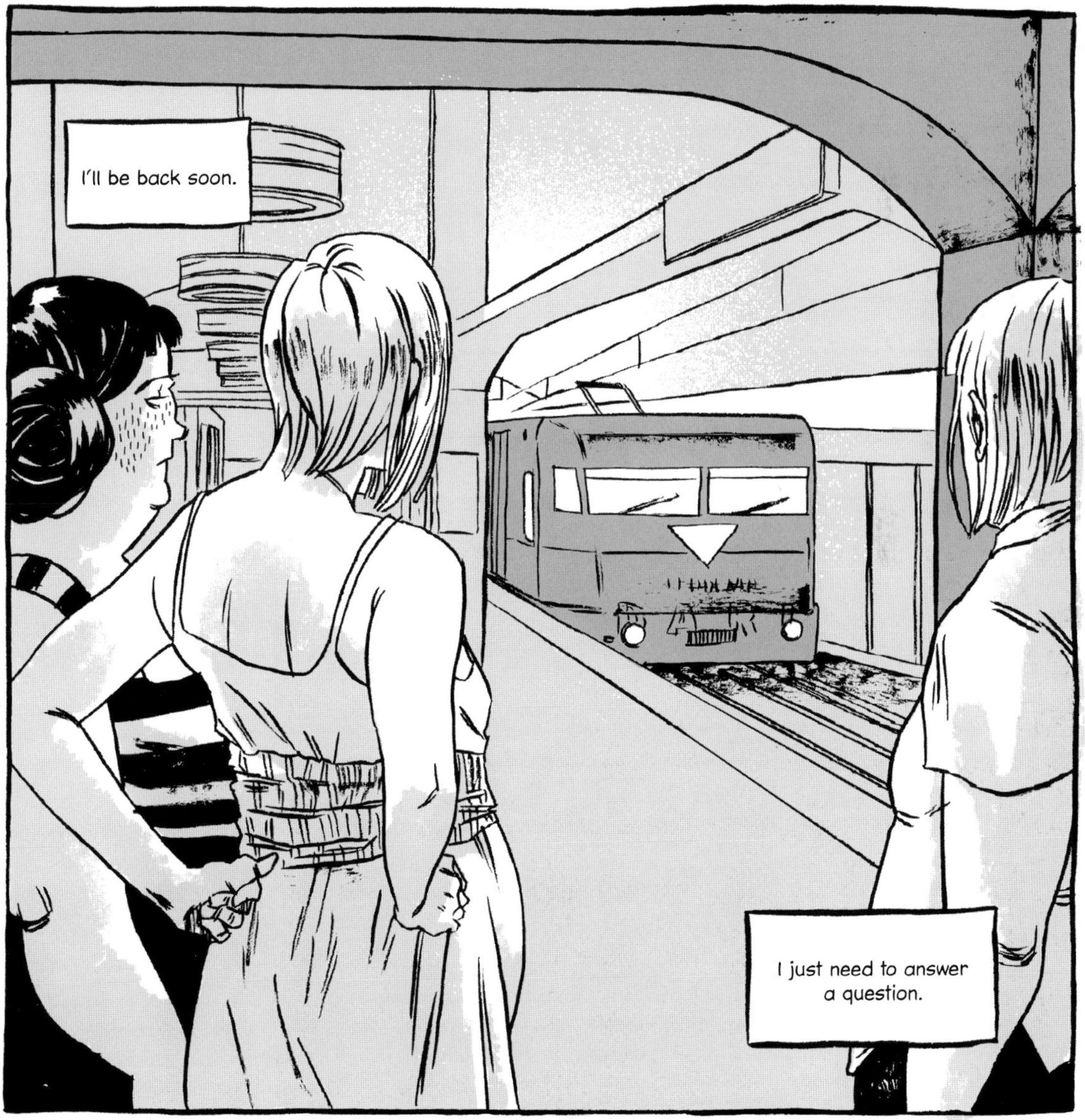
I'll be back soon.
I just need to answer a question.

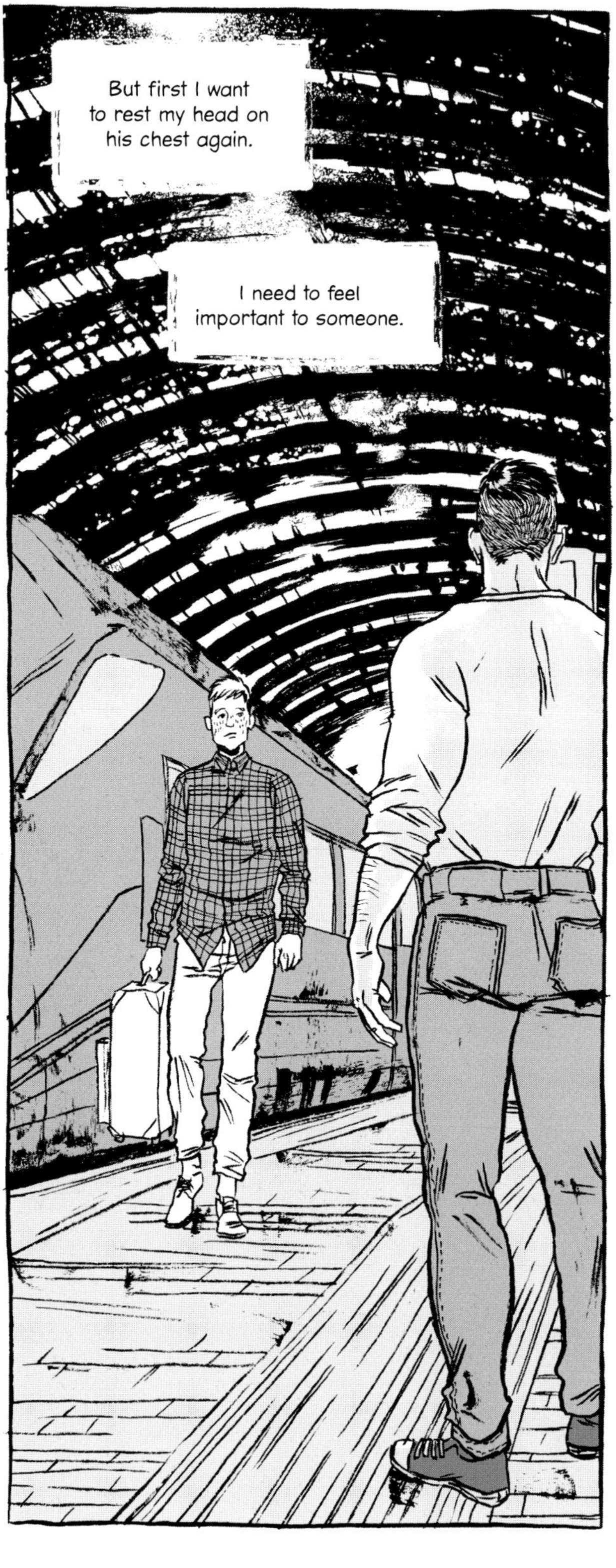
But first I want to rest my head on his chest again.
I need to feel important to someone.

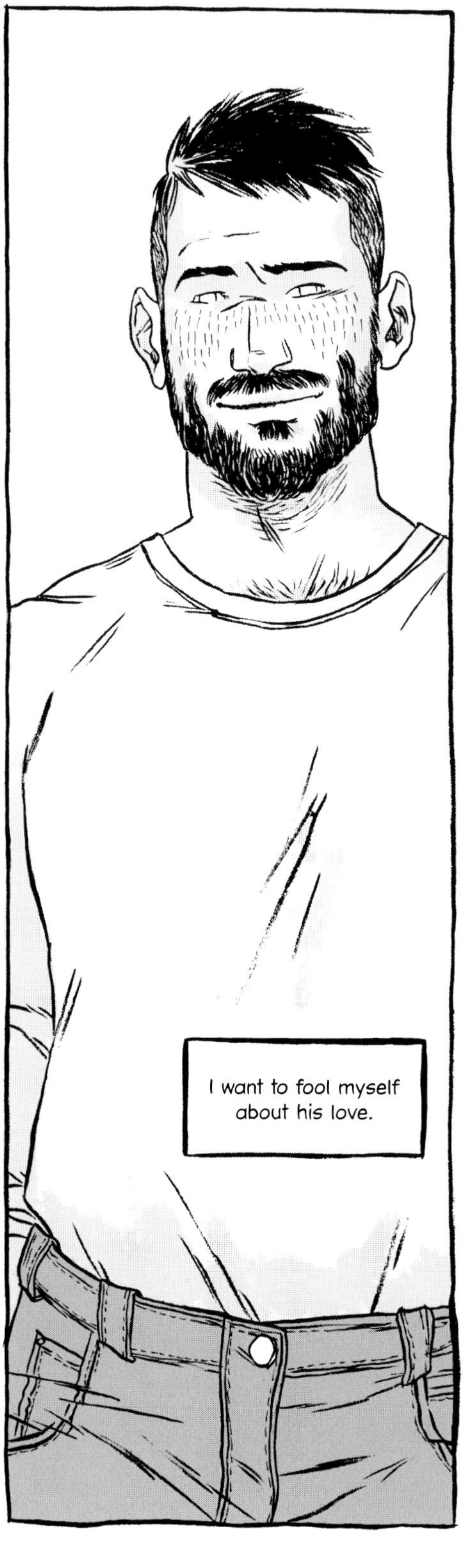
I want to fool myself about his love.

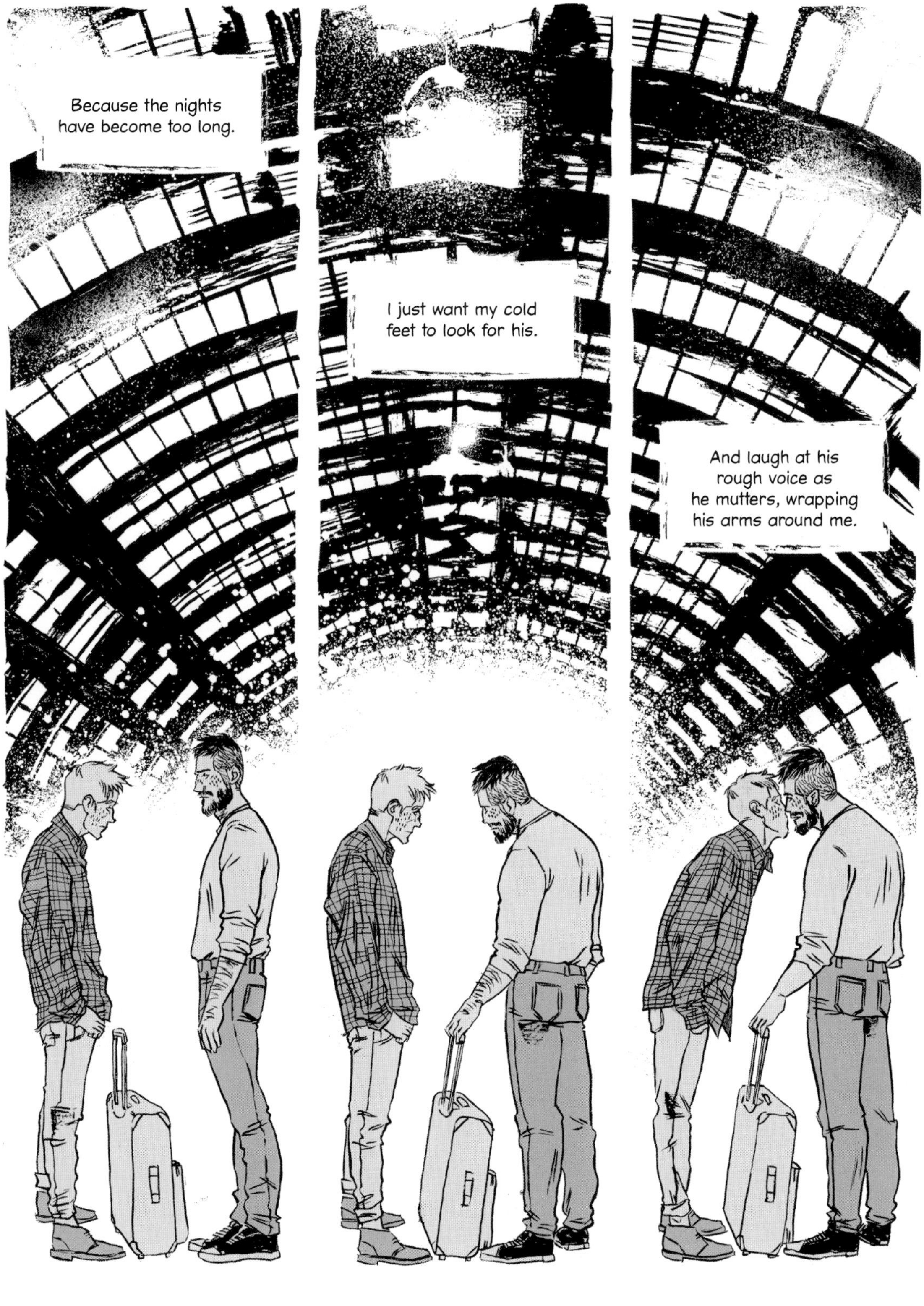
Because the nights have become too long.
I just want my cold feet to look for his.
And laugh at his rough voice as he mutters, wrapping his arms around me.

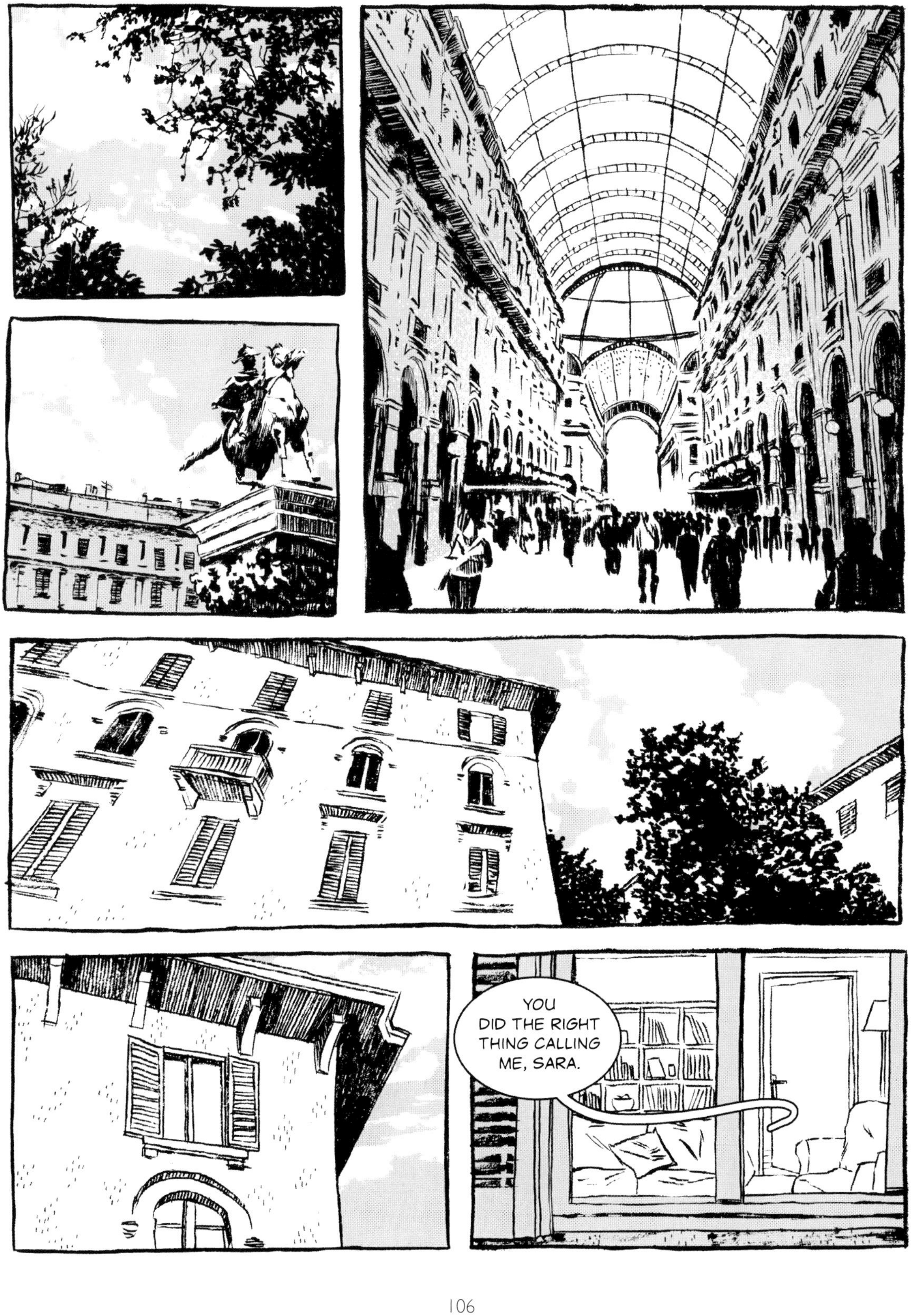
YOU
DID THE RIGHT
THING CALLING
ME, SARA.

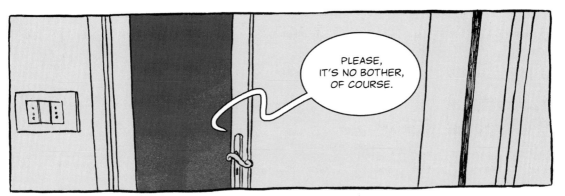

PLEASE,
IT'S NO BOTHER,
OF COURSE.

YES...BUT
HOW IS SHE
NOW?

I GET IT,
I GET IT.

JUST
HOW BAD
IS IT?

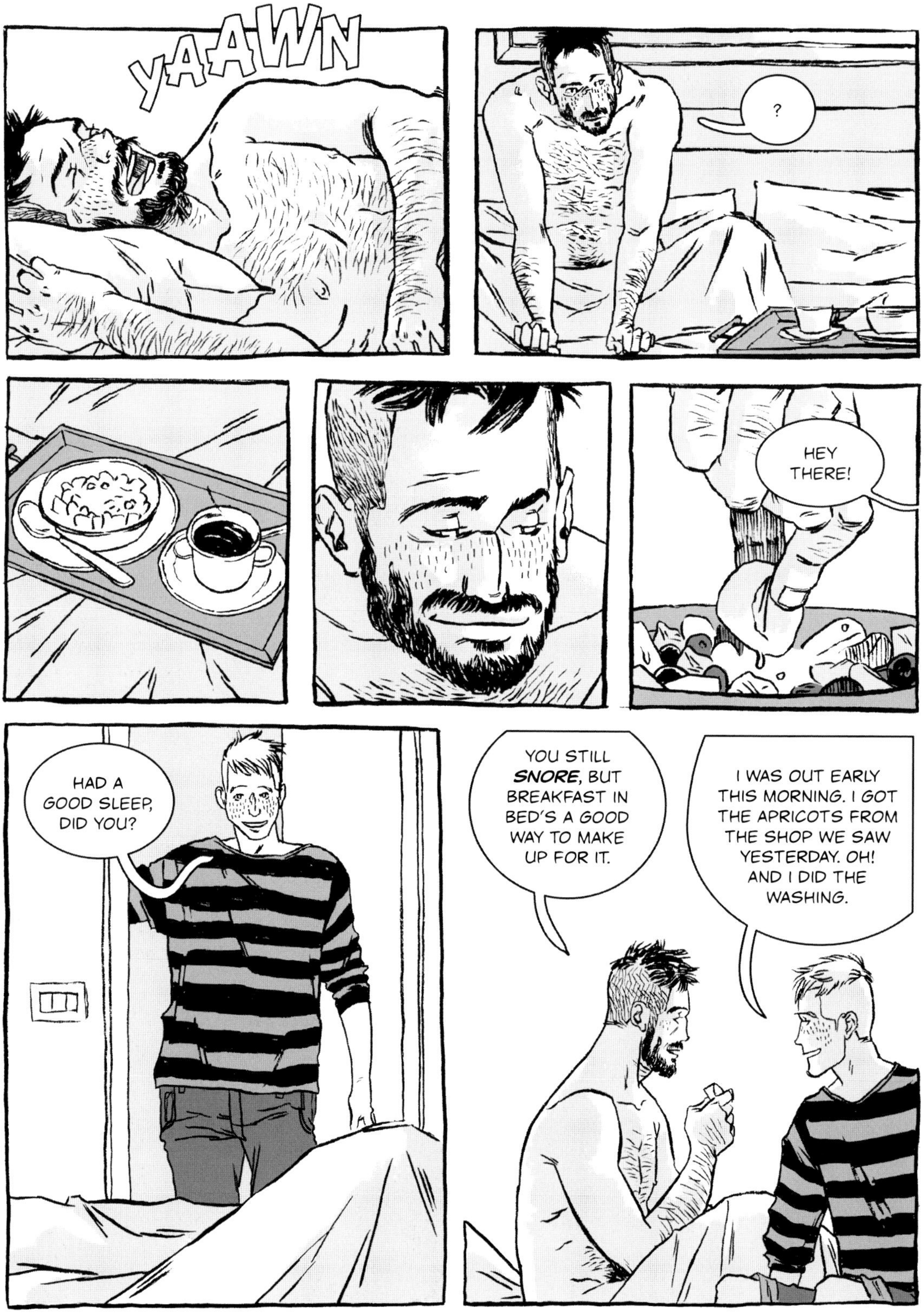
YAAWN
?
HEY THERE!
HAD A GOOD SLEEP, DID YOU?
YOU STILL SNORE, BUT BREAKFAST IN BED'S A GOOD WAY TO MAKE UP FOR IT.
I WAS OUT EARLY THIS MORNING. I GOT THE APRICOTS FROM THE SHOP WE SAW YESTERDAY. OH! AND I DID THE WASHING.

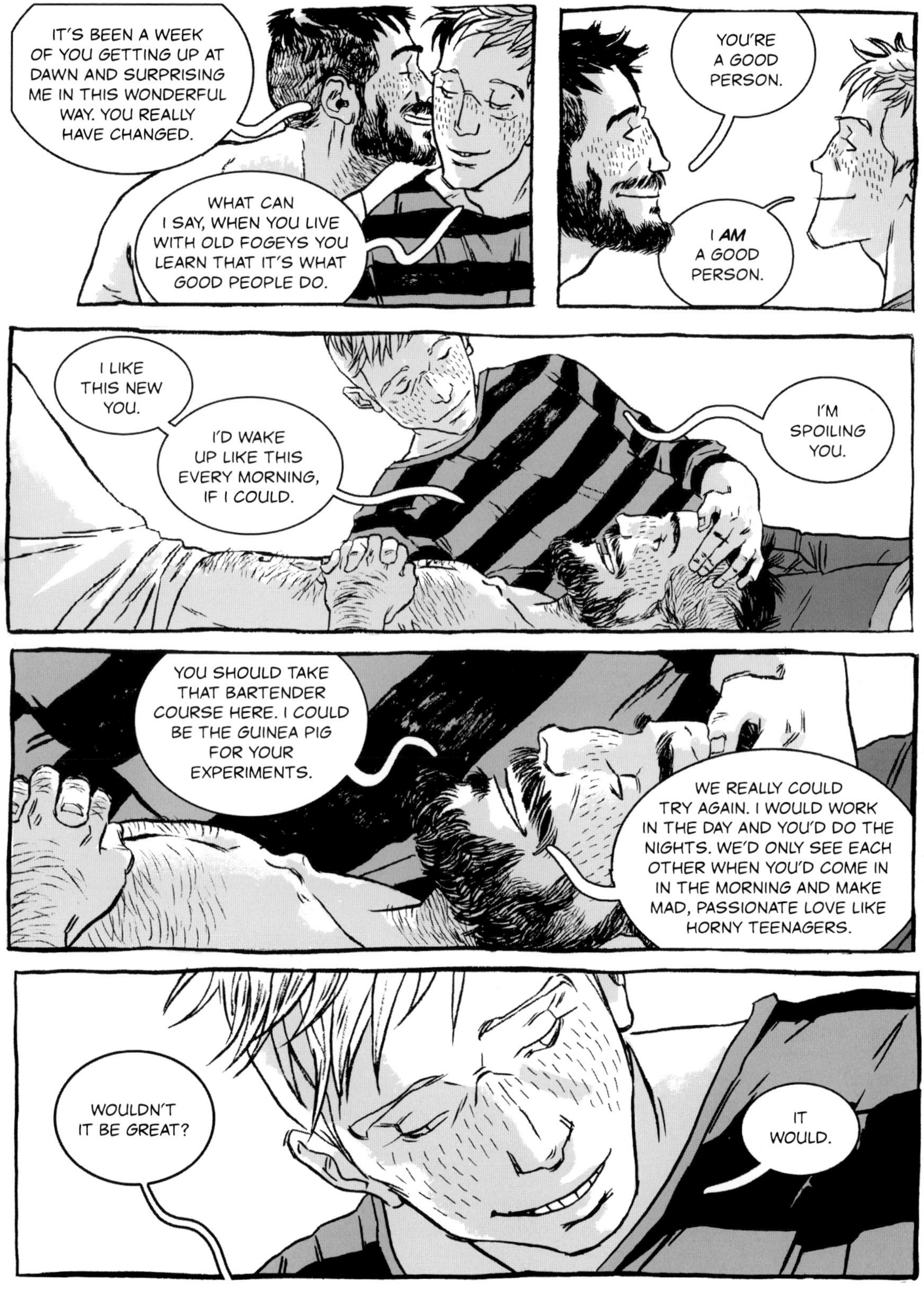
IT'S BEEN A WEEK OF YOU GETTING UP AT DAWN AND SURPRISING ME IN THIS WONDERFUL WAY. YOU REALLY HAVE CHANGED.
WHAT CAN I SAY, WHEN YOU LIVE WITH OLD FOGEYS YOU LEARN THAT IT'S WHAT GOOD PEOPLE DO.
YOU'RE A GOOD PERSON.
I *AM* A GOOD PERSON.
I LIKE THIS NEW YOU.
I'D WAKE UP LIKE THIS EVERY MORNING, IF I COULD.
I'M SPOILING YOU.
YOU SHOULD TAKE THAT BARTENDER COURSE HERE. I COULD BE THE GUINEA PIG FOR YOUR EXPERIMENTS.
WE REALLY COULD TRY AGAIN. I WOULD WORK IN THE DAY AND YOU'D DO THE NIGHTS. WE'D ONLY SEE EACH OTHER WHEN YOU'D COME IN IN THE MORNING AND MAKE MAD, PASSIONATE LOVE LIKE HORNY TEENAGERS.
WOULDN'T IT BE GREAT?
IT WOULD.

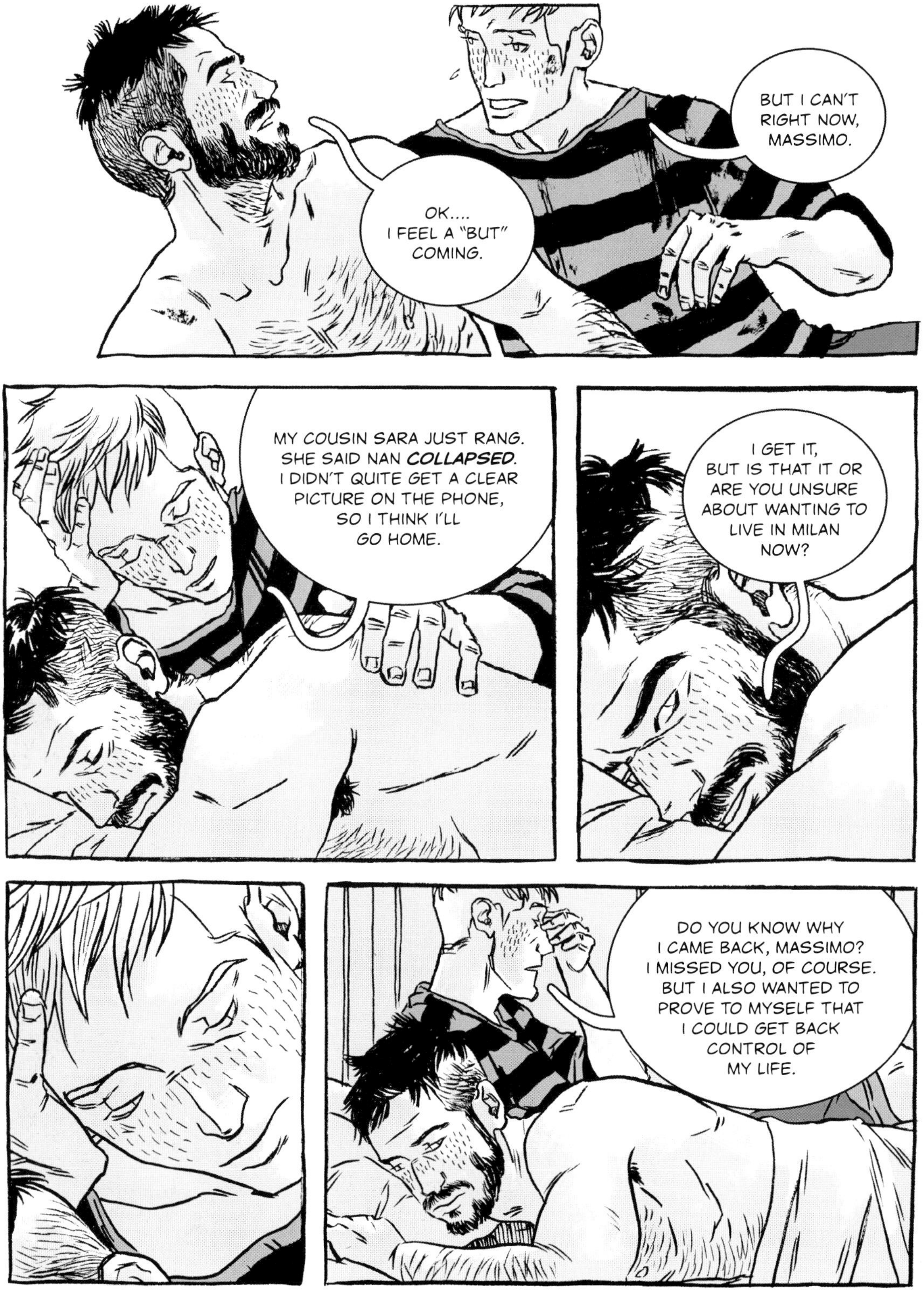
BUT I CAN'T RIGHT NOW, MASSIMO.
OK.... I FEEL A "BUT" COMING.
MY COUSIN SARA JUST RANG. SHE SAID NAN **COLLAPSED**. I DIDN'T QUITE GET A CLEAR PICTURE ON THE PHONE, SO I THINK I'LL GO HOME.
I GET IT, BUT IS THAT IT OR ARE YOU UNSURE ABOUT WANTING TO LIVE IN MILAN NOW?
DO YOU KNOW WHY I CAME BACK, MASSIMO? I MISSED YOU, OF COURSE. BUT I ALSO WANTED TO PROVE TO MYSELF THAT I COULD GET BACK CONTROL OF MY LIFE.

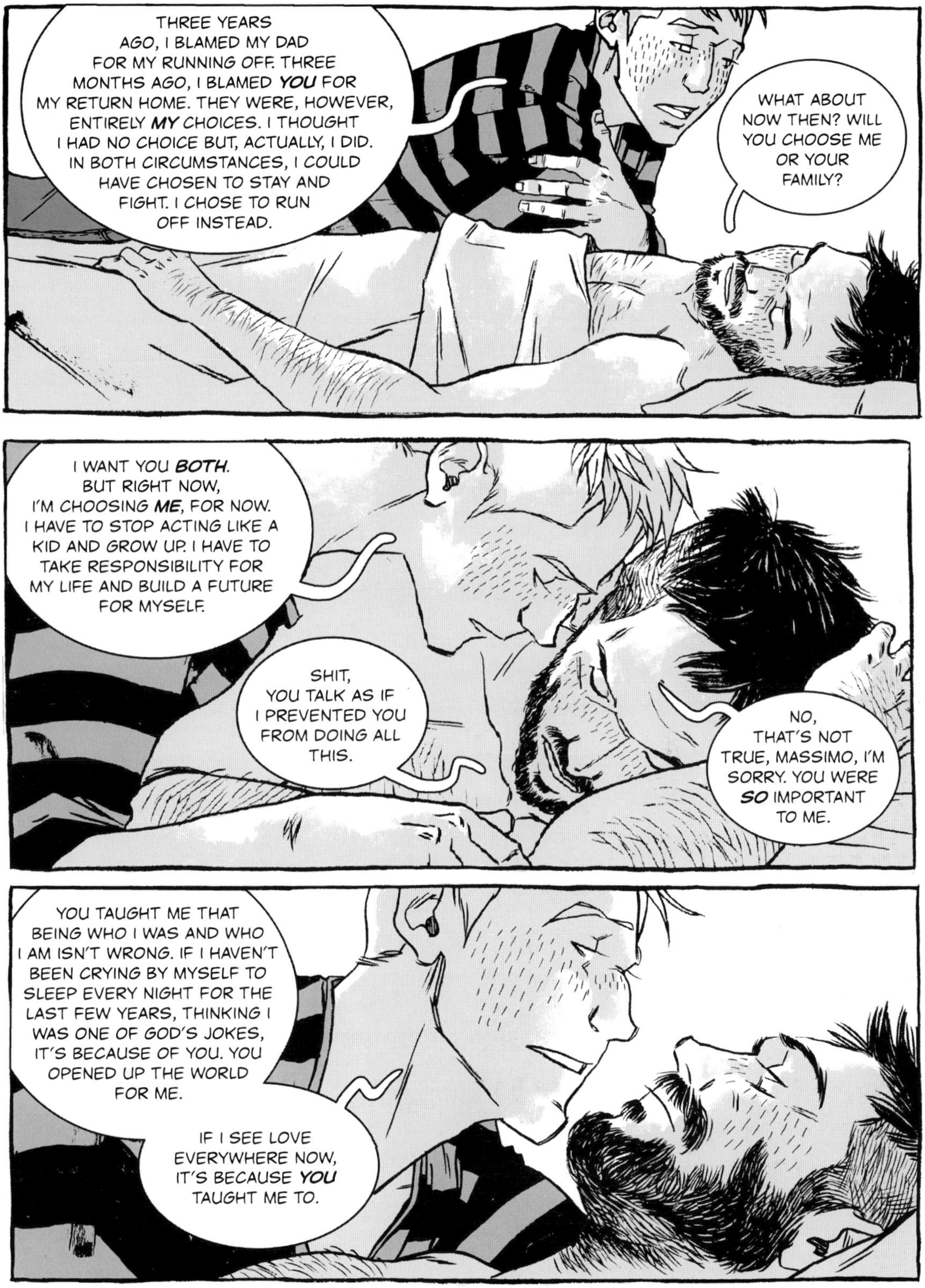
THREE YEARS AGO, I BLAMED MY DAD FOR MY RUNNING OFF. THREE MONTHS AGO, I BLAMED *YOU* FOR MY RETURN HOME. THEY WERE, HOWEVER, ENTIRELY *MY* CHOICES. I THOUGHT I HAD NO CHOICE BUT, ACTUALLY, I DID. IN BOTH CIRCUMSTANCES, I COULD HAVE CHOSEN TO STAY AND FIGHT. I CHOSE TO RUN OFF INSTEAD.
WHAT ABOUT NOW THEN? WILL YOU CHOOSE ME OR YOUR FAMILY?
I WANT YOU *BOTH*. BUT RIGHT NOW, I'M CHOOSING *ME*, FOR NOW. I HAVE TO STOP ACTING LIKE A KID AND GROW UP. I HAVE TO TAKE RESPONSIBILITY FOR MY LIFE AND BUILD A FUTURE FOR MYSELF.
SHIT, YOU TALK AS IF I PREVENTED YOU FROM DOING ALL THIS.
NO, THAT'S NOT TRUE, MASSIMO, I'M SORRY. YOU WERE *SO* IMPORTANT TO ME.
YOU TAUGHT ME THAT BEING WHO I WAS AND WHO I AM ISN'T WRONG. IF I HAVEN'T BEEN CRYING BY MYSELF TO SLEEP EVERY NIGHT FOR THE LAST FEW YEARS, THINKING I WAS ONE OF GOD'S JOKES, IT'S BECAUSE OF YOU. YOU OPENED UP THE WORLD FOR ME.
IF I SEE LOVE EVERYWHERE NOW, IT'S BECAUSE *YOU* TAUGHT ME TO.

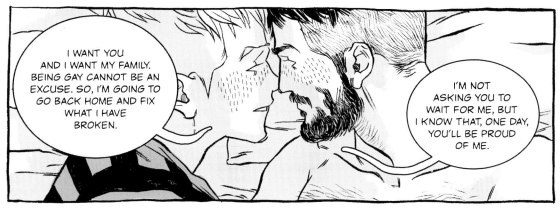

I WANT YOU AND I WANT MY FAMILY. BEING GAY CANNOT BE AN EXCUSE. SO, I'M GOING TO GO BACK HOME AND FIX WHAT I HAVE BROKEN.

I'M NOT ASKING YOU TO WAIT FOR ME, BUT I KNOW THAT, ONE DAY, YOU'LL BE PROUD OF ME.

I DON'T KNOW: WHAT IF I CAME TO VISIT EVERY NOW AND THEN...

WHILST YOU'RE BUSY BECOMING A GOOD MAN?

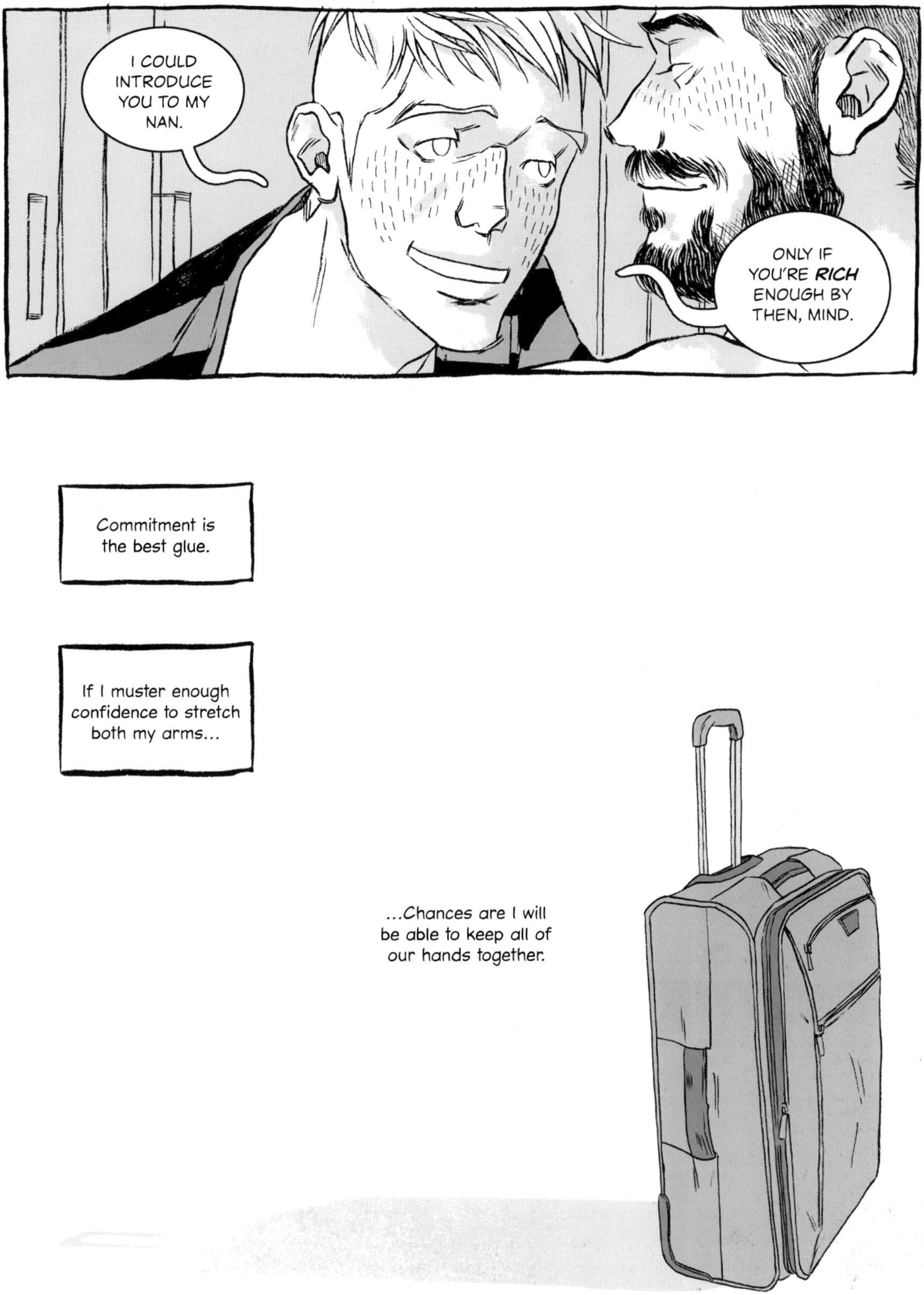
I COULD INTRODUCE YOU TO MY NAN.
ONLY IF YOU'RE **RICH** ENOUGH BY THEN, MIND.
Commitment is the best glue.
If I muster enough confidence to stretch both my arms...
...Chances are I will be able to keep all of our hands together.

KIDNEY FAILURE?

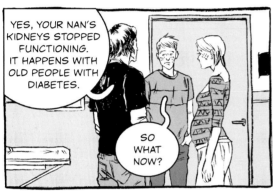

YES, YOUR NAN'S KIDNEYS STOPPED FUNCTIONING. IT HAPPENS WITH OLD PEOPLE WITH DIABETES.

SO WHAT NOW?

IF SHE WERE YOUNGER, DIALYSIS, AND A TRANSPLANT, BUT YOUR NAN'S OVER NINETY YEARS OF AGE. THAT WOULD MEAN OVERTREATMENT, SO...

RIGHT, I GET IT.

THE SIGNS WERE THERE, SHE JUST COLLAPSED ALL OF A SUDDEN.

WOULD YOU LIKE TO SEE HER? AUNTIE B'S IN THERE, THOUGH.

WHO CARES ABOUT AUNTIE B.

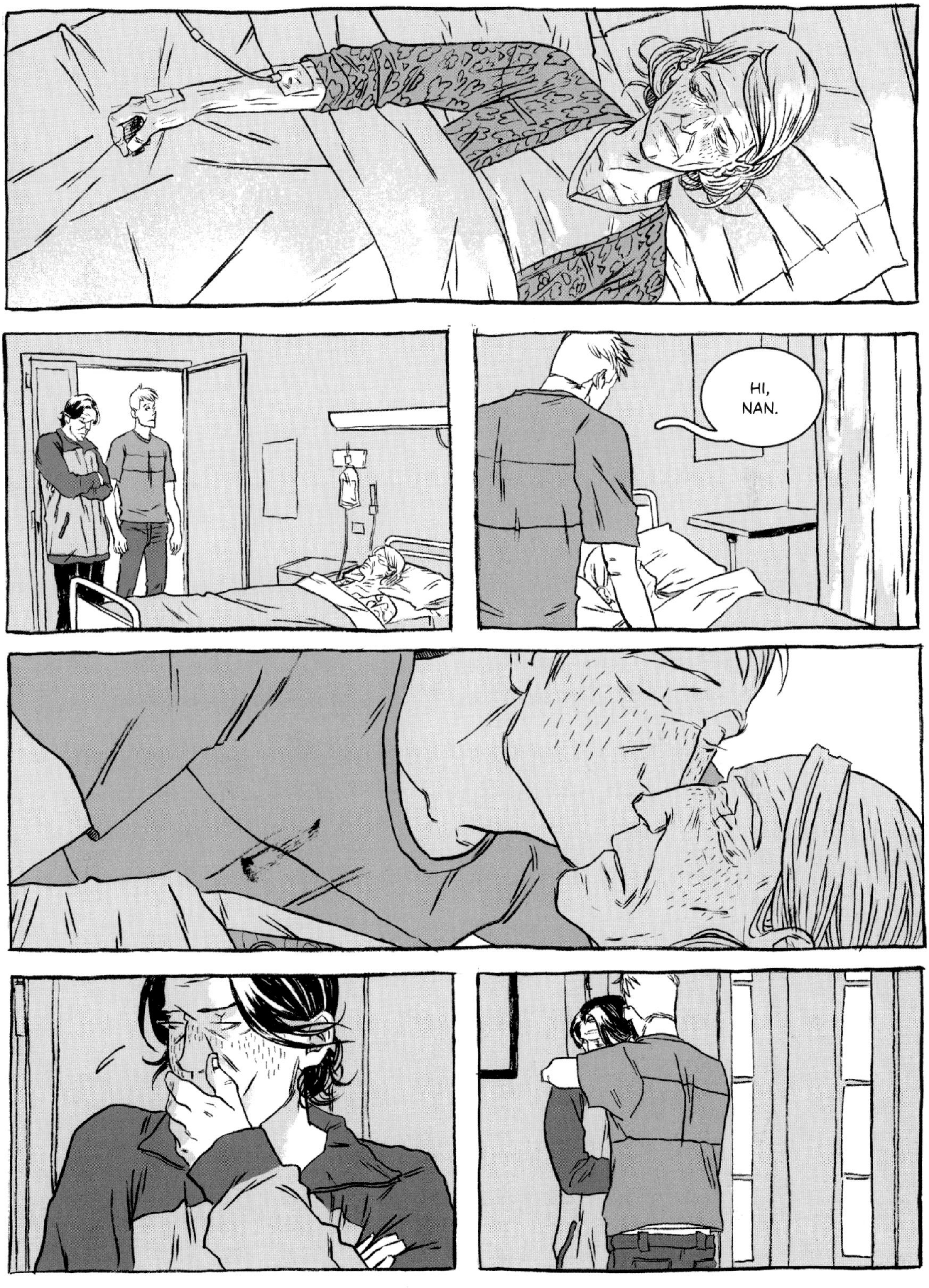
HI, NAN.

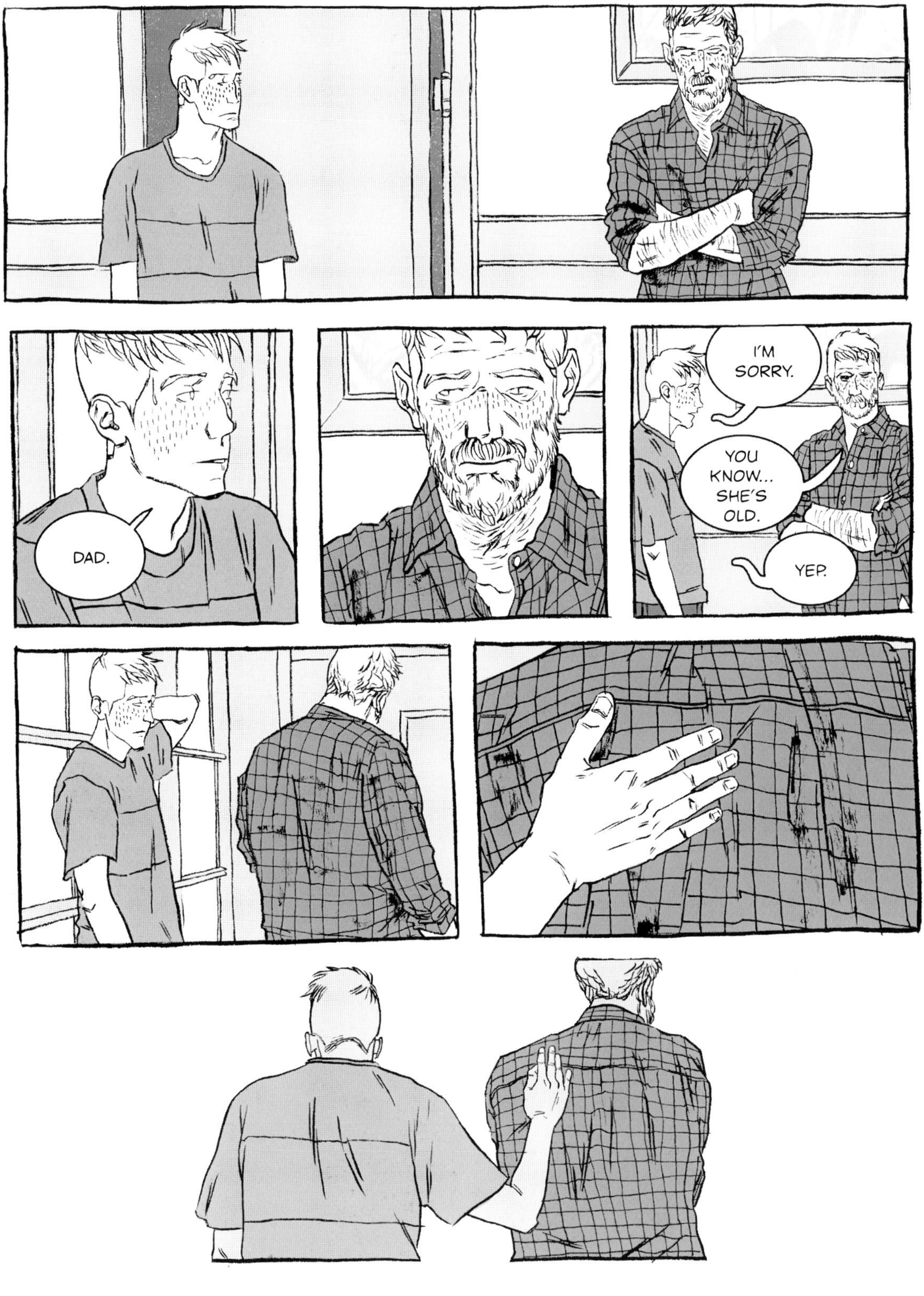
DAD.
I'M SORRY.
YOU KNOW... SHE'S OLD.
YEP.

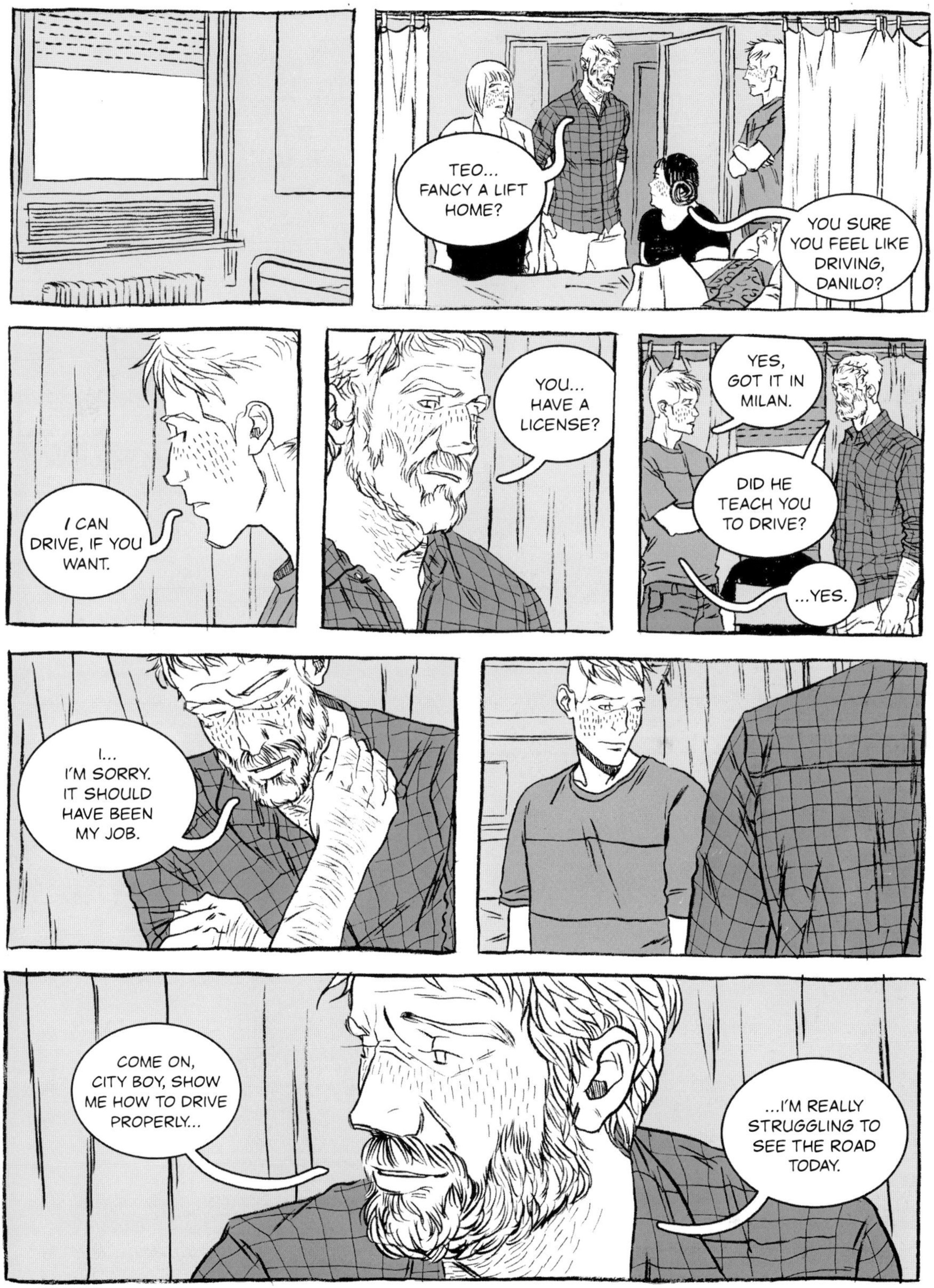
TEO... FANCY A LIFT HOME?
YOU SURE YOU FEEL LIKE DRIVING, DANILO?
I CAN DRIVE, IF YOU WANT.
YOU... HAVE A LICENSE?
YES, GOT IT IN MILAN.
DID HE TEACH YOU TO DRIVE?
...YES.
I... I'M SORRY. IT SHOULD HAVE BEEN MY JOB.
COME ON, CITY BOY, SHOW ME HOW TO DRIVE PROPERLY...
...I'M REALLY STRUGGLING TO SEE THE ROAD TODAY.

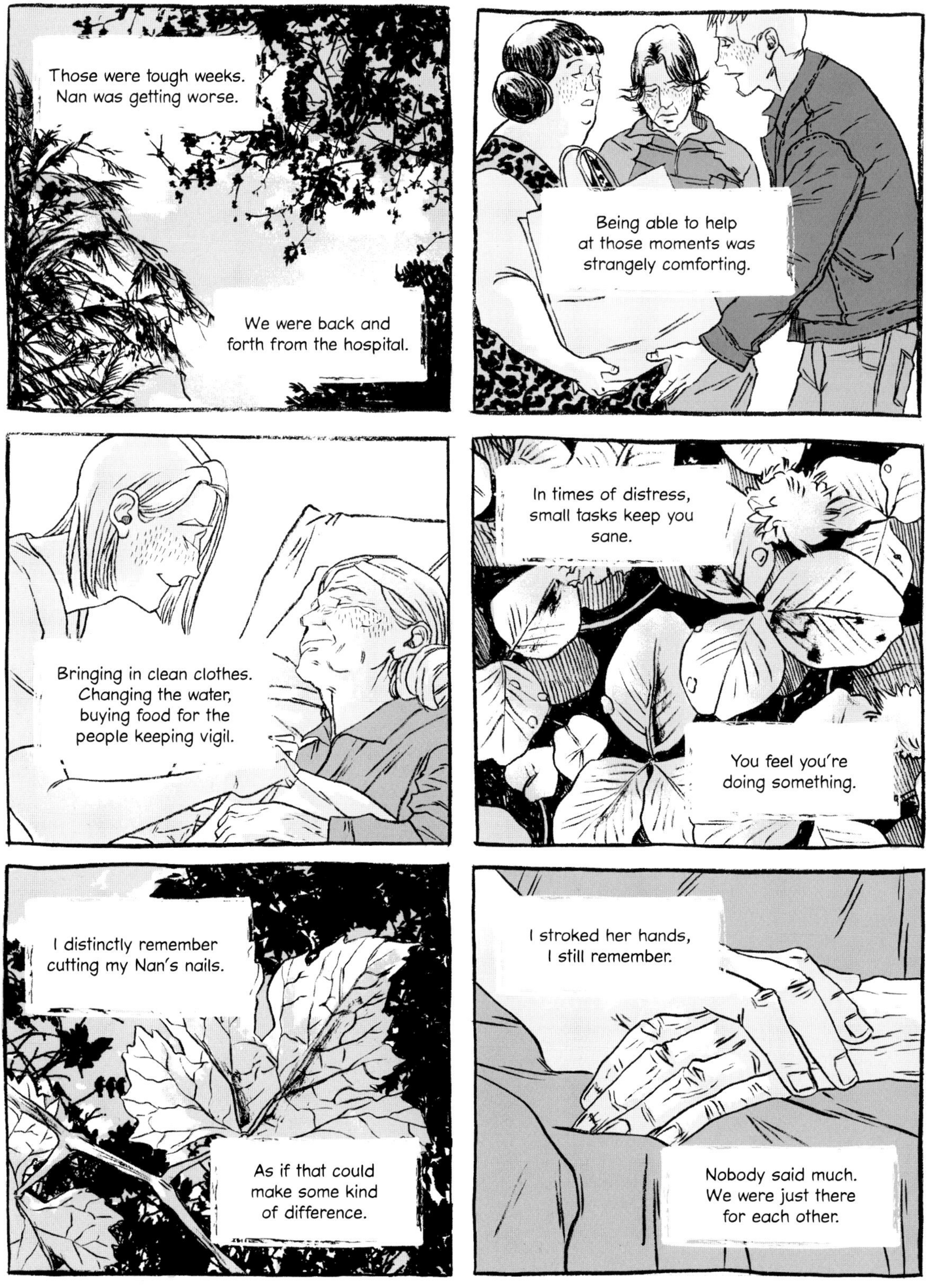
Those were tough weeks.
Nan was getting worse.
We were back and forth from the hospital.
Being able to help at those moments was strangely comforting.
Bringing in clean clothes. Changing the water, buying food for the people keeping vigil.
In times of distress, small tasks keep you sane.
You feel you're doing something.
I distinctly remember cutting my Nan's nails.
As if that could make some kind of difference.
I stroked her hands, I still remember.
Nobody said much. We were just there for each other.

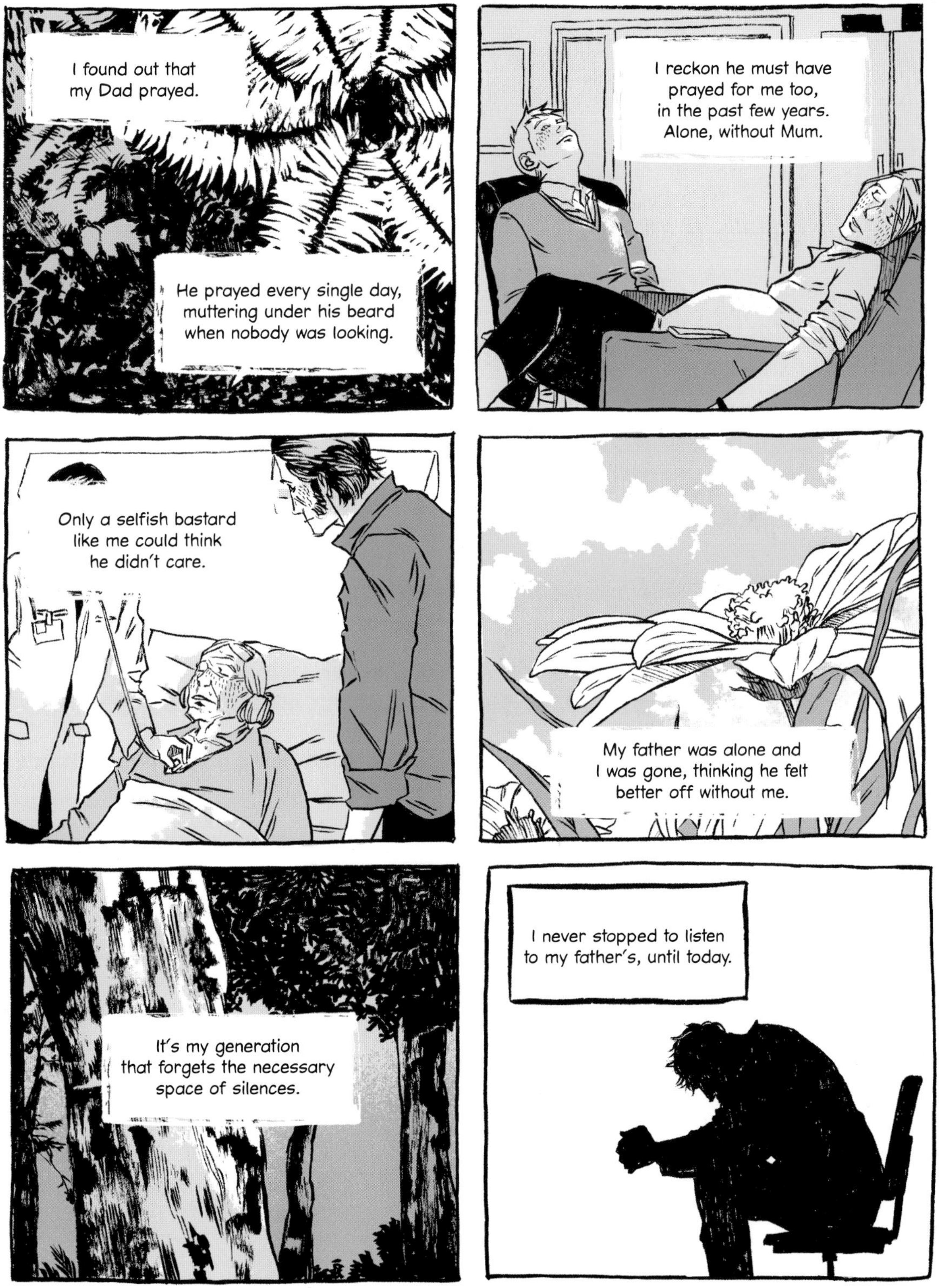
I found out that my Dad prayed.
He prayed every single day, muttering under his beard when nobody was looking.
I reckon he must have prayed for me too, in the past few years. Alone, without Mum.
Only a selfish bastard like me could think he didn't care.
My father was alone and I was gone, thinking he felt better off without me.
It's my generation that forgets the necessary space of silences.
I never stopped to listen to my father's, until today.

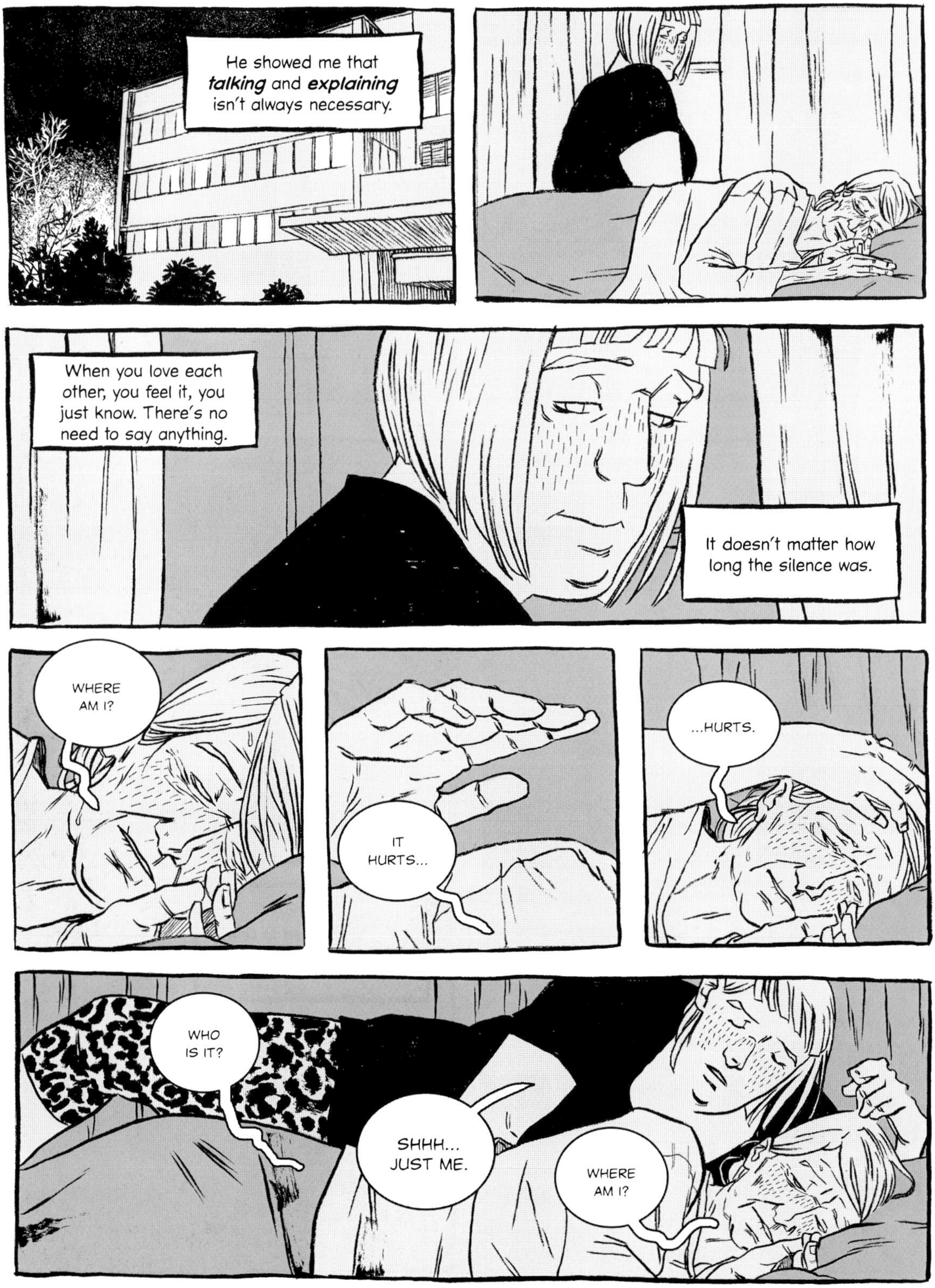

He showed me that ***talking*** and ***explaining*** isn't always necessary.
When you love each other, you feel it, you just know. There's no need to say anything.
It doesn't matter how long the silence was.
WHERE AM I?
IT HURTS...
...HURTS.
WHO IS IT?
SHHH... JUST ME.
WHERE AM I?

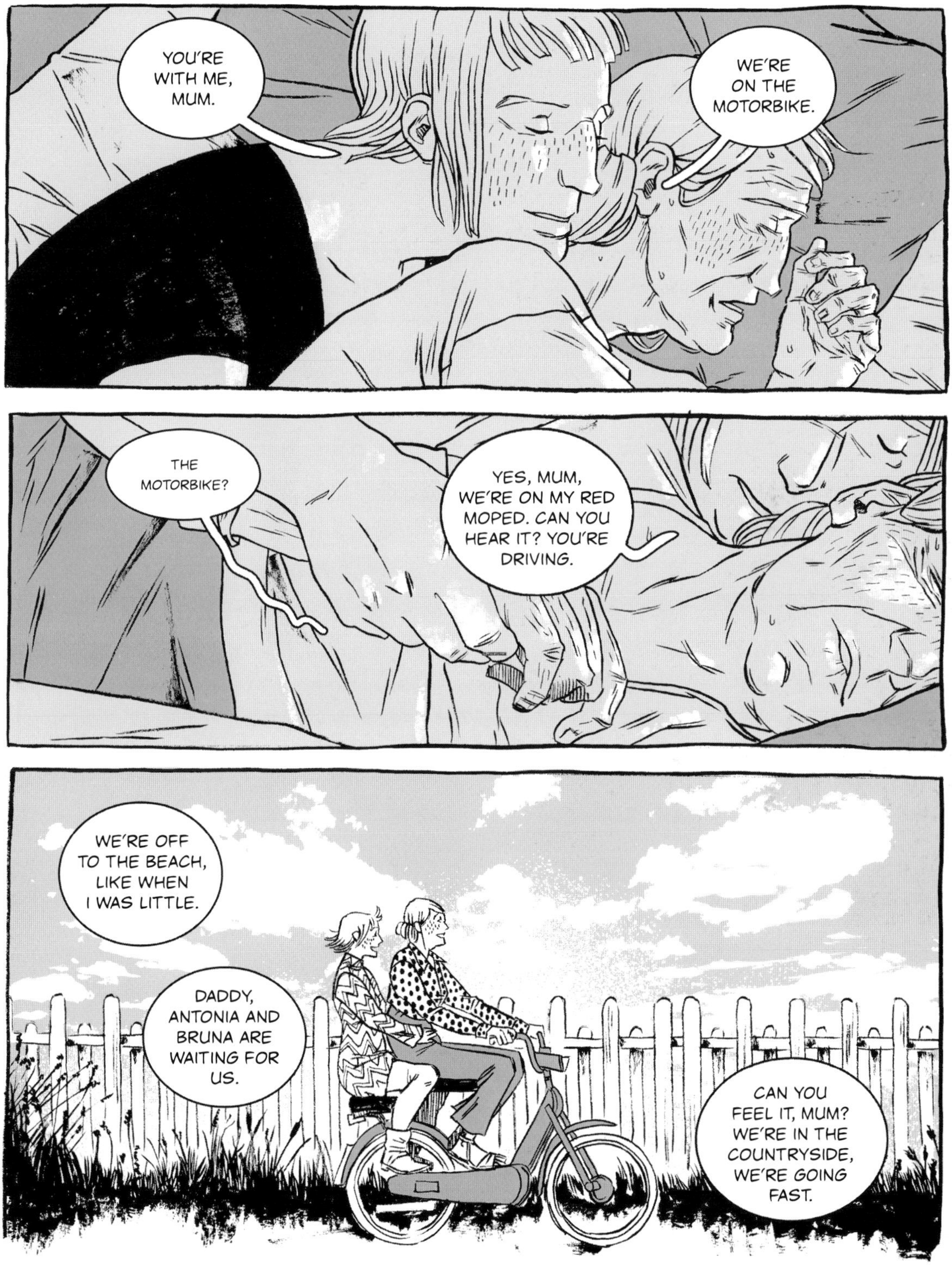
YOU'RE WITH ME, MUM.
WE'RE ON THE MOTORBIKE.
THE MOTORBIKE?
YES, MUM, WE'RE ON MY RED MOPED. CAN YOU HEAR IT? YOU'RE DRIVING.
WE'RE OFF TO THE BEACH, LIKE WHEN I WAS LITTLE.
DADDY, ANTONIA AND BRUNA ARE WAITING FOR US.
CAN YOU FEEL IT, MUM? WE'RE IN THE COUNTRYSIDE, WE'RE GOING FAST.

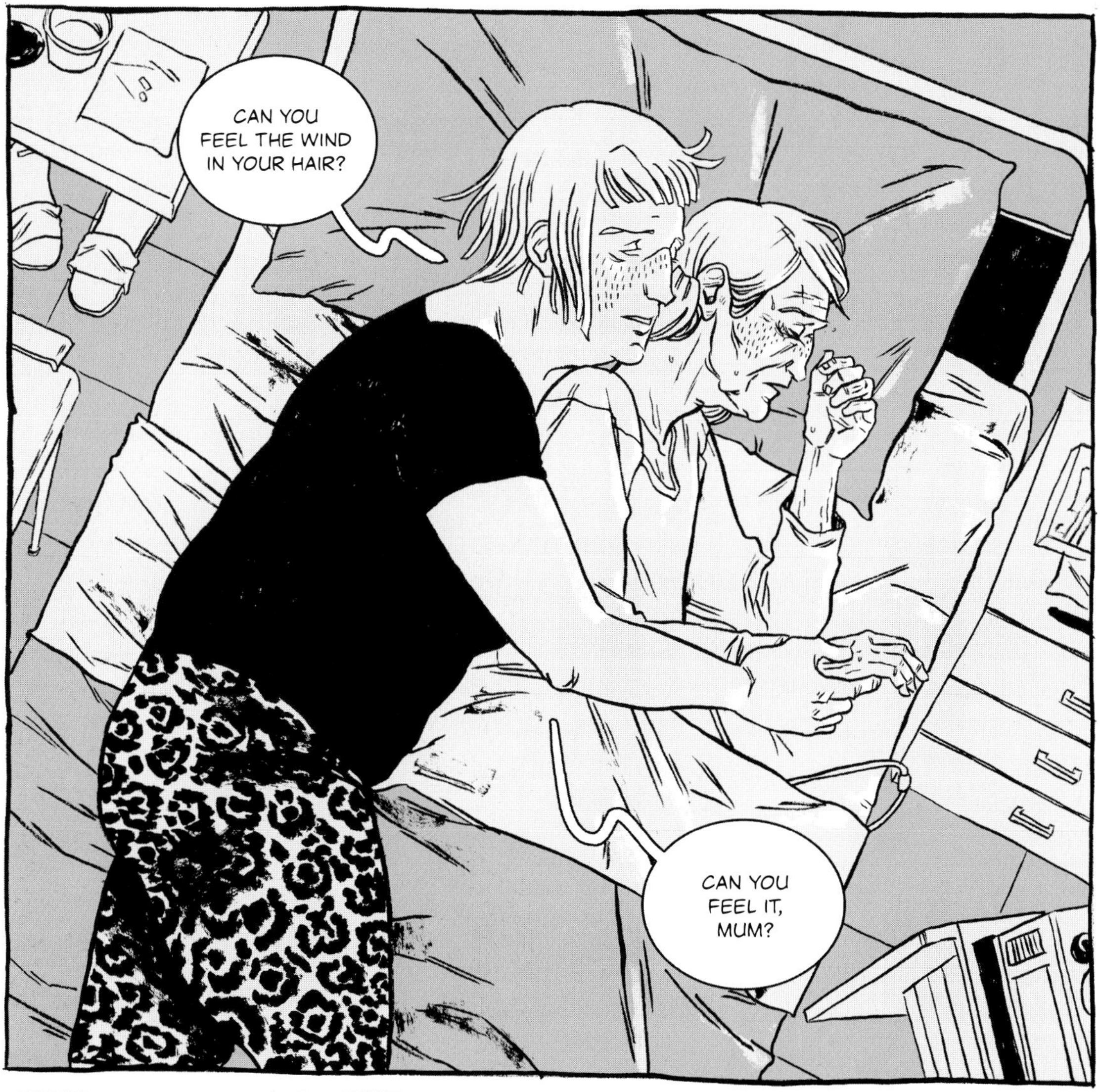
CAN YOU FEEL THE WIND IN YOUR HAIR?
CAN YOU FEEL IT, MUM?

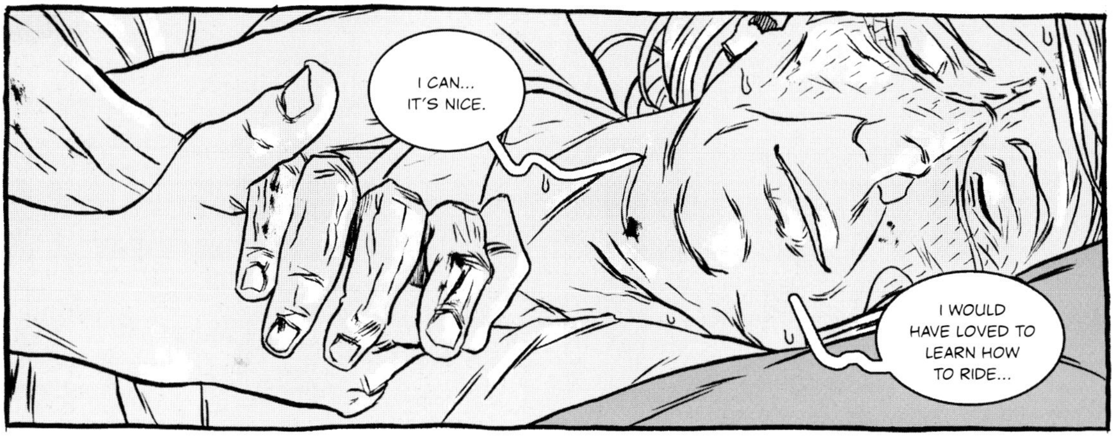
I CAN... IT'S NICE.
I WOULD HAVE LOVED TO LEARN HOW TO RIDE...

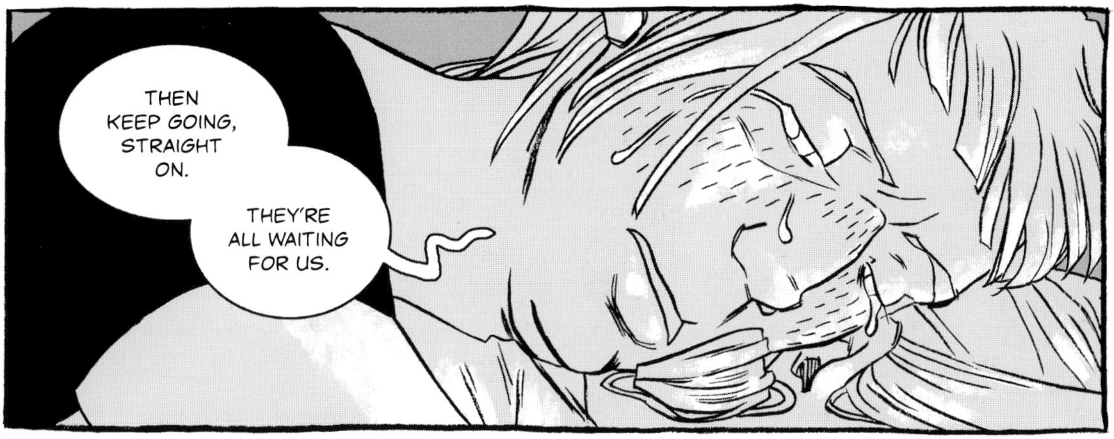
THEN KEEP GOING, STRAIGHT ON.
THEY'RE ALL WAITING FOR US.

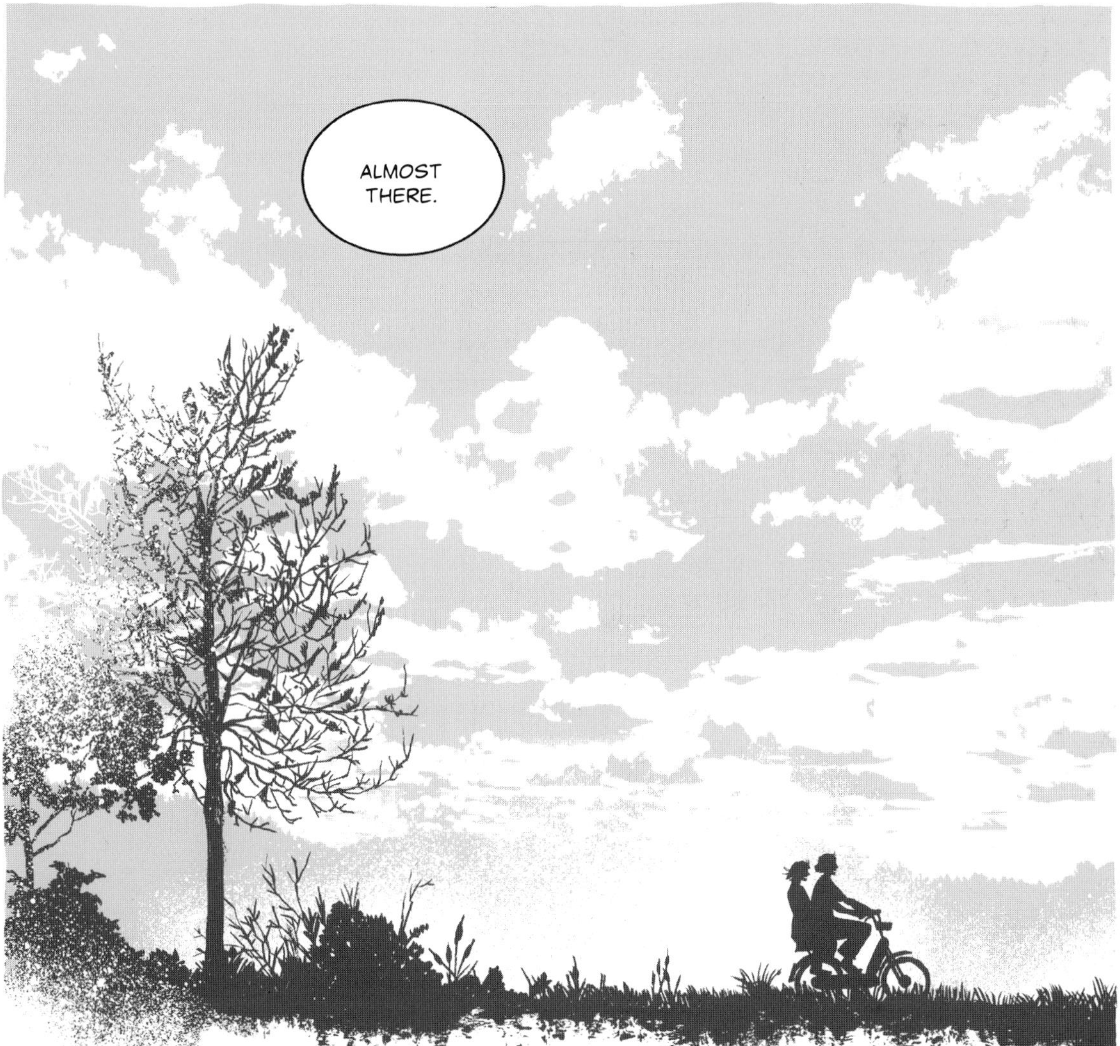
ALMOST THERE.

Auntie B. says we're all apples.

And families are like trees heavy with fruit.

When we're ripe, we just *fall off* and *leave*.

I can't remember my other grandparents.
I was too young when they died.

But when my Nan Tonia left the tree,
I was there. I was there that day.

I thanked all of my mistakes
and my cowardly choices.

If it hadn't been for them,
I wouldn't understand.
I wouldn't be here today.
I wouldn't feel such a great part of you.
Part of us.

So now, as I follow my path,
my hands are still warm from
all the shoulders I hugged.

This is the right way,
I'm here and it's enough,
and it doesn't matter
how I got here.

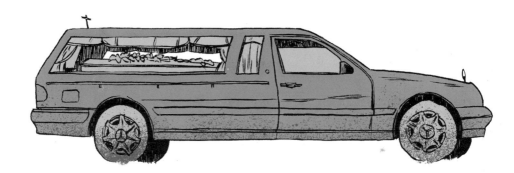

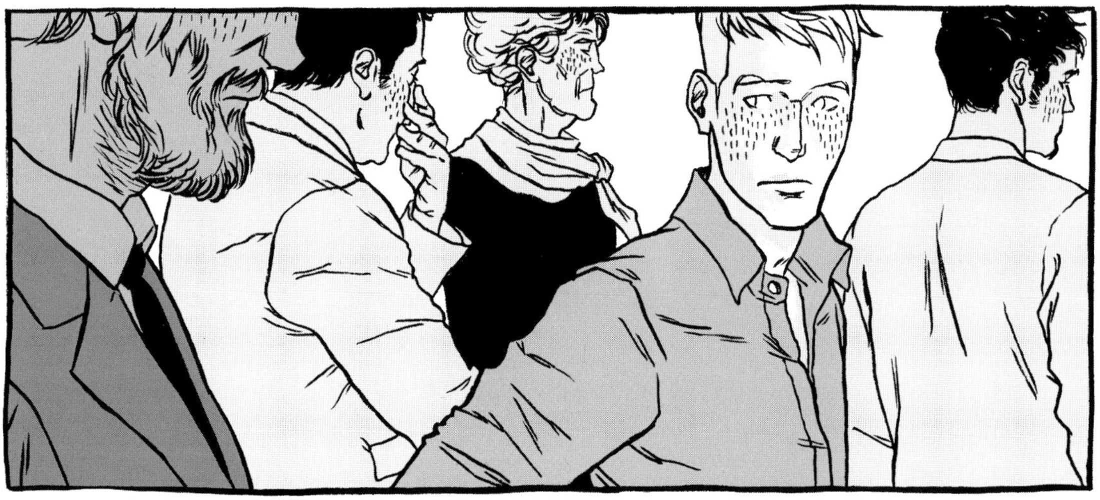

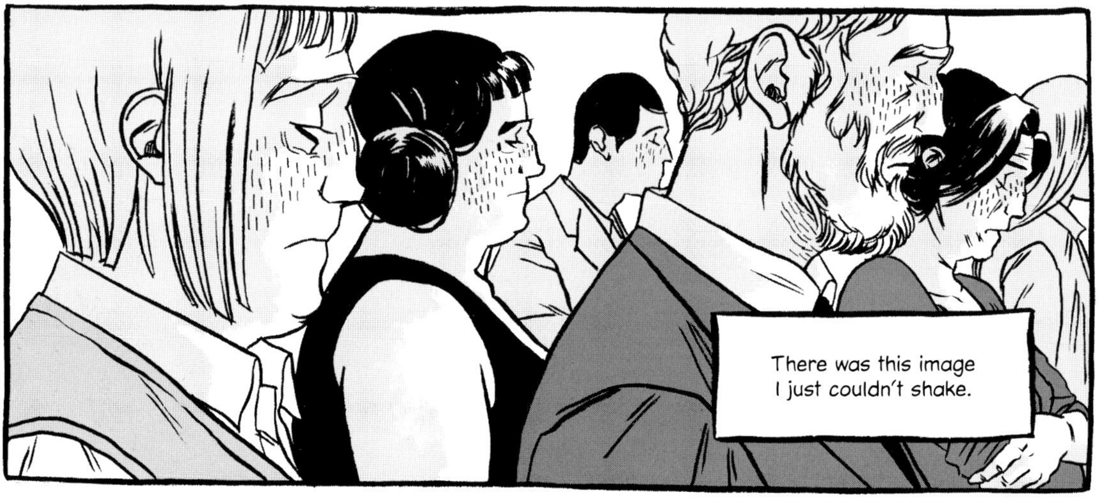
There was this image
I just couldn't shake.

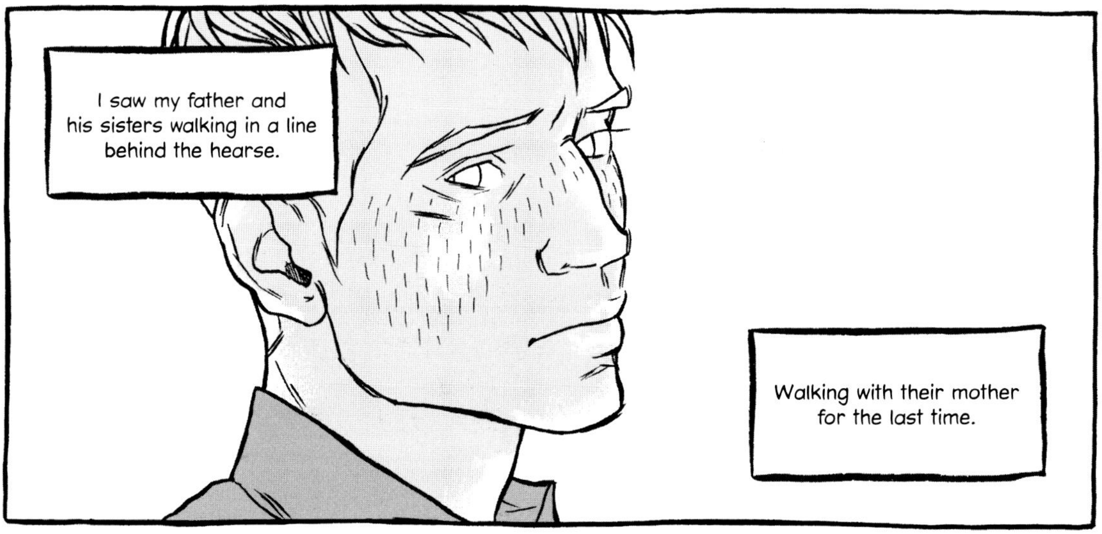
I saw my father and
his sisters walking in a line
behind the hearse.
Walking with their mother
for the last time.

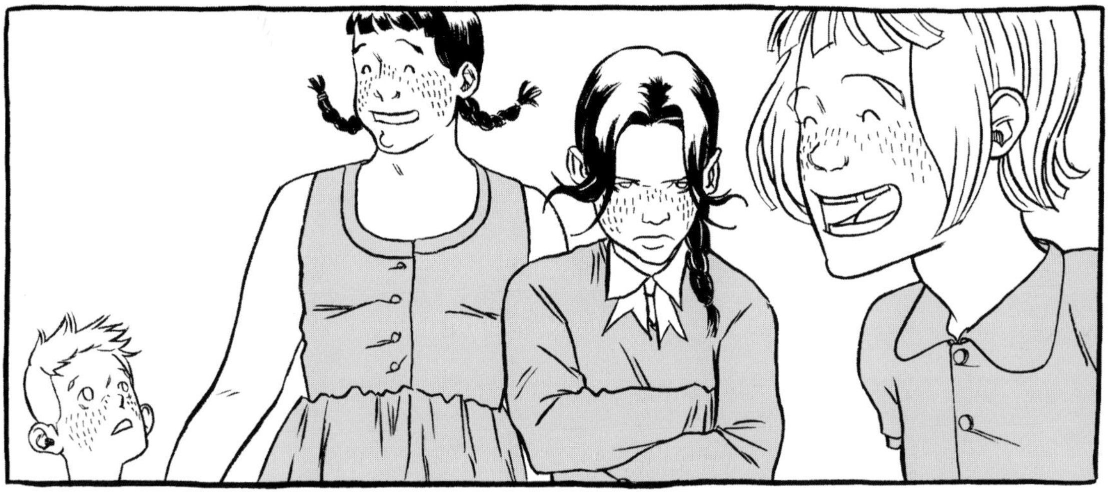

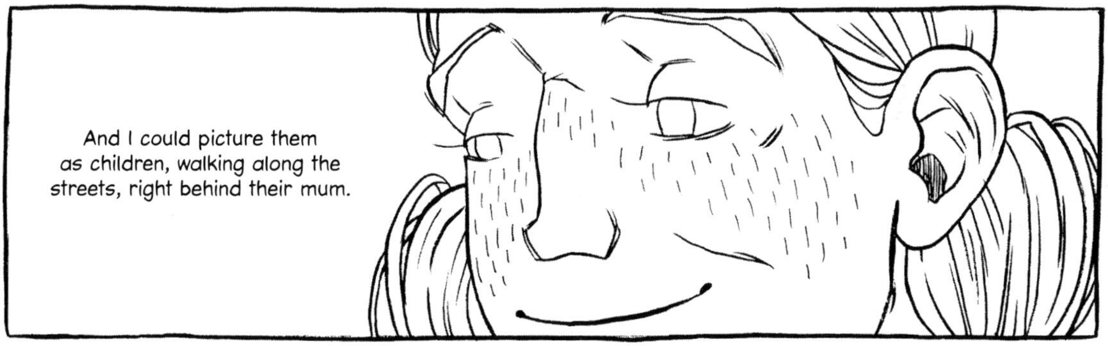
And I could picture them as children, walking along the streets, right behind their mum.

I could feel just how much
Nan Tonia loved the four of them.

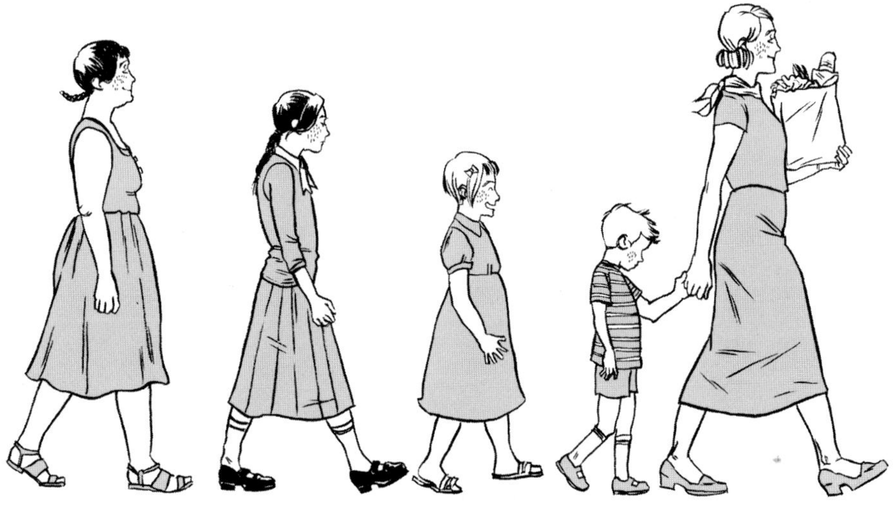

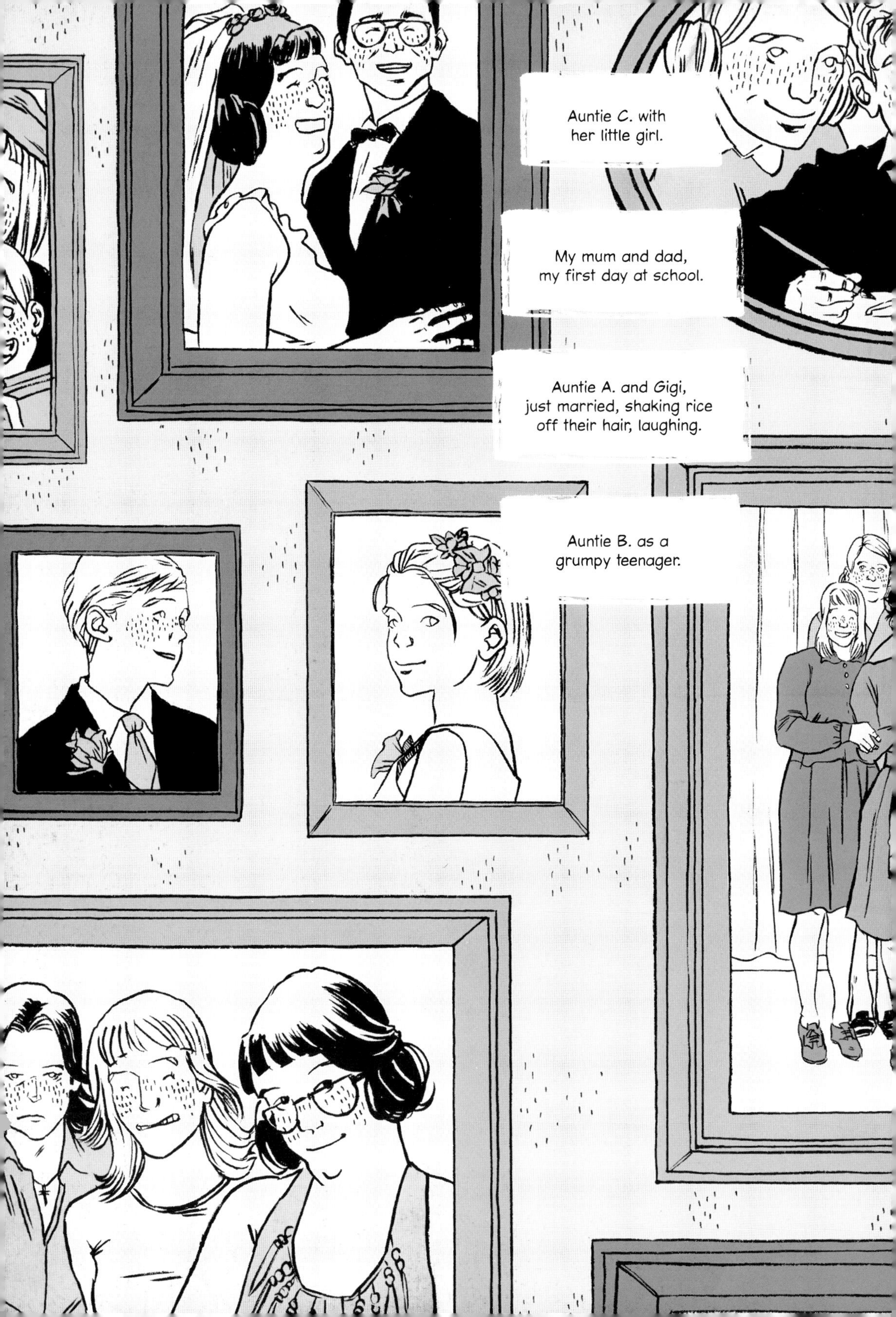
Auntie C. with her little girl.
My mum and dad, my first day at school.
Auntie A. and Gigi, just married, shaking rice off their hair, laughing.
Auntie B. as a grumpy teenager.

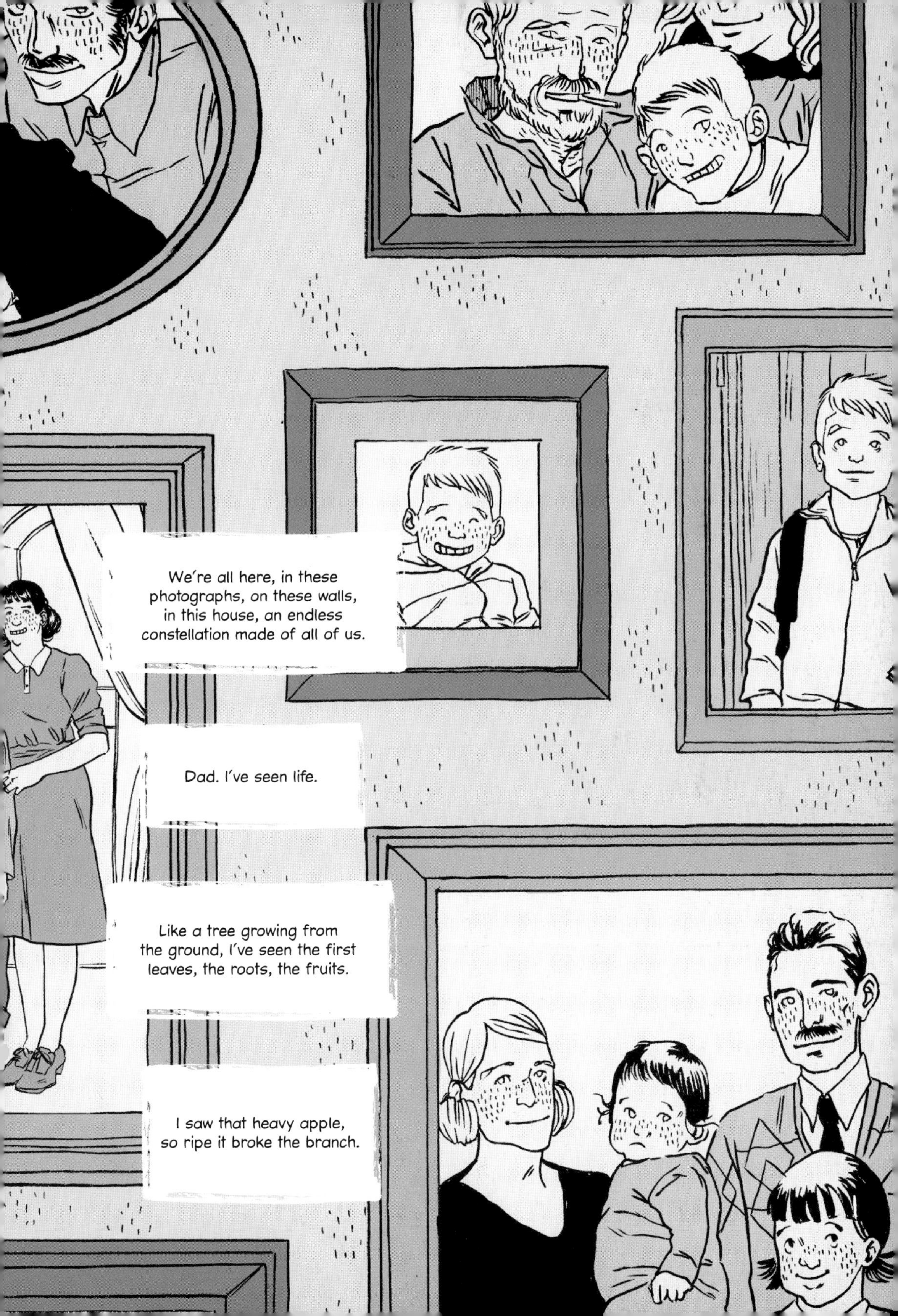
We're all here, in these photographs, on these walls, in this house, an endless constellation made of all of us.
Dad. I've seen life.
Like a tree growing from the ground, I've seen the first leaves, the roots, the fruits.
I saw that heavy apple, so ripe it broke the branch.

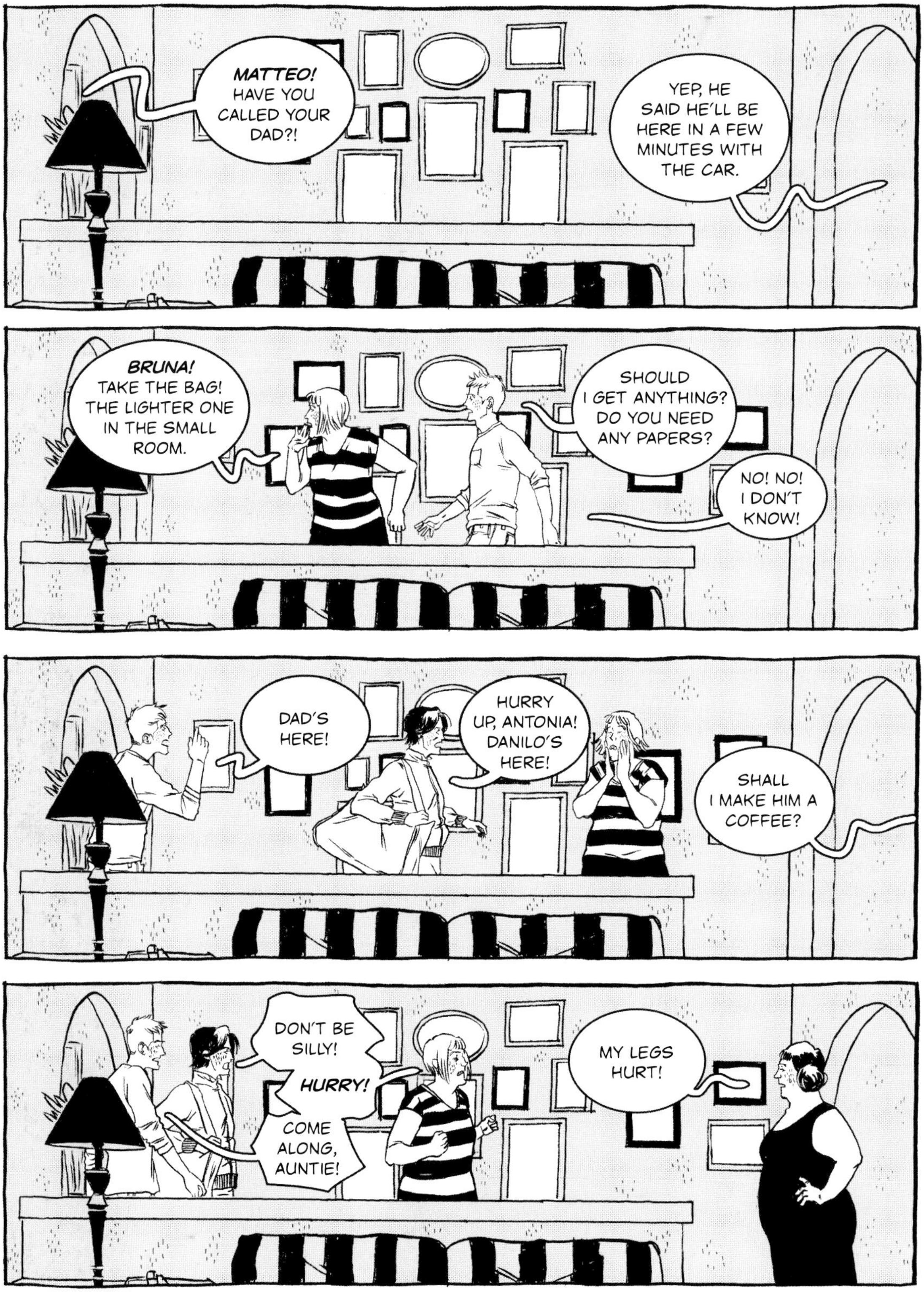
MATTEO! HAVE YOU CALLED YOUR DAD?!
YEP, HE SAID HE'LL BE HERE IN A FEW MINUTES WITH THE CAR.
BRUNA! TAKE THE BAG! THE LIGHTER ONE IN THE SMALL ROOM.
SHOULD I GET ANYTHING? DO YOU NEED ANY PAPERS?
NO! NO! I DON'T KNOW!
DAD'S HERE!
HURRY UP, ANTONIA! DANILO'S HERE!
SHALL I MAKE HIM A COFFEE?
DON'T BE SILLY!
HURRY!
COME ALONG, AUNTIE!
MY LEGS HURT!

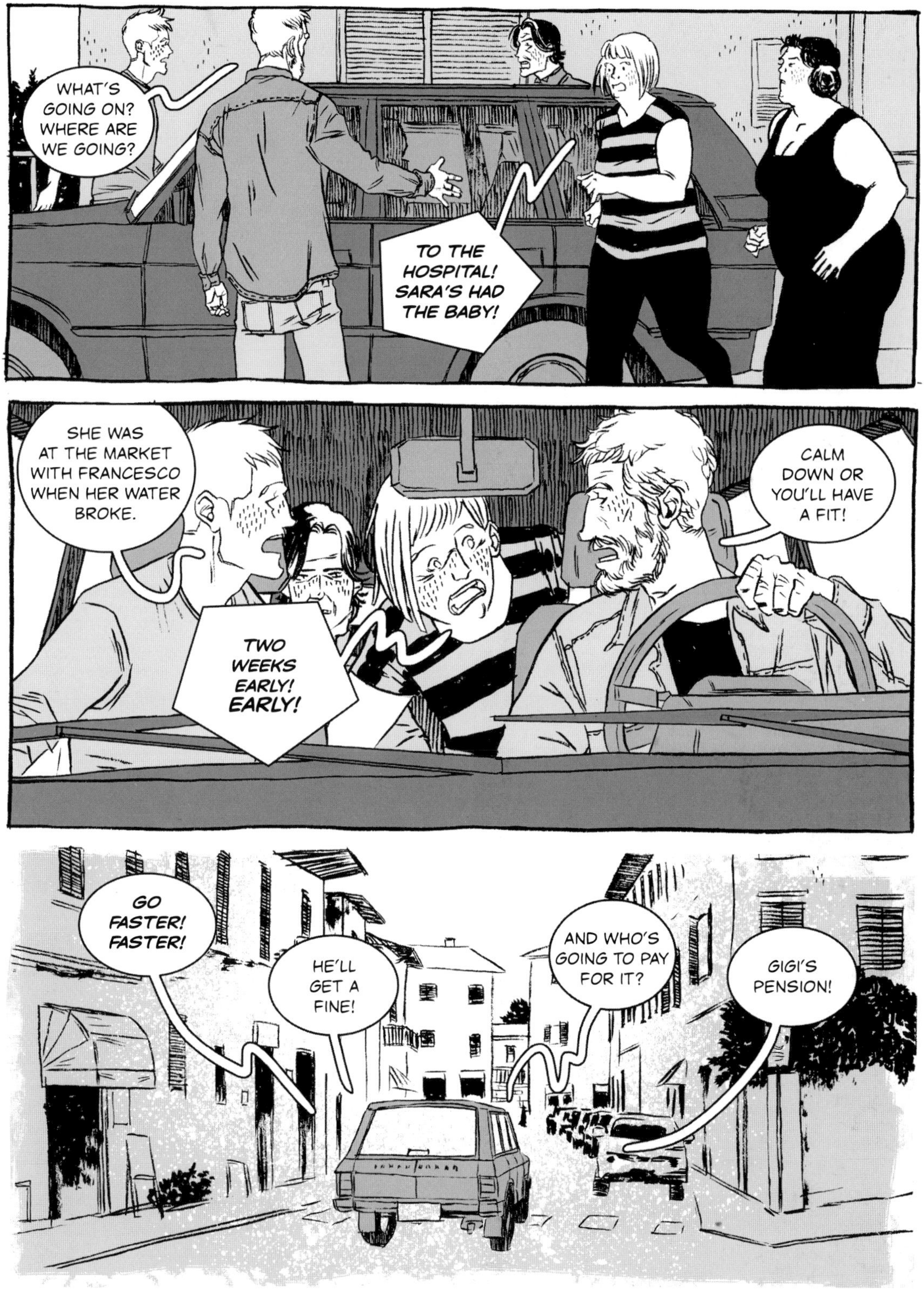
WHAT'S GOING ON? WHERE ARE WE GOING?
TO THE HOSPITAL! SARA'S HAD THE BABY!
SHE WAS AT THE MARKET WITH FRANCESCO WHEN HER WATER BROKE.
TWO WEEKS EARLY! EARLY!
CALM DOWN OR YOU'LL HAVE A FIT!
GO FASTER! FASTER!
HE'LL GET A FINE!
AND WHO'S GOING TO PAY FOR IT?
GIGI'S PENSION!

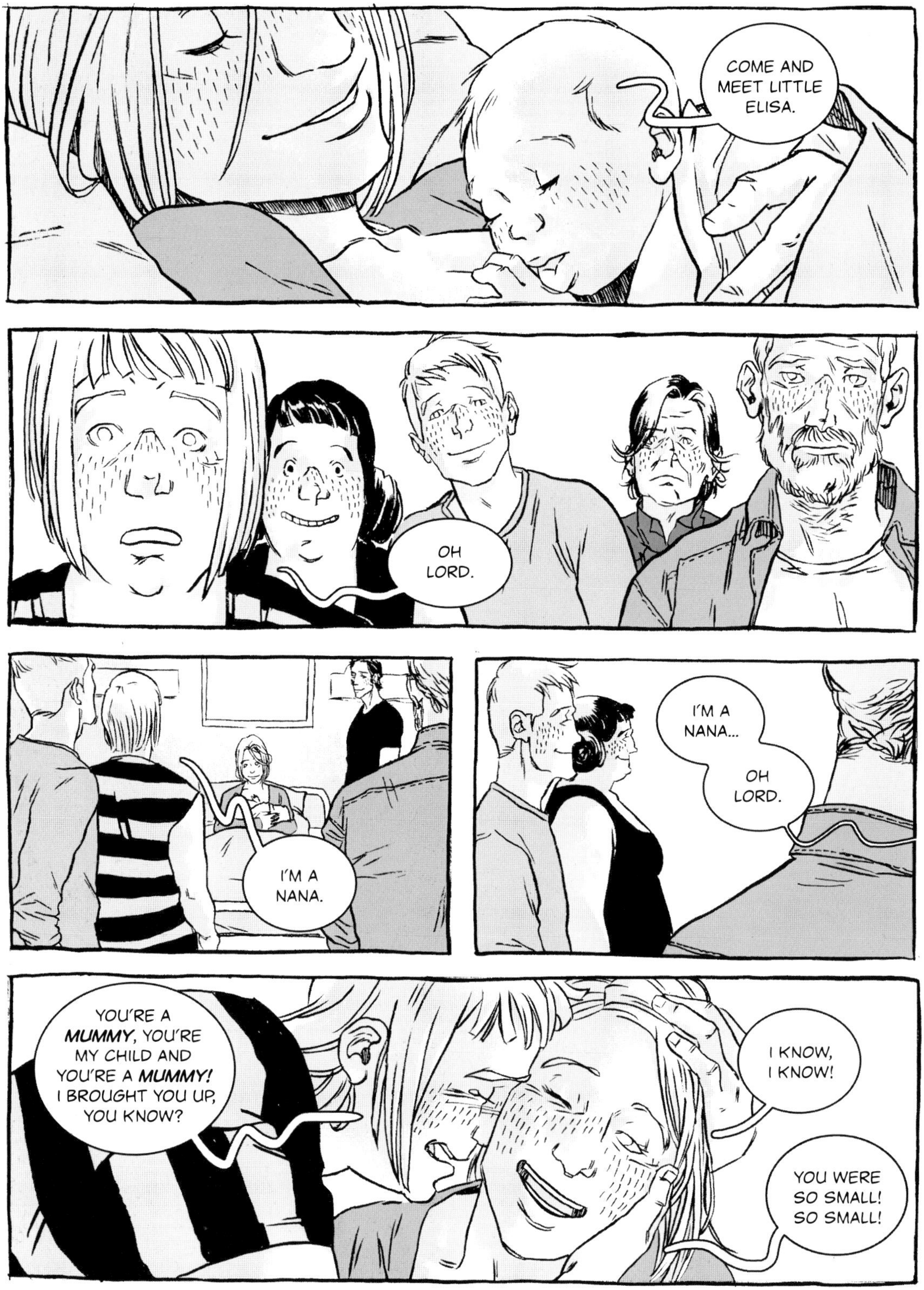
COME AND MEET LITTLE ELISA.
OH LORD.
I'M A NANA.
I'M A NANA...
OH LORD.
YOU'RE A **MUMMY**, YOU'RE MY CHILD AND YOU'RE A **MUMMY!** I BROUGHT YOU UP, YOU KNOW?
I KNOW, I KNOW!
YOU WERE SO SMALL! SO SMALL!

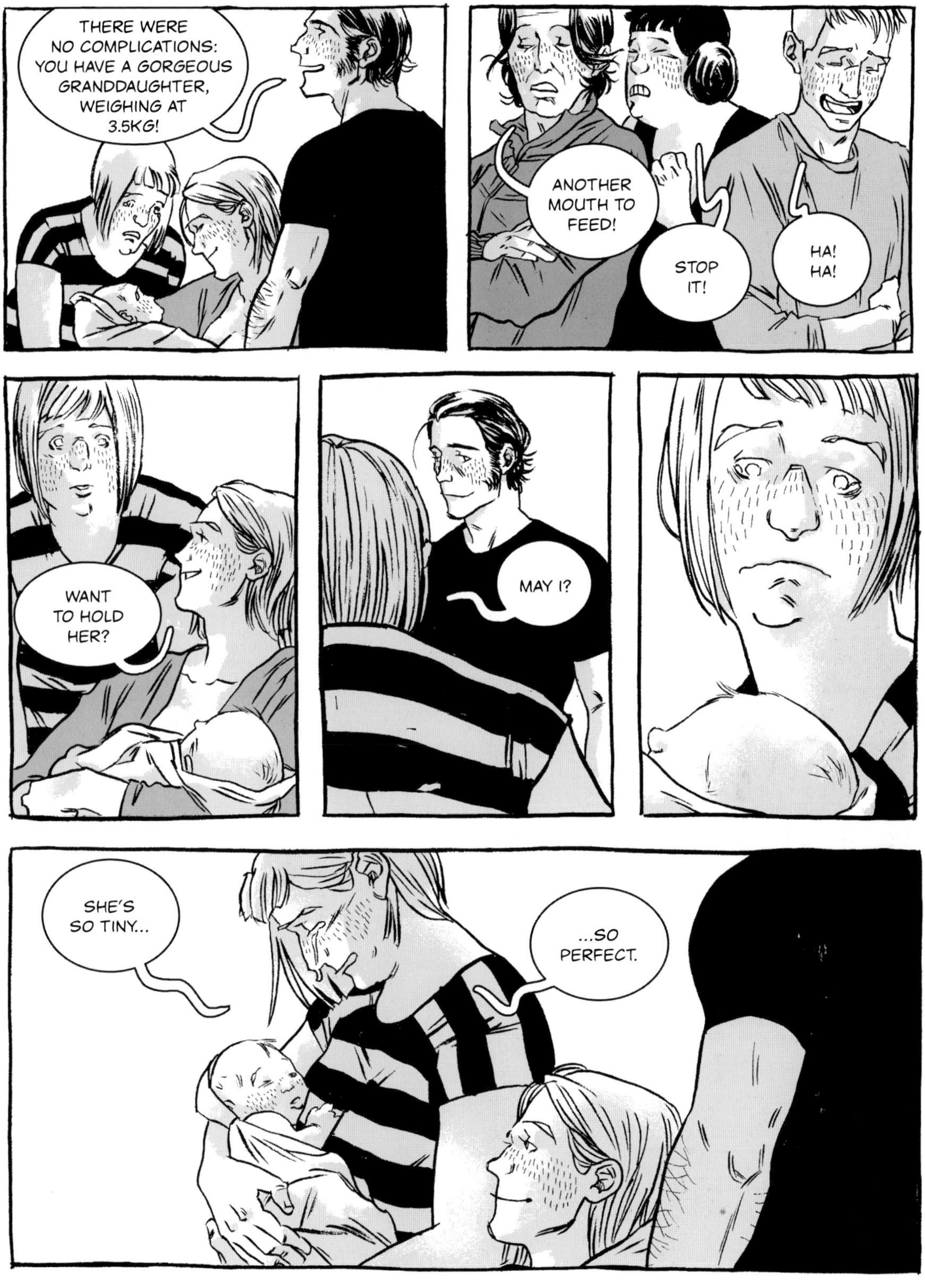
THERE WERE NO COMPLICATIONS: YOU HAVE A GORGEOUS GRANDDAUGHTER, WEIGHING AT 3.5KG!
ANOTHER MOUTH TO FEED!
STOP IT!
HA! HA!
WANT TO HOLD HER?
MAY I?
SHE'S SO TINY...
...SO PERFECT.

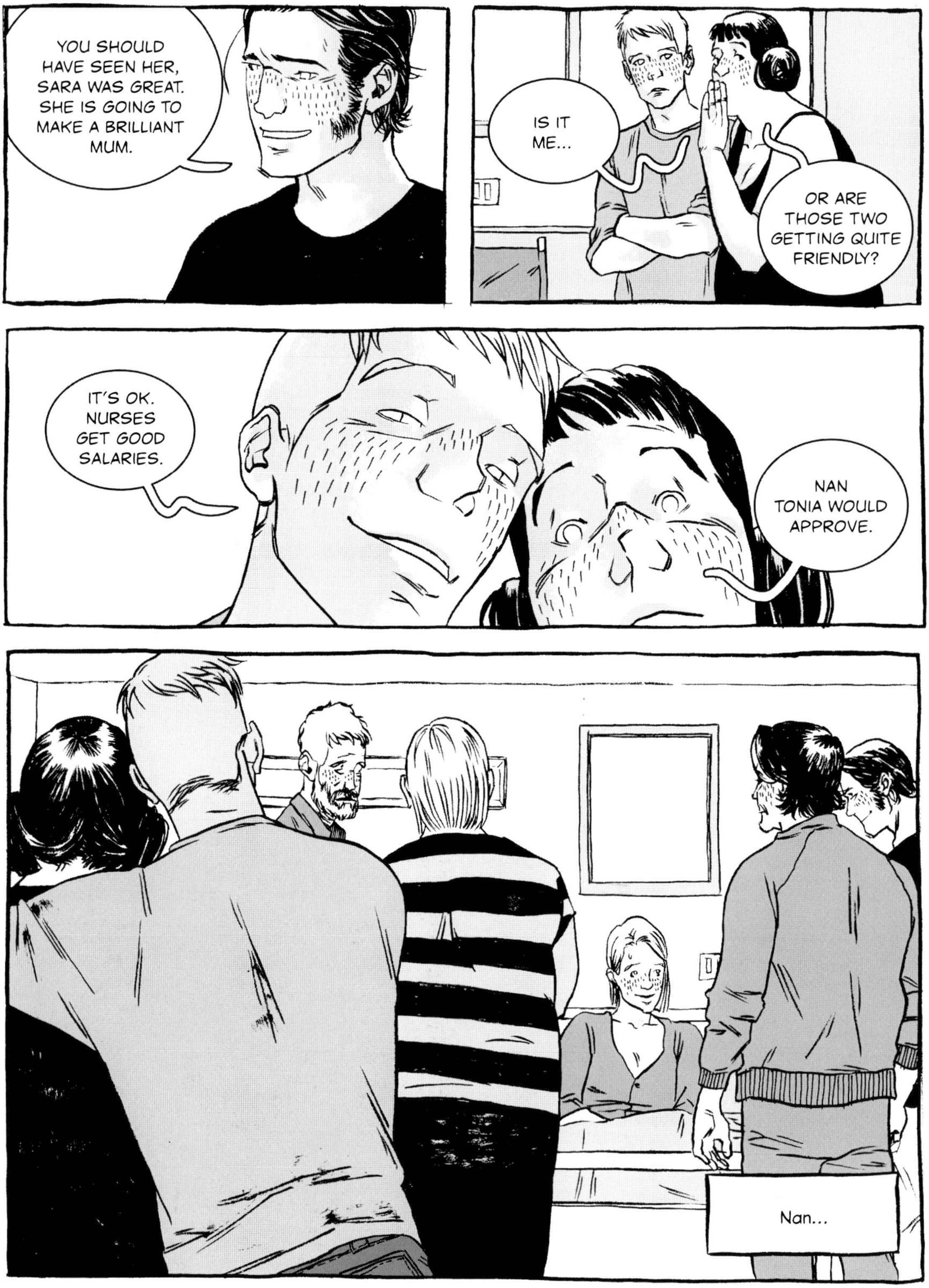
YOU SHOULD HAVE SEEN HER, SARA WAS GREAT. SHE IS GOING TO MAKE A BRILLIANT MUM.
IS IT ME...
OR ARE THOSE TWO GETTING QUITE FRIENDLY?
IT'S OK. NURSES GET GOOD SALARIES.
NAN TONIA WOULD APPROVE.
Nan...

I wonder if Auntie C. saw herself twenty years ago...

...wondering whether perhaps Sara, too, would have to protect her little girl from the world's evil eye.

We'll be there, this time, Auntie.

All of us.

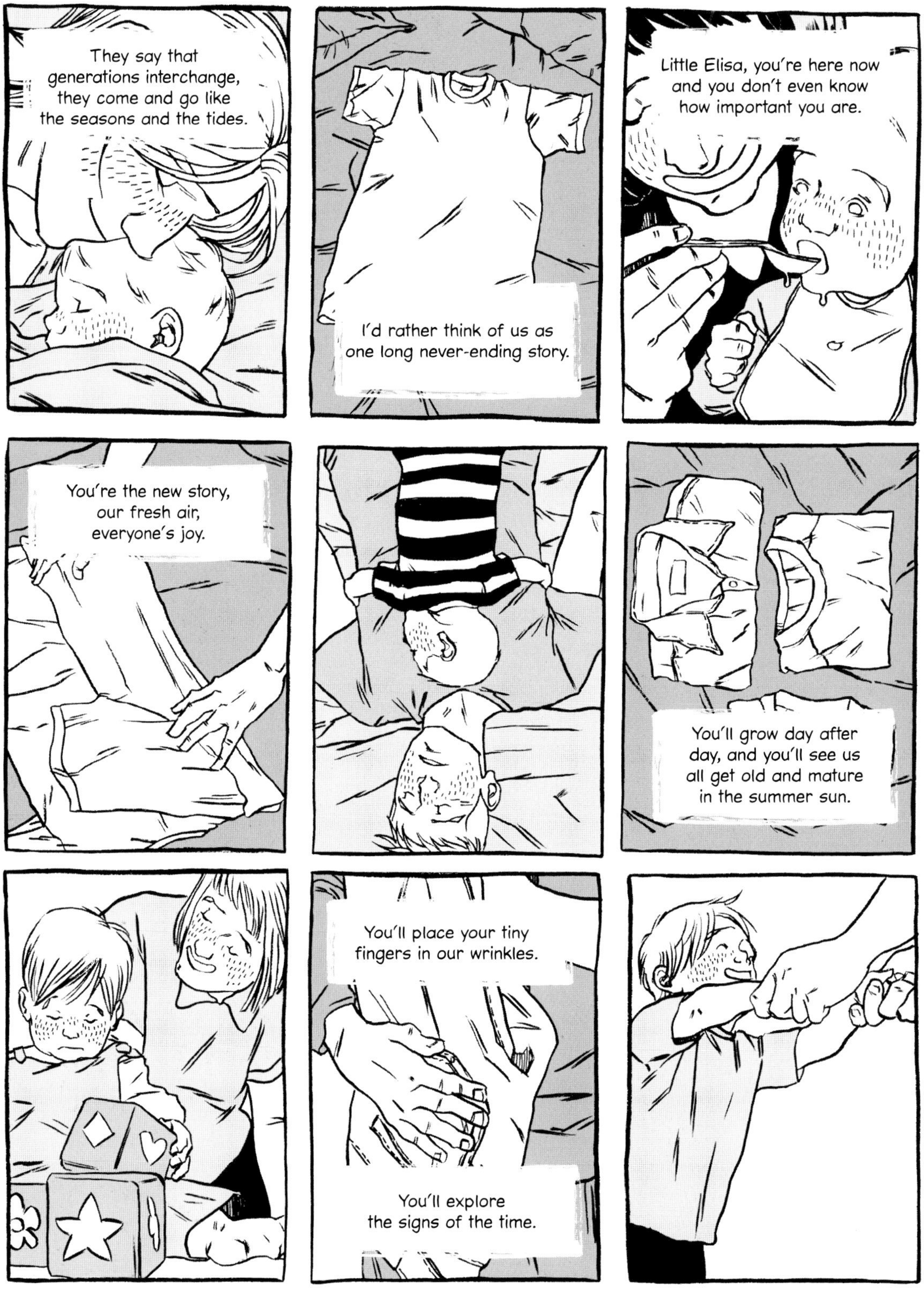
They say that generations interchange, they come and go like the seasons and the tides.
I'd rather think of us as one long never-ending story.
Little Elisa, you're here now and you don't even know how important you are.
You're the new story, our fresh air, everyone's joy.
You'll grow day after day, and you'll see us all get old and mature in the summer sun.
You'll place your tiny fingers in our wrinkles.
You'll explore the signs of the time.

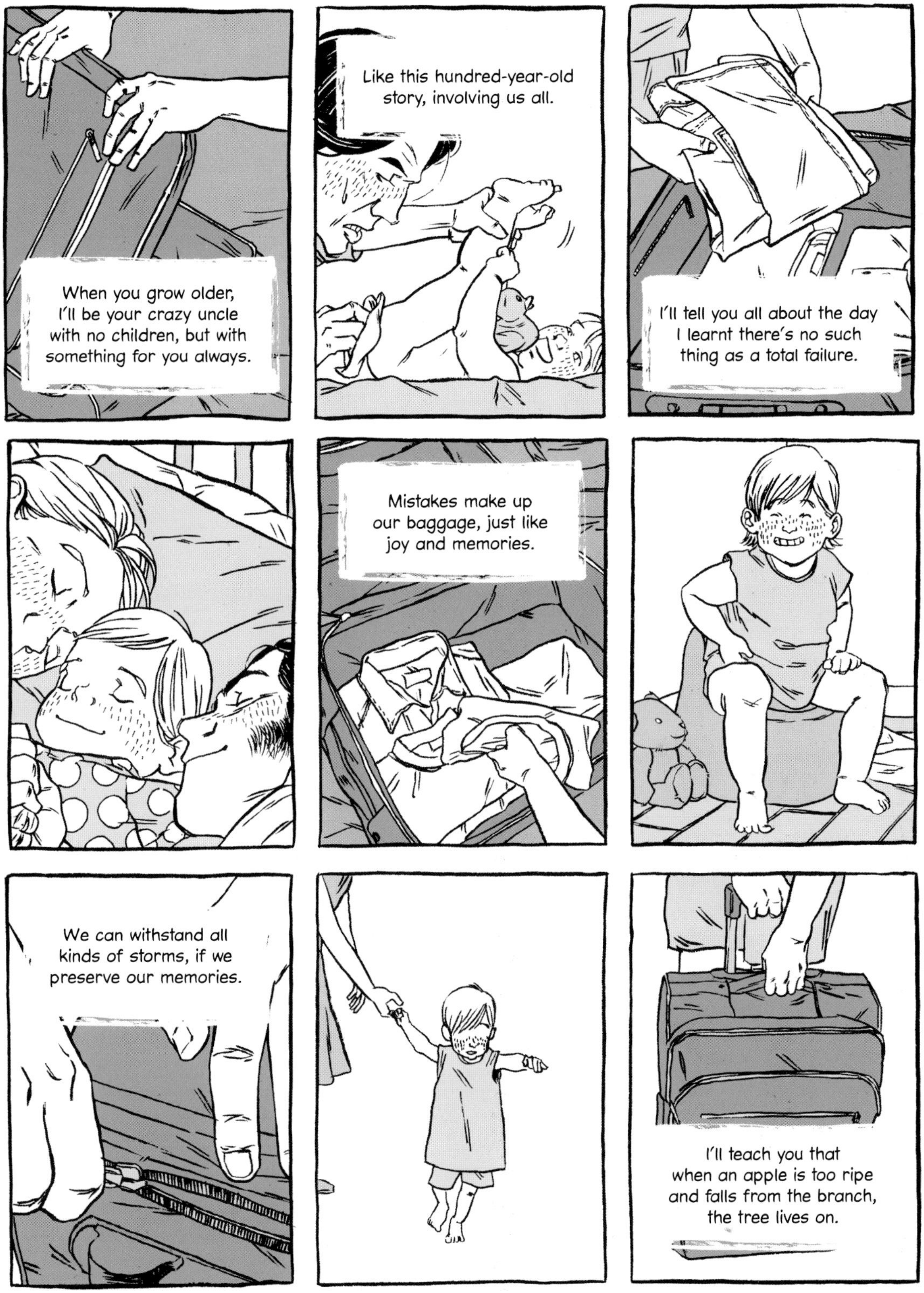
When you grow older, I'll be your crazy uncle with no children, but with something for you always.
Like this hundred-year-old story, involving us all.
I'll tell you all about the day I learnt there's no such thing as a total failure.
Mistakes make up our baggage, just like joy and memories.
We can withstand all kinds of storms, if we preserve our memories.
I'll teach you that when an apple is too ripe and falls from the branch, the tree lives on.

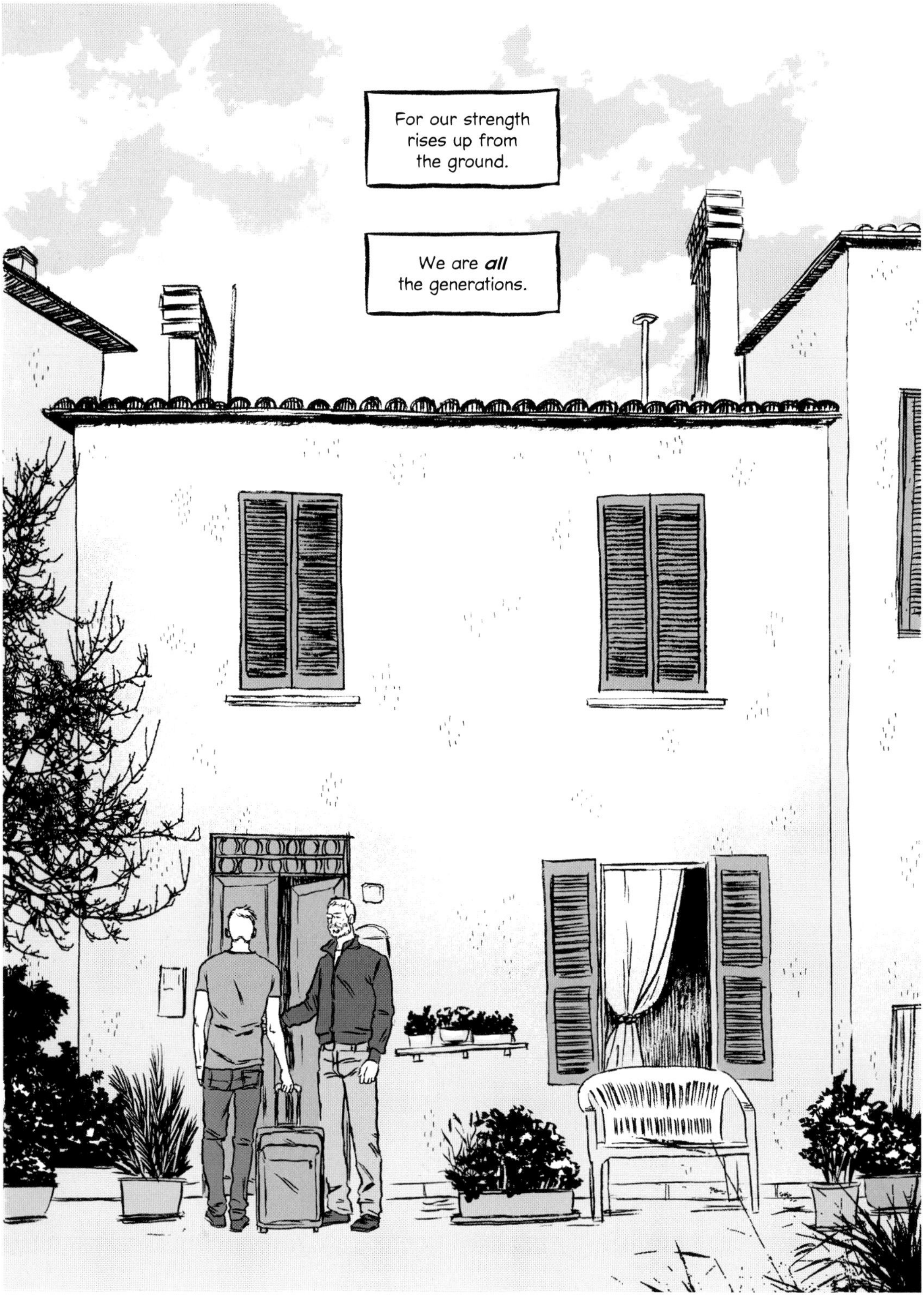
For our strength rises up from the ground.
We are ***all*** the generations.

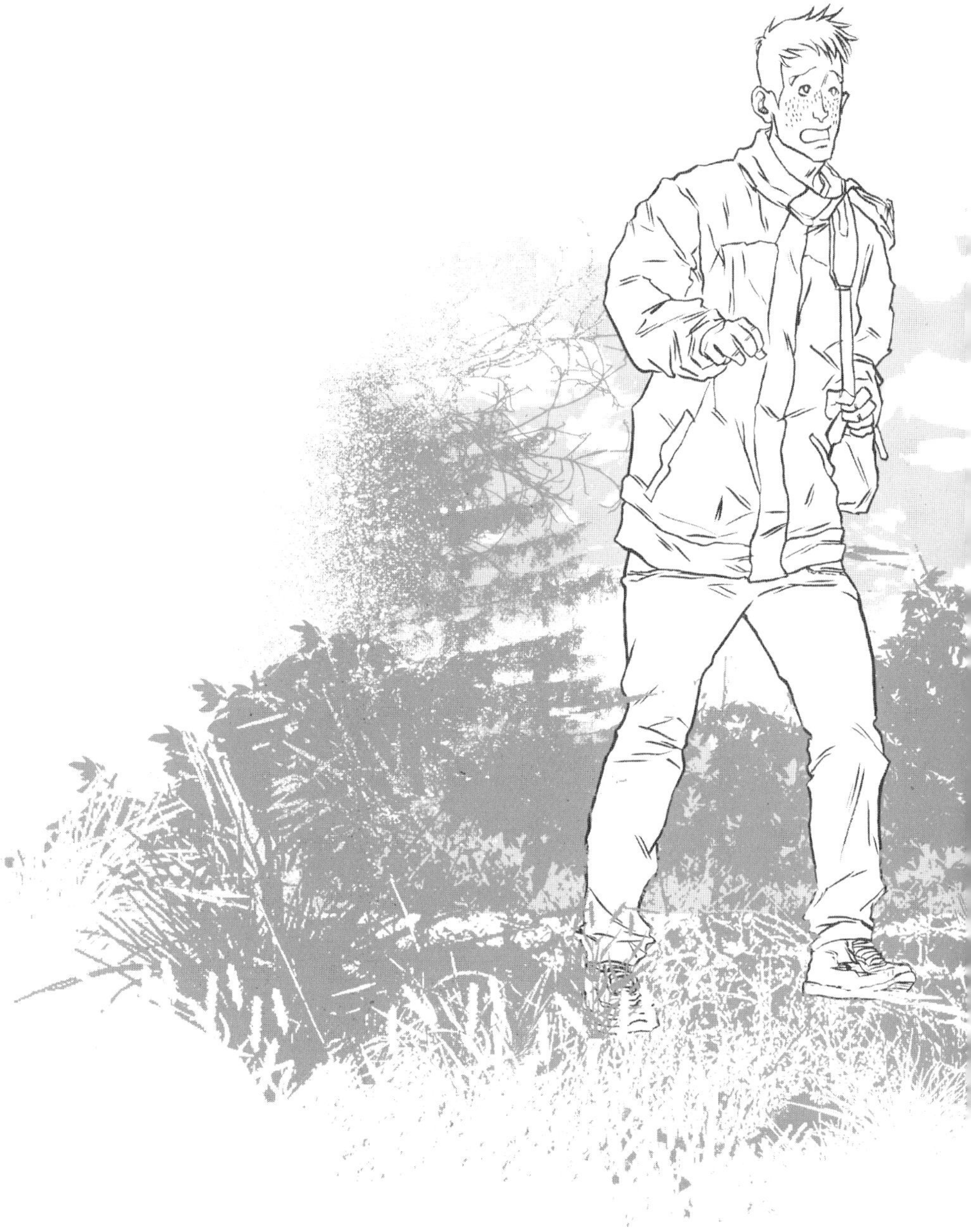

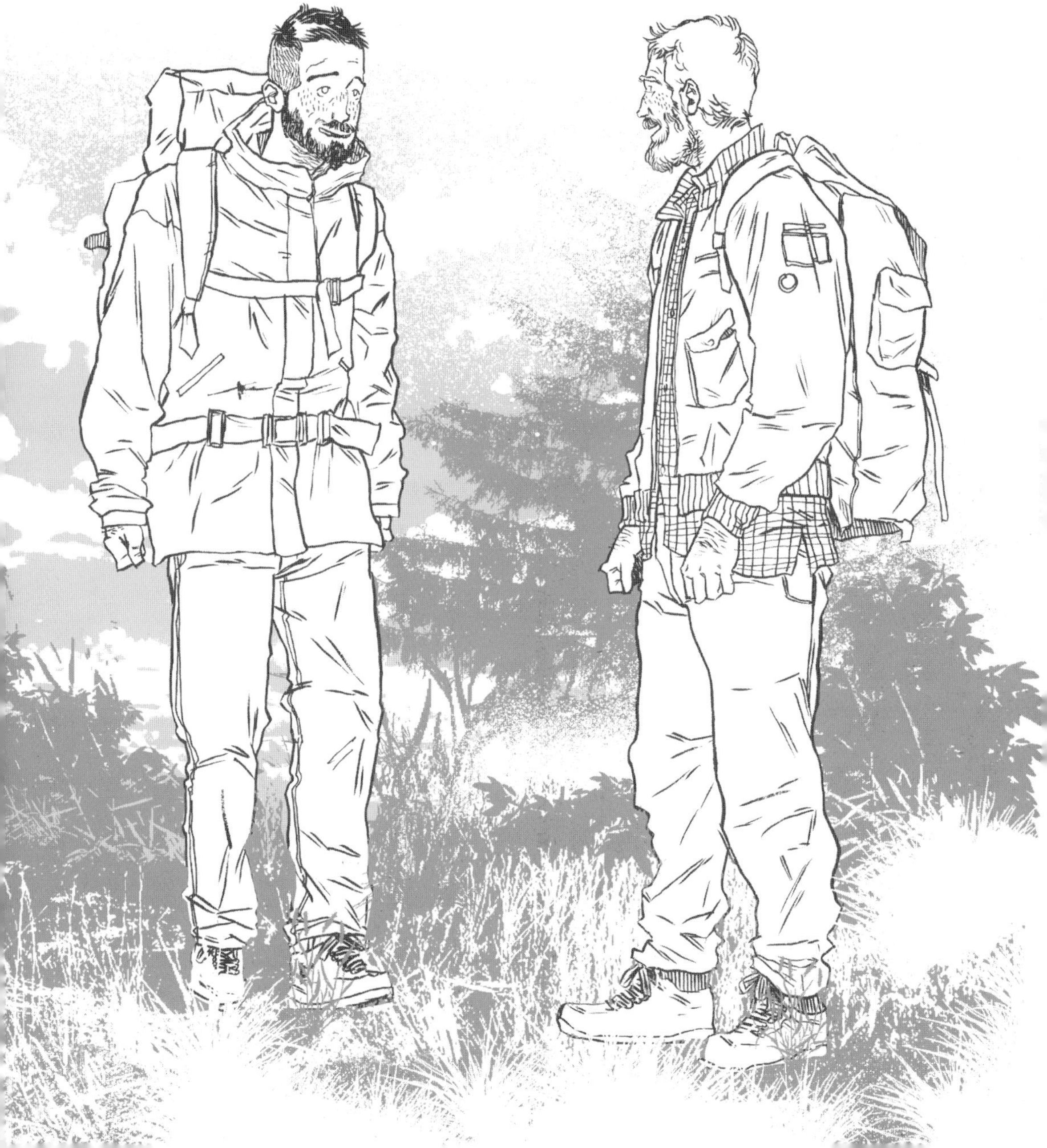

ABOUT THE AUTHOR

Flavia Biondi was born in Castelfiorentino, Italy (in the province of Florence). She received a bachelor's degree in Comics & Illustration from the Academy of Fine Arts in Bologna, and was one of the co-founders of the Bologna-based publishing collective *Manticora Autoproduzioni*. Her first published work came out in 2012 in the *Manticora* anthology book **Sindrome**.

Generations is the fourth of her graphic novels published in her native Italy, and her first to be published in English.

Cliff, the BAO Publishing logo,
interpreted by Flavia Biondi.